Amazing Tales
from times gone by

Amazing Tales
from times gone by

STRANGE BUT TRUE: extraordinary stories from 5000 years of human history

PUBLISHED BY THE READER'S DIGEST ASSOCIATION LIMITED
LONDON • NEW YORK • SYDNEY • MONTREAL

Extraordinary stories from 5000 years of human history

Historical events have shaped all of us over the course of the centuries. The past influences our present and helps us to forsee the future. But stories from history are often far more than simply educational – many are more thrilling than anything the most imaginative author could invent. Some of the events in this book took place in ancient times, while others occurred as recently as the last generation.

We have chosen stories of murder and mayhem, of mighty struggles for power, of liars and devious deceptions, of mysterious disappearances and miraculous meetings, of magnificent women, outrageous rogues and brave adventurers. Find out how legends arose, the astonishing heritage left by our ancestors, how the fickle hand of fate can change the course of history and how brilliant inventions have transformed our lives.

In tales from ancient times, discover whether King Solomon lived up to his reputation for wisdom and the technological secret that made Viking raids so swift and deadly. Meet the Alpine countess who was reviled for her ugliness and learn why Russia's visionary tsar Peter the Great worked as a shipwright in Amsterdam. In the modern era, there are the lives of a chic Frenchwoman who was a deadly double agent during the Second World War and a low-born girl who led a bandit crew and became a democratically elected member of India's parliament.

Each tale is accompanied with quotes from contemporaries or commentators and most include supplementary fact boxes to enhance understanding.

Kings, queens, aristocrats, warriors, artists, inventors, adventurers, murderers, courtesans, spies, rogues and tycoons; their stories are all here, united by the impact they made on history.

The Editors

Contents

Solving the mystery

Pushing back the frontiers

Rogues and adventurers

The legacy of our ancestors

11 Arbitrary acts of fate

12 They changed the world

Murder
and
mayhem

1

Death
in the jungle

Did the followers of Jim Jones, leader
of the People's Temple, really follow his
example and take their own lives in the
Guyanan jungle in a carefully orchestrated
communal suicide? Or was 'Jonestown'
the scene of the perfect mass murder.

Jim Jones and his sect,
the People's Temple,
settled far from civilisation
in the Guyanese jungle.
Few, except his former
followers, had any inkling
of the terror of the regime
that he presided over.

Late on the afternoon of November 18, 1978, Jim Jones, leader of the People's Temple, gathered the members of his sect in an assembly hall in the Guayanan jungle. He announced that they were not about to do another drill: this time it was the real thing. For a long time the inhabitants of 'Jonestown' had been regularly practising suicide by drinking Kool Aid together, knowing that one day the scarlet liquid would contain poison.

That day, the drink was lethal. Babies and small children, the first to be given the draft, died as their parents watched. Audio tapes made at the time indicate that there was little resistance; one or two women raised their voices in protest, but were shouted down by the crowd. The adults then followed their leader to their deaths, some by swallowing the drink and others with injections of potassium cyanide.

DRAMA AT THE AIRPORT

At around the same time, at the airstrip at Port Kaituma – in the northwest of Guyana not far from the border with Venezuela – a delegation of American politicians, reporters and other US citizens under the leadership of Congressman Leo J. Ryan was preparing to take a flight back to the capital, Georgetown. On November 17–18 they had visited the nearby commune of 'Jonestown', in its tropical jungle surroundings. They were there to get a first-hand impression of conditions at the settlement, where members of the sect known as the People's Temple had been living since the mid-1970s. Around a dozen of the estimated 1200 inhabitants, who were mainly Americans, had decided to return home and waited by the runway for the planes to arrive.

At about 5.10 pm, two aircraft, a single-engined Cessna and a Twin Otter, landed. The small Cessna boarded six passengers and taxied to the start of the runway ready for take-off. Suddenly, one of the occupants pulled a gun and fired at the other passengers. Almost simultaneously, a tractor with a trailer drove straight onto the airstrip and a group of men opened fire on the members of the delegation, who were about to board the Otter. The shooting went on for five minutes, until the unknown gunmen melted back into the jungle, leaving five people including Congressman Ryan dead and six seriously wounded.

Late that night, two men arrived in Port Kaituma and reported that 408 people had been killed at 'Jonestown'. Units of the Guyanese army who searched the commune on the morning of November 19 found the bodies. But the massacre had actually claimed the lives of more than twice as many victims as first reported: 913 people.

AN ALL-POWERFUL FATHER FIGURE

The chain of events that led to the death of Ryan and his companions had begun almost exactly a year before. On November 13, 1977, in San Francisco, Ryan read an article about the mysterious death of a member of the People's Temple. The man decided to leave the sect but was crushed to death by a train the next day. Ryan questioned former members of the People's Temple and their relatives and found evidence of serious human-rights violations against a number of individuals. Time and again, the name 'Jonestown' cropped up. It was alleged that many were being held against their will at the commune in the Guyanese jungle. After months of research, Ryan was granted permission by the White House to visit the commune accompanied by an official delegation of politicians, press representatives and relatives of sect members. He planned to question the leader of the sect, a man named Jim Jones, about the allegations that had been made.

'He will be a Messiah.'

JIM JONES' MOTHER
ON HER SON

The People's Temple sect was founded by the Reverend James ('Jim') Warren Jones in the mid-western state of Indiana in the mid-1950s. His motives were initially honourable and even visionary. He aimed to create an ideal society in which all people were equal, everyone had enough to eat and no-one was discriminated against because of the colour of their skin. Although he was white, Jones attracted a large number of African-Americans to his sect. The numbers of his followers grew rapidly, and the People's Temple became known for finding jobs for the unemployed and helping people to kick drug dependency.

To his followers, Jones, barely 30 at the time, was a charismatic father figure. But, over the years, he began to reveal a darker side to his character. He was unfaithful to his wife, took drugs and flew into fits of rage – he once shot at his best friend after a disagreement. Jones came to regard himself as a miracle faith healer and offered his services to cancer patients, often with apparently successful results. In 1965 he prophesied a 'nuclear holocaust' and from then on was constantly in search of a place where he thought he and his followers could survive the impending nuclear catastrophe. Jones first found such a haven in California; later he moved to Hawaii, then Brazil and finally to Guyana, where in 1974, the People's Temple acquired an estate of 120 hectares. At the end of 1977 Jones moved into the eponymous 'Jonestown' with several hundred of his followers.

HELL ON EARTH

The remote spot in the jungle was ideally suited to Jones' purpose. Here, in complete isolation, he could fully exploit techniques of indoctrination that he had developed over the previous decades. An excellent student of human nature, Jones was expert at bending people to his will without using physical violence and making them psychologically dependent. One of his principal methods was to exploit people's fears. Members of the People's Temple would sign over to the sect all their worldly possessions, including their pension entitlements. Accordingly,

Ghostly relics of the massacre: syringes containing traces of potassium cyanide were found among the piles of bodies.

This couple escaped by the skin of their teeth – just days before they had managed to evade the surveillance system in operation at 'Jonestown.'

anyone who left the sect could face financial oblivion. Yet an even stronger compulsion was the fear of failure. Jones encouraged the view that anyone who quit the People's Temple would be regarded as a traitor. On returning to bourgeois society, they would believe themselves to be a failure twice over.

Jones' regime of psychological terror also came to include physical violence. Even the children, 276 of whom were on the roll-call of the dead, were not spared. They were expected to work like slaves and might be punished with electric shocks for indulging in ordinary childish behaviour. It was not unknown for children to be savagely beaten in front of their parents or to be thrown into a well after first being told that there were poisonous snakes waiting for them.

Adults were prevented from making a bid for freedom by armed guards posted around the perimeter of the commune. According to Jones' teachings, the guards were there for the protection of the inhabitants of 'Jonestown', since enemies lurked everywhere. One day they would strike, and then the only way out for the People's Temple would be that which the garrison of the fortress at Masada in Israel had opted for almost 2000 years before: communal suicide.

WHAT REALLY HAPPENED?

Key questions about the event have never been satisfactorily answered. Was it a mass suicide, a mass murder, or possibly even both? And there have been frequent rumours of CIA involvement.

Several pieces of circumstantial evidence point to the murder theory. Many corpses had puncture marks on parts of the body that could not have been reached by people injecting themselves, for instance between the shoulder blades. Many victims including Jones himself had gunshot or crossbow-bolt wounds. There was a huge difference between the number of dead originally reported and the final tally: 408 as opposed to 913. Did more than 500 people manage to flee into the jungle, before being hunted down and shot, their bodies dragged back to the compound? There was a discrepancy in the number of victims and the estimated number of residents of 'Jonestown': up to 1200. Did some of the cult members murder their fellows and escape into the jungle?

A later series of mysterious deaths were associated with the massacre. All the victims had a connection to the People's Temple. Nine days after 'Jonestown', San Francisco Mayor George Moscone and Supervisor Harvey Milk were assassinated. Both had received financial support from Jones while he was in San Francisco and were involved in an investigation into their involvement in the disappearance of People's Temple funds. Jeanne and Alan Mills, cult members who had defected before the move to Guyana, were found murdered almost a year after the 'Jonestown' massacre. They had written a book about the People's Temple and believed that they would be killed.

The US Federal archives alone hold more than 8000 documents on the massacre at 'Jonestown', most of which are still classified. They probably hold the key to what really happened in the isolated jungle compound.

Mass suicides

October 1994
53 members of the Order of the Solar Temple were found dead; 48 of them in Canada and five in Switzerland. The bodies showed signs of gunshot wounds and the marks of lethal injections.

March 1997
Police uncovered the bodies of 39 members of the Heaven's Gate sect in a luxurious villa in California. They were thought to have drunk a deadly cocktail of vodka and sleeping pills.

March 2000
200 followers of the Ugandan sect known as Movement for the Restoration of the Ten Commandments apparently took their own lives in a ritual act of self-immolation.

A
mass murder
raises baffling questions

The massacre of the innocents is perhaps
the most terrible crime recorded in the Bible.
The man who ordered the slaughter, Herod,
King of Judea, was undoubtedly a bloodthirsty
tyrant – and had a motive for his actions. But
do the historical facts really add up?

Matthew's Gospel tells how three wise men from the East
came to Jerusalem after receiving news of the birth of Jesus.
They claimed to have been following a star and now wanted to
pay homage to the newborn King of the Jews. Herod summoned
the wise men and questioned them about the appearance of the
star – from which he was able to calculate the child's age.
Alarmed at the news of a possible rival to his throne, Herod
asked them to let him know as soon as they found the child,
so that he too could come and worship him. The wise men
continued their journey, still guided by the star.

TWO DREAMS
When the wise men came to the house in Bethlehem
where the infant Jesus and his parents, Mary and Joseph,
were staying, they began to worship the child and present
him with valuable gifts. The next morning they planned
to return to Jerusalem to inform Herod of the child's
whereabouts. But in a dream God instructed them to avoid
Herod and return home. Hardly had they left when Joseph

also had a dream. The Angel of the Lord told him to take his wife and son and go to Egypt as Herod was planning to hunt down the child and kill him. Alarmed, Joseph fled with his family.

In Jerusalem, Herod waited for the return of the wise men and their report. It soon became clear that he had been deceived. Enraged, he issued the order that all male children of two years old and under in Bethlehem were to be killed – a policy which would guarantee to rid the king of his potential rival. But by the time the massacre began, Jesus, Joseph and Mary were safe in Egypt. Shortly afterwards, Herod died and they were able to make their way back to Judea.

The infanticide in Bethlehem, as imagined by the illustrator of a 19th-century Bible.

BIBLE STORY OR HISTORICAL FACT?

Historians have found little evidence beyond Matthew's Gospel to support the story of the infanticide. But the incident does fit with what is known of Herod's character. A brutal, pragmatic politician, he was quite prepared to use murder as a final resort. He had even ordered the assassination of members of his own family, as he suspected treachery and intrigue everywhere.

At least three of his 14 sons – the product of a total of ten marriages – were killed on Herod's orders along with his favourite wife Miriam and her mother Alexandra.

POWER BASED ON ROMAN PATRONAGE

Herod's fears were entirely justified. His power, like that of his father, Antipater, was based on securing the goodwill of powerful patrons in Rome. In 63 BC, the Romans had occupied Syria and gained control of the neighbouring territory of Palestine. The politicians and high priests of Judea immediately began ingratiating themselves with the Romans, vying with one another to govern the country on behalf of their new masters. One of those most active in seeking Roman approval was Antipater.

He was an Idumaean, from a tribal state to the south of Palestine. In 47 BC, Julius Caesar entrusted him with control over Judea. When, following Caesar's murder in 44 BC, civil war erupted in Rome, Judea was also thrown into chaos and Antipater was killed by a local political opponent.

Herod left an architectural legacy of far more lasting significance than his political exploits. He reconstructed Jerusalem and a number of temples, especially the great temple of the Jews in Jerusalem, were remodelled or completely rebuilt.

MAINTAINING A HOLD ON POWER

After the murder of his father, Herod made a bid for power. Following his father's example, he made overtures to Mark Antony, now in command in Rome. He offered him such an enormous sum of money that the Roman was prepared to install Herod in his father's place immediately.

But it was not long before Herod was called upon to defend his newly won power. The Parthians, a warlike people from Persia, overran Palestine, expelled Herod and appointed one of their own as ruler of Judea. Herod refused to surrender. He battled his way to Rome, where he made it clear to the senators that he was prepared to spend large sums of money to secure their help. In response to his bribery, Herod was officially named King of the Jews and returned to Palestine with their blessing and a contingent of Roman troops. After a series of further struggles,

Herod finally managed to overcome his enemies both at home and abroad. His empire became almost as great as that of King David, the great hero of early Jewish history.

Herod was obsessed with maintaining his hold on power. He owed his position to his close relationship with Rome, but among his subjects, he had many enemies. Jews resented his interference in their religious affairs – he had taken over the appointment of a high priest, and filled the Jewish high tribunal with his own supporters. Pious Jews never accepted him as a legitimate ruler – they thought he was a pagan usurper of the Jewish throne. At the same time, pagans perceived him as a Jew who played favourites with his Jewish subjects.

> *'I'd rather be Herod's pig than Herod's son.'*
>
> EMPEROR AUGUSTUS

With so many out to get him, Herod believed he was justified in using any means to eliminate a rival. Such reasoning could well have supplied him with a motive for the infanticide at Bethlehem. As someone who had fought so hard for his kingdom, he was predisposed to see the birth of Christ as a declaration of war against his own authority.

WEIGHING THE EVIDENCE
So did the infanticide at Bethlehem actually take place? Although Herod may have had the capacity – and motive – to do so, it seems unlikely that he did order the slaughter. He died in 4 BC, before the birth of Jesus – a chronological inconsistency that would seem to absolve him of the charges. But the discrepancy is actually the result of an error made by the 6th-century monk Dionysius when he devised the Christian calendar and miscalculated Christ's date of birth.

Perhaps more significant is the fact that only the Gospel of St Matthew includes the infanticide. A Roman philosopher of the 4th century, Ambrosius Theodosius Macrobius, gives the earliest reference to the event outside the Bible: 'When Augustus heard that Herod, King of the Jews, had ordered all the boys in Syria under the age of two years to be put to death and that the king's son was among those killed, he said, "I'd rather be Herod's pig than Herod's son."' As Macrobius places the massacre in Syria, and combines it with the separate killing of one of Herod's sons, some historians have argued that the account is independent. But it is likely that, given the popularity of Matthew's Gospel and the spread of Christianity, it was taken from Matthew.

> *'I shall pass through the land of Egypt and all the first-born shall perish.'*
>
> GOD TO MOSES IN THE OLD TESTAMENT

INFANTICIDE IN EGYPT AND ROME

Although Herod's alleged massacre seems to derive exclusively from St Matthew, similar incidents are described elsewhere in the Bible and in the writings of early historians.

The Old Testament tells how Moses and the Israelites were enslaved by a Pharaoh who refused to let them return to the Promised Land. As a consequence, God visited ten plagues upon Egypt to force Pharaoh to change his mind. The worst of these was the final plague: 'Around midnight', God told Moses, 'I shall pass through the land of Egypt and all the first-born shall perish, from the eldest son of the Pharaoh on his throne to the eldest son of the serving maid sitting behind her mill.' The cruel judgment was duly enacted: neither the Pharaoh nor his lowliest servant was spared the loss of a child. The last loss was too much for him to bear and Pharaoh was forced to swallow his pride. Moses and the Israelites were allowed to leave Egypt and set off on their exodus back to the Promised Land.

Another parallel comes from Rome, shortly before the birth of the future Emperor Augustus, in 63 BC. A number of miracles had indicated that something momentous was about to happen. Rumours abounded that the natural world was about to produce a new king to rule

Herod's Roman friends

Julius Caesar
As Governor of Judea in 47 BC, Herod first backed Julius Caesar.

Cassius
After Caesar's murder in 44 BC, Herod switched his support to Caesar's assassin Cassius.

Mark Antony
In 42 BC, when Cassius had been eliminated, he ingratiated himself with Mark Antony.

Octavian
Following Mark Antony's defeat at the battle of Actium in 31 BC, Herod changed sides once again, becoming Octavian's representative in Judea.

When Herod heard of the quest of the three wise men, he asked his scribes where the birth of the King of the Jews might have taken place. They quoted the prophet, Micah, who had foretold that a new ruler of Israel would come out of Bethlehem.

over the Roman people. The senators became alarmed, fearing the demise of the Republic if they lost control of the succession. So they resolved that no boy born in that year should be permitted to survive. Although the measure was intended to save the Republic from being supplanted by a king, there was discord as a result of the ruling and the resolution of the Senate was overturned. Every man whose wife was pregnant hoped that it would be his son who would be the prophesied ruler and bring his family renown, power and honour.

A final example of an event that could be regarded as an infanticide took place in Rome under the despotic Emperor Nero, who reigned from AD 54–68. Fearful of conspiracies against him, Nero had many of his citizens placed under arrest, and their children driven out of the city and then killed, either by poisoning or starvation.

SOLVING THE PUZZLE

So in ancient times, the motif of the murder of children was just one – but a potent example – of an arsenal of accusations that might be used against tyrants and despots. And many rulers were ready to kill in order to hang onto their hard-won power.

In Judea there was no shortage of people who had scores to settle with Herod. 'I know that the Jews will celebrate my death with an outpouring of joy,' the king is reputed to have said, shortly before his death. It is entirely plausible that his dissatisfied Jewish subjects wanted to blacken his memory by ascribing to him a particularly monstrous deed.

Another possibility is that if a massacre did take place, it was on too small a scale to rate a historical mention. Some of the early churches suggested that as many as 64,000 children had been murdered on Herod's orders. But given the size of Bethlehem and the surrounding area, it is unlikely that more than a few dozen children could have been killed.

It is also possible that the early Christians of Palestine created the myth. The alleged murder plot and the miraculous escape of Jesus and his family showed their Saviour in a uniquely favourable light – as a divine figure whom even the most evil ruler could not touch.

Hung, boiled and **beheaded**

The death penalty – inflicted in a wide variety of barbaric ways – was a common feature of life in past centuries.

A mother found guilty of murdering her child is bound and thrown into a river. Drowning was a widespread method of execution for women.

On the evening of August 5, 1621, an accused criminal trotted along next to the hangman. She had not the slightest awareness of her guilt. But with a single shove, she had killed a heavily pregnant farmer's wife, a capital offence that, according to the law, could only be atoned for through death. Yet in this case the enforcement of the death sentence must have struck even the Leipzig public executioner who carried it out as unusual. For the accused was a cow.

Cases of this kind were not uncommon: in 1403, at Mantes in France, a sow was hanged for eating a child. In

1474 a cockerel that had had the temerity to lay an egg – incontrovertible proof that it must be in league with the Devil – was put to death. And because the executioner then discovered two more eggs in its body cavity, the corpse of the dastardly bird was also burned. That the 'cockerel' might simply have been a hen with a cockerel's plumage was never considered. In 1665, the hangman of Merano, in northern Italy, carried out a death sentence for sodomy – but not against the guilty man, who was merely condemned to serve as a galley slave – but against the calf that the accused sodomite had supposedly 'seduced'.

Although these cases appear ludicrous to us, they are examples of the medieval concept of justice. It was irrelevant whether or why the culprit had been motivated to commit an unlawful act. What was important was the need to avert the wrath of God – in the form of failed harvests, famines or storms – that would inevitably ensue if a sin was left unatoned. So the death penalty did not just ensure law and order; it was also a means of keeping peace with God.

With the advent of technology, new execution devices were developed – such as the electric chair which aimed to kill criminals more humanely.

AN ORDINARY PROFESSION?

Whatever the motivation behind capital punishment, someone still had to carry out the sentence. And although he killed legally, the social position of the executioner was on a par with that of an outlaw. The ostracism was so extreme that any contact with an executioner was taboo. In 1546, a man who had dared to drink in the company of a hangman was expelled from his guild. Shamed, the man killed himself.

On the other hand, public executions offered a superb, if horrifying, piece of public theatre. An especially grisly execution took place in Vienna in 1463. Wolfgang Holzer had become too closely involved in an internecine dispute among members of the ruling Habsburg dynasty and had been condemned to die. As the condemned man was led to the scaffold, the assembled crowd bayed insults at him, flung mud at him and tugged at his hair. The executioner then cut open the man's chest while he was still alive and tore out the heart, which he held up to the howling mob. Finally, he cut the heart into four pieces, which were displayed at the gates and approach roads to the city as a warning to others.

BLOODLUST AND COMPASSION

Did executioners take any pleasure from their duties? The public executioner in Dresden claimed he could lead a man who had been beheaded by the hand for a few metres. The Elector of Saxony was keen to verify this for himself. So when the next beheading took place, the executioner stuck a piece of turf on the neck stump of his victim to staunch the flow of blood, and walked hand in hand with the beheaded man. The Elector ennobled the hangman and granted him the land on which he and his victim had promenaded. In the late 15th century, the Hamburg executioner dispatched 75 pirates in an hour. He strung them up six at a time, a practice that was later prohibited, as it didn't provide enough entertainment.

In other cases there was evidence of a degree of compassion shown by the executioner. A small bag of gunpowder would be tied under the chin of a person condemned to be burnt at the stake to shorten his suffering. And one of the main reasons for blindfolding miscreants before they died was to stop the executioner from being troubled by pangs of conscience. He would not have to look into a person's eyes as they begged for mercy. For if an

Methods of execution

Breaking on the wheel
Victims were tied onto a cartwheel, after first having their legs and arms broken.

Drowning
Used mainly as a way of executing women. The condemned was trussed up, thrown in the water and pushed under with poles.

Boiling
In the reign of Henry VIII, poisoners were put into a vat of water that was gradually heated to boiling point.

Halifax Gibbet
The principle behind the first mechanical execution device was later adopted in the guillotine. The falling blade was designed to kill quickly and painlessly.

executioner failed to carry out an sentence, he might be pursued by a howling mob, outraged at the loss of their afternoon's entertainment. He would lose his position, and at worst he might also pay with his life.

RAISED FROM THE DEAD

Hundreds of bizarre myths and legends surround the death penalty. The 'hanged man who thawed' was executed in the bitter winter of 1681 and cut down to be dissected for medical research. In the warmth of the dissecting room, he not only thawed out but came back to life. According to the principle that a person could only be punished once for the same crime, he was then freed to enjoy his reprieve.

Stories like these flourished around places of execution. Splinters of wood from gallows were thought to prevent warts, while the blood of a beheaded person, if drunk while warm, could cure epilepsy. Only with the Enlightenment in the 18th century did the idea of the death penalty start to be challenged. Gradually, in certain cases, it was superseded by imprisonment. Yet even the philospher Immanuel Kant

While one thief was being hanged, his 'colleagues' picked the pockets of the onlookers.

believed that the most serious of crimes should be answered with the most serious of penalties. When the first general proscriptions of the death penalty were issued, wrongdoers were made to perform forced labour or transported, tantamount to condemning a person to death by instalments.

The death penalty is still in force today in more than 70 countries, including the superpowers of China and parts of the USA. The world's oldest punishment has lost none of its power to terrify.

The bloody countess

In the 17th century, a Hungarian noblewoman was held responsible for the deaths of hundreds of young women. Did Elisabeth Báthory have her victims killed so she could use their blood to prolong her fading beauty – or was her behaviour provoked by sheer sadism?

On a freezing night in December 1610, the Chief Imperial Prosecutor of Hungary and his troops stormed the castle at Cachtice, in response to rumours of dreadful deeds being enacted within its walls. They came upon its countess in the process of torturing several girls. Reports that young women were being murdered at the castle seemed to have been confirmed in the most terrible way.

A detail of a painting by Istvan Czok shows Elisabeth in the aftermath of one of her torture sessions at Castle Cachtice. It implies the involvement of rather more than the handful of 'assistants' who were actually convicted of helping her.

WAS ELISABETH A BORN SADIST?

Born in 1560 to one of Hungary's noblest families, the Báthorys, the young Elisabeth was considered a radiant beauty. In 1572, she married Count Francis Nádasdy, to whom she bore six children. An intelligent woman who could read and write in four languages, it also seems likely that she had violent sexual fantasies from an early age. The families of both Count Nádasdy and his wife had a history of violence and the Báthorys in particular may have been inbred. Her husband may have known of Elisabeth's sadistic tendencies and it is claimed that an aunt introduced her to the idea of flagellation, using an instrument of torture that her husband had once used when interrogating his Turkish prisoners.

Although Elisabeth became notorious for the harsh punishments that she meted out to her female servants, her behaviour was not at first seen as a sign of a disturbed personality. But following her husband's death in around 1604, when Elisabeth was in her forties and her beauty was fading, rumours of killing sprees began to circulate.

THE LEGEND OF THE BLOODY COUNTESS

Elisabeth's taste for blood was apparently aroused by a seemingly innocuous event. She wore her hair elaborately arranged and it would be regularly dressed by a servant. But on this occasion, the maid who was brushing her hair pulled it too hard. Enraged, the countess struck her in the face so violently that she began to bleed from her mouth and nose. A few drops of blood fell on the countess's hand which she wiped away. But when she looked at the hand, the spots where the blood had fallen appeared more youthful. As a result, it was said, she conceived the ghastly idea of rejuvenating her entire body with young girls' blood.

At first content with gathering blood from her victims' veins, Elisabeth developed a craving for ever greater quantities. An 'Iron Maiden', designed to impale a body on hundreds of steel spikes, was said to have been built for her. The blood was collected and channelled directly into the countess's bathtub. Whenever Elisabeth wished to refresh her complexion, the torture was repeated with a fresh batch of girls.

THE DEVELOPMENT OF A MONSTROUS OBSESSION

Though several accounts of torture tally with the legend, they probably misinterpret the countess's motives. In the 17th century, sadistic perversions would only have been ascribed to men. Elisabeth's behaviour was attributed to her vanity, but in reality it seems to have been the pleasure she gained from watching the suffering of others that lay at the heart of her behaviour. Although her husband and family knew of her perversion, they did nothing to stop it.

The torture took place at all of Elisabeth's homes but especially at Cachtice, in the Carparthian mountains. The castle was ideally equipped for keeping her activites secret. It had a mighty keep, dark underground passages and dungeons. There she was surrounded by a throng of female servants who would be summoned on the pretext of performing a small task. They would then be bound and tortured by the countess's helpers or by Elisabeth herself. Initially, the torture was confined to sticking needles under the maids' fingernails or cutting them with scissors. But Elisabeth soon progressed to more violent behaviour, including beating her victims with whips.

At first, the victims were probably peasant girls, but women of higher birth were also involved. It was the fashion for girls from respectable but impoverished homes to be sent to aristocratic courts to acquire social skills and be raised in a manner befitting their status. Elisabeth apparently took full advantage. Parents were told that their daughter had eloped with a lover or died of an illness. Visits by family members were discouraged.

As more girls started to disappear, rumours began to circulate. It was even alleged that some girls from aristocratic families had been kidnapped on Elisabeth's orders.

The countess committed most of her depraved acts at Cachtice Castle. It was said that the people who lived nearby hated her so much that she could only leave with an armed escort.

INVESTIGATING THE RUMOURS

But it was only when the parish priest of Cachtice and some Viennese monks lodged complaints about cries that had been heard at the castle that the rumours were investigated. The emperor, Matthew II, assigned Chief Imperial Prosecutor Thurzo to find out what had been going on and he and his soldiers entered the castle on December 29, 1610. Thurzo himself noted seeing only one body on the night that he searched Cachtice, although one of his lieutenants reported finding bodies or parts of bodies throughout the castle. They also found girls who were still alive and their testimony was heard. A large number of torture devices were also discovered.

A contemporary portrait of Countess Nádasdy shows a graceful and attractive woman. Was it the urge to keep her looks that later drove her to commit torture and murder?

Between 1611 and 1614, when Elisabeth died, more than 300 people were interrogated, but the countess herself was never brought to a formal trial. A number of 'assistants' confessed under torture by Thurzo that they had helped to procure victims and take part in sadistic acts. All had served Elisabeth for many years, one as nurse to her children. Three were executed by being burnt alive barely a week after Thurzo and his men entered Cachtice Castle.

But Elisabeth escaped the death penalty. Her high birth seems to have guaranteed her survival. Executing her would have required the enactment of a special statute to strip her of her royal immunity. It is also likely that Thurzo did not want to strain relations with neighbouring Transylvania, which was governed by Elisabeth's nephew, Gabriel. Her punishment was to be walled up in a suite of rooms in her castle, with only slits left for food. Here she died miserably in the summer of 1614.

The
struggle
for power

2

The
terror from
the north

Even their enemies admired the audacity of the Vikings. Aided by their seamanship and advanced naval technology, their brutal lightning raids sent shock waves throughout Europe for more than 200 years.

The boats used by the Vikings were fast, manoeuvrable and shallow-hulled, so did not require deep harbours to land.

Gazing out to sea, the monks of Lindisfarne were amazed by the sight before them. In boats with carved dragons on their prows, crews of heavily armed Vikings headed for the peaceful island at speed. As soon as they landed, it was clear that the new arrivals were bent on destruction. The monastery was swiftly pillaged of its treasures.

This, one of the first reliably documented attacks carried out by Scandinavian invaders, received the greatest attention in political and ecclesiastical circles. Alcuin, once a monk at Lindisfarne, who had become a scholar at the court of Charlemagne, learned of the raid and made mention of it in his letters to Rome, giving June 8, 793, as the date of the attack. It is often considered to be the beginning of the age of the Vikings, whose sea-launched raids were to terrorise much of Europe.

A NEW NAVAL TECHNOLOGY

Though the inhabitants of the British Isles were accustomed to raids, never before had an enemy arrived without warning from the open sea – a tactic thought to be impossible with the ships in use at the time. But the Vikings were experienced sailors, known to have used an instrument similar to the compass long before it was introduced to the rest of Europe from Arabia at the end of the 12th century. The terrifying appearance of the warships incorporated important technical features that made them potent weapons both at sea and on landing.

In contrast to the broad-beamed merchant ships they used for trading, the Viking dragon boat was a longboat propelled both by oars and by a large square sail. The sturdy hull, made from oak timbers, made the ship seaworthy and resilient – even in the rough waters of the North Sea. They could reach top speeds of up to 20 knots and had a shallow draught of only 1.5 metres. This enabled them to beach quickly on sandy shores and along stretches of coast where there were no harbours – a decisive advantage when carrying out surprise attacks.

Nor were areas further inland safe from the Vikings. The collapsible mast of the boat could be taken down in less than two minutes, meaning that they could sail under river bridges as they progressed inland. In addition to these technological advantages,

The monastery at Lindisfarne was founded by St Aiden in AD 635 and settled by monks from his community at Iona in Scotland. It promoted Christianity throughout the north of England. The renowned Lindisfarne Gospels were probably made at the monastery in the early 700s.

the crews of Viking longboats were very highly motivated. The oarsmen were not spurred on by the whip, but by the prospect of a share of the booty.

STRIKING OUT FROM THE HEARTLANDS

The people collectively known as the Vikings came from Sweden, Norway, Iceland and Denmark. In their home territory, a land of fjords, mountains and stony soils, they lived by farming and herding livestock. The majority of the populace led a harsh and simple life. From the Scandinavian heartlands they spread both north and west. They ventured further than any European people before them and in their travels greatly expanded the bounds of the known world.

In the accounts of contemporaries, the Vikings appear as fearsome warriors whose very appearance instilled fear in other peoples. Yet these descriptions are almost certainly based on the exaggerated accounts of survivors of Viking raids. The stories of wild-haired filthy savages who wore horned helmets and drank from cups made from the skulls of their enemies are far from the historical truth. The Vikings who settled in England were in fact renowned for the frequency with which they bathed.

It may have been that a series of bitter winters and failed harvests in their home territories impelled the Vikings to undertake their raiding missions. Other historians have suggested the opposite: that mild winters and good harvests led to population growth and the need to seek new lands. They may also have been motivated by a geographical shift in the European

economy. The Mediterranean was declining as an economic centre. In 785, Charlemagne had destroyed the Frisian fleet, which interrupted the flow of many trading goods from central Europe to Scandinavia and may have led the Vikings to come looking for the trade themselves.

THE IMPACT OF THE ATTACK ON LINDISFARNE

The brilliant seamanship that had allowed the landing at Lindisfarne was followed by an attack carried out at lightning speed. The Vikings – in this case probably Norwegians – stormed off the ships bearing broadswords, battleaxes and spears. The abbey's livestock was slaughtered and the carcasses loaded onto the ships.

> *'The harrying of the heathen miserably destroyed God's church by rapine and slaughter.'*
>
> REPORT OF THE LINDISFARNE RAID IN THE ANGLO-SAXON CHRONICLE

The monks could offer little resistance. Several were murdered, some were drowned in the sea and others taken on board the longboats as slaves. The Vikings then plundered the monastery's treasures, finally vanishing off to sea as quickly as they had arrived. News of the attack sent shock waves across Europe. The abbey at Lindisfarne was a centre of Christian culture. The raid was perceived as an attack on civilisation in general, an assault by everything that was barbaric on honourable and civilised Christendom.

Clearly, careful planning had gone into the raid; the Vikings had been certain of the wealth and vulnerability of their target.

Viking colonisations

800
Settlement of the Faroe Islands.

870
Norwegian settlement of Iceland by
Ingólfur Árnason.

882-6
Discovery and settlement of Greenland
by Eric the Red.

1000 onward
Eric the Red's son Leif Ericsson began to
explore the coastlines of Newfoundland
and Labrador. Sailing from Greenland, the
Vikings established the first colonies on
American soil. Violent disputes may have
broken out with the native peoples,
forcing a swift withdrawal.

Ecclesiastical institutions, with their lightly-guarded treasures, were to become a favourite target. Richly-decorated metal artefacts found in Scandinavian graves reflect the astonishing hoards of treasure that the Vikings must have amassed from these soft targets.

TWO CENTURIES OF VIKING RAIDS

Before long, the profitability of pillaging became widely known. Norwegian raiders were joined by raiders from Denmark and Sweden, turning the entire coastline of continental Europe into a danger zone. Their armadas would often comprise over 100 ships. During the 50 years that followed the attack on Lindisfarne, the Vikings launched raids to plunder the British Isles and the sea coasts of the European mainland with increasing frequency. In France, which suffered the greatest proportion of raids, they even advanced as far inland as Paris. Many saw the raids as a fulfilment of the Old Testament prophecy, whereby God would visit a dreadful punishment on men for their sins.

Throughout much of coastal Europe – and even further inland – people became terrified of falling victim to a Viking attack. Soon the news that a flotilla of ships had been sighted was enough to create panic.

In Britain, Viking raids during the 9th century were followed by settlement. As the Viking enclaves expanded, the area under their control came to be known as the Danelaw and comprised an area roughly to the north of a line drawn between London and Chester.

In 1017 Viking influence reached its peak when the Danish king Cnut – King Canute of legend – became king of all England, a distant descendant of those Viking raiders of 200 years before.

From emperor to communist

Pu Yi, the last Emperor of the Qing dynasty, was crowned at the age of two but his life was to take an utterly different course from the one mapped out for him.

The coronation of the infant Pu Yi in the Forbidden City was an event of great spendour. It is here imagined in the film of his life, *The Last Emperor*.

The small boy pushed down hard on the pedals of his bicycle and rang the bell as the deferential crowd on the street parted to clear a path for him. His bodyguards ran close behind him. Although, in the Forbidden City, he faced no danger, his servants knew that they could never let the emperor out of their sight. It seemed unimaginable that little Pu Yi, crowned when still a child, would end his days working as a humble gardener.

THE LAST EMPEROR OF THE LAST CHINESE DYNASTY

In November 1908, a two-year-old boy, Pu Yi, was brought to the Forbidden City in Beijing. A few days later, he was installed on the Dragon Throne and as Xuan Tong, Emperor of China, proclaimed ruler over almost half the world's population. A few weeks before, the previous emperor of the Qing Dynasty, Dezong, had died. His wife, the powerful Dowager Empress Cixi, had just enough time to select a successor before she too passed away.

She chose a young relative, Aisin Gioro Pu Yi. His father, Zai Feng, became prince-regent. During the coronation ceremony, Pu Yi shouted out 'I want to go home!' – and his father replied 'Soon it will all be at an end'.

In the early years of the 20th century, China was beset by troubles. Revolts broke out with increasing frequency and both peasants and intellectuals were involved in the protests. On February 12, 1912, the young Xuan Tong was forced to abdicate and China became a republic. His father's premonition had come true: the office of emperor was indeed at an end.

A PRISONER IN A GOLDEN CAGE

Pu Yi was permitted to stay living in the Forbidden City. A decree guaranteed him favourable treatment and generous expenses. He grew up in luxury behind the high walls of the Imperial Palace,

The Forbidden City lies at the centre of the ancient metropolis of Beijing. Construction started in 1406 and was completed 14 years later. It comprises 800 buildings with 9999 rooms and covers 720,000 square metres.

cut off from his subjects in the same way as his ancestors had been. He was still uniquely privileged. At midday, hundreds of dishes were brought for him, although a weak stomach allowed him to taste only a few of them. A huge retinue of servants at the palace included more than 1000 eunuchs and the young man took great pleasure from giving them the runaround.

In December 1922 Pu Yi married for the first time – taking two women at once to be his wives – a First Wife named Wan Rong, and a Subsidiary Wife called Wen Xiu. Both women quickly found life in the Imperial Palace intolerable. Wen Xiu was granted a divorce from Pu Yi and became a teacher, while Wan Rong initially took refuge in smoking huge quantities of opium and conducting affairs with palace servants, before making her escape from the Forbidden City.

In the same year, a new Subsidiary Wife was found for the young emperor, the 17-year-old Tan Yuling. She became Pu Yi's constant, caring companion and he grew extremely fond of her. Their happiness was shortlived: at the age of 24 Tan Yuling died of typhoid. Pu Yi was devastated by her loss. He kept the urn containing her ashes until his death.

THE FORMER EMPEROR IS TAKEN PRISONER

In 1924, Pu Yi had to leave Beijing following widespread revolts. He took refuge first in the Japanese consulate and then in the treaty port of Tianjin. There, he continued to lead a privileged life under Japanese protection and to dream of being reinstated as emperor. In 1932, Japan occupied the northeast of China and proclaimed it as the state of Manchukuo. On March 1, the Japanese authorities installed Pu Yi as emperor over the region. He reigned over the Japanese puppet state until 1945.

At the end of the Second World War the Soviet Red Army occupied Manchukuo. The Japanese tried to fly Pu Yi to Japan, but he was intercepted and arrested. Although he was treated respectfully, he was forbidden contact with the outside world.

In 1949, following the Communist takeover, Pu Yi was handed over to the Chinese authorities and put under arrest as a war criminal. He no longer enjoyed special privileges and was sometimes forced to share a cell with other prisoners.

The Communists decreed that prison inmates were to be re-educated in the ideology of the new regime. Pu Yi was tested on whether he had read and understood all the Communist texts and could demonstrate that he had become a good Communist himself. After 14 years, when he was deemed to be sufficiently 're-educated', Pu Yi was finally released from prison.

LIFE AS AN ORDINARY CITIZEN OF CHINA

Pu Yi arrived in Beijing early on the morning of December 9, 1959. The next day he reported to the police. He was to be employed as a gardener in the botanical gardens. He moved into a small furnished room in the grounds, which he shared with a bookkeeper. Pu Yi devoted himself to learning the principles of horticulture. He enjoyed his work and, for the first time, there was a degree of normality about his life.

In April 1962 he even married again, this time to a 37-year-old nurse called Li Shuxian. The 200 wedding guests reflected the enormous changes that had taken place during Pu Yi's lifetime. They included members of the former royal family, several Communist Party representatives and colleagues from Pu Yi's work.

Pu Yi's new wife was able to help him with aspects of daily life that he had never learned to master. He did not know how to light a fire or cook a meal; he also managed to lose anything that he was given. Attracted partly by Pu Yi's sheer helplessness, Li Shuxian also shared her husband's sense of humour. Pu Yi now led a very simple life. He loved walking and rediscovered the pleasure that he had enjoyed when riding a bike around the Forbidden City as a child.

But this new contentment was not to last. Shortly after the wedding, Pu Yi was diagnosed with cancer of the kidneys. He was also suffering from high blood pressure, an inflamed prostate gland and anaemia.

NO PEACE FOR THE EX-EMPEROR

Along with the collapse in his health, the political situation in China had again become dangerous for Pu Yi. During Mao Ze-dong's Cultural Revolution, he was seen as the embodiment of corrupt imperial rule and subjected to attacks and threats.

As early as September 1966, a woman phoned him, demanding reparation for the ill treatment that she had allegedly received in the Imperial Palace during his reign. She also demanded that the former emperor should hand back the royalties for his recently published autobiography, as the book had been 'damaging' for the Revolution.

Although it later turned out that the woman had never been employed at the palace, Pu Yi hurried anxiously to the authorities to give back his royalty payment. He asked only to be allowed to keep a small part of it to pay for his medical treatment. Such was the public persecution of Pu Yi at this time that even Mao Ze-dong felt obliged to defend the former emperor against the hate campaign being waged against him.

Nevertheless, the attacks on the old man

After the terrors of imprisonment and 're-education', the former emperor found fulfilment in his work as a gardener.

Child rulers

Tutankhamun
The young Pharaoh reigned from c.1347 to 1339 BC and died at the age of 18. His almost untouched tomb was found in 1922.

Henry IV
In order to ensure the royal succession, the Holy Roman Emperor Henry III had his son Henry IV chosen as king at just four years old. His untimely death two years later saw a six-year-old monarch ascend the throne.

Louis XIII
After the murder of his father, Louis XIII ascended the French throne at the age of 9. His mother acted as Regent for him until he came of age. The two kings who succeeded him, Louis XIV and Louis XV, were both enthroned at the age of five.

continued remorselessly. In December, 1966, Pu Yi had to go into hospital again. Members of the Red Guards, the driving force behind the Cultural Revolution, threatened to storm the hospital and turn him out of his room. As a result, he had to be moved to another hospital with less sophisticated facilities. There, his condition grew worse. On the evening of October 16, 1967, the doctors informed his wife that the former emperor would not last the night. Along with other family members, she kept watch at his bedside, until Pu Yi died at half-past two in the morning. Two days later, the body of the last Emperor of China was cremated.

THE EMPEROR'S LIFE ON FILM

Thirty-one years after his death, Pu Yi's fate was once more at the centre of public attention, this time in the West. In his film *The Last Emperor,* the Italian director Bernardo Bertolucci captured the life of the emperor who was 're-educated' into a Communist on celluloid.

The film and documents in which Pu Yi recorded events in his life, portrayed him as a pawn of more powerful forces, but many have pointed out that he had a strong interest in minimising the significance of his political role. Had he been seen as a ruler, not a gardener, he would most likely have been executed.

Mohammed Ahmed el-Sayyid Abdullah was not the first or the last to claim the title of Mahdi, or Chosen One – but his meteoric career certainly left its stamp on history.

The Mahdi –
a holy warrior
in the Sudan

Unjust and corrupt Egyptian rule and growing discontent among the ordinary people prepared the ground in 19th-century Sudan for the coming of an Islamic Messiah as prophesised in the Koran.

Mohammed Ahmed el-Sayyid Abdullah came from nowhere to lead a victorious *jihad* (holy war) against his country's oppressors. His career reached its apogee with the fall of Khartoum, in 1885, an event in European eyes more notable for the tragic death of the celebrated British Major-General Charles Gordon, or Gordon Pasha, who fell leading the defence of the capital. For the next 13 years, the theocratic regime established by the Mahdi and his successor maintained Sudanese independence until a well-equipped Anglo-Egyptian force defeated the hitherto invincible Mahdist hordes at Omdurman in 1898.

THE SEEDS OF REVOLT

The story began many decades earlier, in 1821, when the Egyptians started to expand deep into Sudan, extending the area under their control to almost as far south as the Equator. The colonisation brought misery and discontent. In the north, farmers were driven to bankruptcy by high taxes, but when they moved south to try trading in ivory and slaves, they fared no better. Under pressure from Europe, the Egyptians suppressed the slave trade, while ensuring that they enjoyed rich pickings from ivory dealing. Even worse for many Sudanese, they began to bring in Westerners to fill key positions in their administration.

The most notable of these was Charles Gordon, who had been governor of the southern province of Equatoria until ill-health forced him to resign. But within a few months he returned as Governor General of the entire country. He was a reformer whom many Sudanese came to admire, but he could do nothing to quell their intense and growing hatred of the Egyptians.

Revolt was in the air: what it needed was a leader. The man who filled the role was Mohammed Ahmed. From 1871, inspired by the memory of his great grandfather, a respected religious leader, he journeyed through Sudan, preaching an end to Egyptian rule and a return to the values set out in the Koran. Gradually he recruited an army of fanatical followers until, ten years later, he was ready to proclaim himself the Mahdi. His sheer charisma overcame the tribal divisions that until then had prevented any chance of unity. Under the banner of *jihad*, the Mahdi and his forces began a triumphant progress.

JIHAD IN THE SUDAN

The news finally stirred the Egyptians into action, but the first troops sent out from Khartoum to arrest the Mahdi withdrew in confusion at the strength of the opposition. A second force, and then a third was hacked to pieces. When the 6000-strong garrison of El-Obeid capitulated in early 1883, the south was completely cut off from Khartoum. With no prospect of supplies and reinforcements, it was a matter of time before the governors of the isolated provinces would be forced to surrender.

By now, the British were heavily involved in Egypt, having intervened to put down a nationalist revolt. But they refused to intervene in the Upper Nile, so the Egyptians were left to fend for themselves. They assembled a 15,000-strong army under Colonel William Hicks and marched south. Guides who had gone over to the Mahdi led Hicks and his men to a grim fate. Exhausted and dying of thirst, they were encircled and massacred. Only 300 escaped. Hicks himself fell on the battlefield.

The Egyptian position in Sudan was now desperate. The Mahdi marched north on Khartoum itself, while, still determined to avoid open involvement, the British decided on a total withdrawal. Gordon was sent back to Khartoum to organise the evacuation. But, believing that he had a moral duty to protect loyal Egyptians and Sudanese, he prepared instead to defend the capital, convinced that public opinion at home would force the despatch of a relief force in time to save the situation.

THE FALL OF KHARTOUM

The siege that followed lasted for ten months. Towards the end of the year, food supplies ran out. The Nile was falling and one side of the city was now open to attack. On January 5, 1885, the Mahdi ordered a final assault. Within six hours Khartoum had

The dervishes, whose fanaticism in battle greatly contributed to the success of the Mahdist revolt, wore distinctive flowing white robes.

fallen. Massacre, rape and looting followed. Among the victims was Gordon himself. He, against the Mahdi's express orders, was speared to death on the staircase of the governor's palace, his head cut off, and his body thrown down a well.

Just two days later, the advance guard of the Anglo-Egyptian relief force ran into a hail of hostile fire and turned back down the Nile. Lord Wolesley, the British commander-in-chief in Egypt, ordered a complete withdrawal. At home, William Gladstone, the Liberal Prime Minister who had dispatched Gordon to Egypt, was booed and hissed by a mob at Downing Street. A furious Queen Victoria telegraphed: 'To think that all this might have been prevented and many precious lives saved by earlier action is too fearful.' Gladstone's soubriquet of GOM (Grand Old Man) was swiftly transformed into MOG (Murderer of Gordon).

A THEOCRACY'S RISE AND FALL

The Mahdi did not live long to savour his victory. He died of typhus just six months after the fall of Khartoum. Some said it was a punishment from God for having taken Gordon's life. The task of establishing a government fell to his deputies – the three caliphs chosen in emulation of the prophet Muhammad. In 1891, Abdallahi ibn Muhammad emerged as the undisputed leader and named himself the Khalifa (successor).

The regime survived until 1898, when the British sent another Anglo-Egyptian force. It was commanded by General Sir Herbert Kitchener who had served in Wolesley's expedition 13 years before and learned much from the disaster. Battle was joined on September 1, 1898, outside Omdurman. Some 8000 British regulars and 17,000 Egyptian and Sudanese soldiers took on the Khalifa's 50,000-strong army. Despite the charges of wave after wave of fanatical dervishes, superior Anglo-Egyptian firepower led to their complete rout in just a few hours – the battle started around dawn and finished at about 11.30 in the morning. The Khalifa escaped but perished in battle the following year.

The British triumph was complete. Barbarously, they dug up the Mahdi's corpse and threw it into the Nile. Yet what he had achieved during his relatively brief career could not be banished from history. Indeed, his memory still lives on in Islam today.

Father and son at war

Frederick (centre) was attracted to all the areas of interest that his father (right) despised. Violent disagreements would often flare up between them.

Prince Frederick of Prussia, later celebrated as Frederick the Great, was cultured and artistic. His stern and practical father was known as the 'Soldier King'. As the prince grew older the two clashed repeatedly. The prince became so frustrated that he conceived a grand escape plan – aided by his friend – Lieutenant von Katte.

At seven o'clock on the morning of November 6, 1730, a roll of drums echoed around the courtyard of the fortress at Küstrin (known today as Kostrzyn in western Poland). The bodyguard of Frederick William I of Prussia encircled the condemned man, Lieutenant Hans Hermann von Katte. Above him, a voice begged for von Katte's forgiveness. From his cell in the fortress, Crown Prince Frederick of Prussia was forced to watch the execution of his friend. The lieutenant replied, 'I know of nothing for which you require my forgiveness', and the prince fainted from shock and grief. By the time he had recovered, von Katte had been beheaded. The king was without mercy – von Katte's breach of trust in aiding and abetting the Prince in his attempt to escape the hated parental home was too much to forgive.

A FATHER AND SON AT WAR

But why did the prince want so desperately to escape? Disagreements between fathers and sons were hardly unknown in royal families. Prince Frederick loved music and philosophy. In contrast, his father's main focus of interest was the army. He believed that a powerful military force was the basis of a nation's strength. Funding his army required considerable expenditure – and his own father, Frederick I, had almost bankrupted the kingdom with his predilection for the arts and culture, another reason why the Soldier King was not prepared to allow his son to indulge in such frivolous pastimes.

The unfortunate prince was only able to pursue his musical interests in secret.

He believed that the prince should acquire an interest in administration and economics. He called him 'an effeminate chap' and subjected him to humiliating beatings. The sensitive Prince Frederick, stifled by his father's stern demands, longed to get away. Neither was willing to give ground, and as a result the young Frederick could see only one solution: escape.

THOUGHTS OF ESCAPE

While planning his escape, the Prince enquired of the British ambassador whether he would be welcome in England. But the British government was not enthusiastic about getting drawn into a private dispute between members of the Prussian royal family. So Frederick looked to Paris. Although Prussia was then on the brink of war with France, Frederick scarcely seemed to consider that a flight by the Crown Prince into enemy territory would provoke a scandal. But he knew he could never hope to evade his father's strict surveillance on his own. He needed an accomplice or, better still, a good friend.

A WILLING ACCOMPLICE

Lieutenant von Katte, a dashing officer of the royal bodyguard, loved adventure. He cheerfully boasted of being the Crown Prince's best friend. Together, they hatched a succession of escape plans. Von Katte's ideas had a theatrical flavour: a clandestine meeting with the English ambassador took place under the castle gate at midnight. His romantic notion of conspiracy did little to ensure that the matter was kept secret. The whole court soon knew of Frederick's plans and they were openly discussed, since no one took them seriously. It seemed unlikely that they would ever be put into practice. Nor did that seem to be the young men's intention. He and von Katte refined every last detail of the escape without ever settling on a date for it – until the king's actions led the conspirators to put their plan into action after all.

THE DIE IS CAST

Out of the blue, Frederick William announced to the court that he intended to show his son the wider world. The prince would accompany his father on a journey through the German principalities to learn the skills of diplomacy. Enchanted by the idea, Frederick forgot all thoughts of escape. But the period of harmony with his father was brief. Stringent security on the trip kept the prince under constant supervision. When the king reprimanded him in public, at Freudenstadt, in western Germany, it was the last straw. He had to get away – it was now or never. A glance at the map showed him that in a few days'

The first kings of Prussia

Frederick I
On January 18, 1701, Elector Frederick III of Brandenburg crowned himself Frederick I, 'King in Prussia.' His love of splendour and the arts almost ruined his country's finances.

Frederick William I
Laid the financial, administrative and military foundations for the expansion of the Prussian state.

Frederick II
Known as Frederick the Great, he made Prussia into a major European power, above all in the three wars he fought over Silesia. Internally, his reign was characterised by an openness to the ideas of the Enlightenment and by absolutist rule.

time, their route would take them close to the French border. Surely he would never again be presented with such a favourable opportunity to flee?

Von Katte, accompanying the royal party as a member of the guard, had received money and jewels over the long months of planning. He was responsible for supplying the prince with fresh horses during the escape. Frederick's only concern now was how to evade his minders. He bribed one of the king's pages to come along with the horses. Everything was now in place.

The royal party stopped for the night at the village of Steinfurt. Because they only had to cover a short distance the next day, the king decided to make a late start. Frederick saw his chance. He sent a letter to alert von Katte and the page was instructed to ready the horses for three o' clock in the morning. They reckoned that two hours would be enough to reach the French border. It was unlikely that anyone in the royal camp would have even noticed his absence before he reached France.

THE ESCAPE FAILS

As Frederick waited for his horse, one of the king's spies appeared at his rendezvous with the page. The page lost his nerve and revealed his role in the plot. At first Frederick William was at a loss what to do. As they were still on the road, he decided to delay arresting his son until they returned home.

Frederick quickly sensed that something had gone wrong. Though he had been closely monitored before, now his minders refused to let him out of their sight. Once they had crossed back into Prussia, his fears were confirmed. His father reproached him angrily and ordered that he be thrown in prison. The prince did not try to deny any of the accusations or to conceal the part played by his accomplice. He had sent a warning letter to von Katte and believed that his friend had escaped. In fact, the lieutenant had already been arrested. As he was repeatedly interrogated, the truth began to emerge.

THE KING SHOWS NO MERCY

Frederick William proceeded strictly by the book. A court martial was set up to try the conspirators and a court hearing held on

October 25, 1730. The cautious judges reached agreement. As loyal subjects, they were reluctant to pass judgment on a member of the royal household. They commended him to the mercy of his father, but also let it be known that, in their opinion, the period of detention that Frederick had suffered since his arrest was already punishment enough.

In the case of von Katte, the judges decided on a guilty verdict but put the final sentence into the hands of the king. As a member of the royal bodyguard, von Katte had sworn an oath of loyalty that he had broken. To Frederick William, such an act of betrayal was deserving of the death penalty. With a stroke of his pen the king sealed the fate of his son's friend and a few days later the sentence was carried out.

The imprisoned Prince Frederick is forced to look on as his friend von Katte is led to his execution.

A FRAGILE ACCORD

It was claimed by many that Prince Frederick and von Katte were more than friends and the writer Voltaire implied that Frederick was homosexual. Certainly, his marriage to Elisabeth Christine von Braunschweig-Bevern in 1733 seems to have been primarily a means of atoning for his past behaviour to his father. The union yielded no children and it appears that Frederick largely ignored his wife.

By the late 1730s the prince and his father seem to have reached a peace of sorts. The king gave Frederick the chateau of Rheinsberg. Here he gathered a company of musicians, actors and other artists who made music and performed plays. He also came to form strong opinions about the nature of kingship and in 1739 published a work in which he opposed the views espoused by Machiavelli in *The Prince*.

A GREAT KING

As part of his rapprochement with his father, Frederick at last studied administration and economics. From 1740, when he ascended the Prussian throne, he aimed to make his small nation a major player on the European stage.

To this end, he encouraged its fledgling industries, reformed the taxation system, abolished torture and granted religious freedom. In a series of wars – mainly against the Habsburgs of Austria – he became admired as a military tactician.

'His picture hung in the meanest hovel and the grandest house; he became a legend in his own lifetime.'

THOMAS MANN ON FREDERICK THE GREAT.

Frederick's legacy was political and cultural. He established a civil service with a code based on a respect for law and ethics. Magificent buildings such as the State Opera and St Hedwig's Cathedral in Berlin, and the palace of Sanssouci in Potsdam – a rococo masterpiece – were built under his patronage.

The iconic guerrilla

Ernesto 'Ché' Guevara, an asthmatic Argentinian doctor, was hailed as one of the liberators of Cuba. He ended his days disgraced and out of favour, and was executed in the Bolivian rainforest. Yet he remains for many the quintessential revolutionary.

The city of Havana was buzzing with sheer joy as Cuba's citizens celebrated the deposal of the hated dictator Fulgencio Batista by troops of the liberation army. The revolutionaries had seized control of Havana and on January 8, 1959, they entered the city in a triumphant victory parade. At the head of the parade was Fidel Castro, the 'Lider Maximo' or 'Great Leader' of the country, his brother Raúl, and the hero of the decisive battle, Ernesto 'Ché' Guevara.

THE UNLIKELY REVOLUTIONARY

Ernesto Guevara was not an obvious candidate to become a guerrilla fighter. Born on June 14, 1928, in the Argentinian city of Rosario, his family was upper middle class and he suffered from asthma. But he was not to be constrained either by his background or his illness. He was deliberately unconventional, a sloppy dresser who washed infrequently, with the result that his friends nicknamed him 'pig'. But the young man had another more serious side. When his father's business ventures ran into difficulties, he got a job with the city engineer's department to help the family with its financial problems.

Guevara's own illness was probably an important factor in his decision to study medicine in Buenos Aires. In the winter of 1951, during his time at medical school, he set off with his friend Alberto Granado to travel around South America. On the journey, he came to know the continent and many of its problems and contradictions: peasants scratching a harsh existence from tiny plots of land, despotic landowners, displaced Amerindian peoples and priests who studiously ignored the plight of their flocks in their sermons. 'This aimless wandering around ... has changed me more than I could have imagined,' he confided in his diary. Following this trip, he felt a burning desire to change the world; he now knew what his goal in life was to be.

'Ernesto Guevara gave life to the social Utopias and dreams of an entire generation.'

JORGE CASTAÑEDA, CHÉ'S BIOGRAPHER.

After qualifying as a doctor in 1953, Guevara left Argentina to work in a leprosy ward in Bolivia. Next year he moved to Guatemala where the country's president Jacobo Arbenz Guzmán had instituted a radical programme of land reform. A military coup was organised by the USA to topple Guzmán and Guevara tried to organise resistance against those carrying out the putsch. It was during this period that he became a confirmed communist.

ERNESTO BECOMES 'CHÉ'

Guevara's travels took him ever further north. While working at a hospital in Mexico City, he married a Peruvian woman, Hilda Gadea Acosta, the mother of his daughter Hilda Beatriz. During this time, Guevara came to know Raúl and Fidel Castro. The young Cuban brothers had fled from Batista and were looking for a doctor to join their small guerrilla group. They planned to depose the Cuban ruler, who had been in illegal control in Havana since March 1952, after staging a military coup. Ernesto took up their offer. He became known to his comrades as 'Ché', a term that translates roughly into English as 'mate' or 'comrade'.

On November 25, 1956, Ché Guevara, the Castro brothers and 79 other Cuban exiles boarded the yacht *Granma*. The crossing to Cuba was nightmarish, with the ship in constant danger of foundering. When the exhausted group finally made landfall on December 2, 1956, they were discovered by a coastguard ship and came under attack from the Cuban airforce. Then, on December 5, they became involved in a firefight with the dictator's troops. Just 15 guerrillas escaped from the fierce skirmish and withdrew into the Sierra Maestra.

From the mountains, the small band, led by the Castro brothers and Ché Guevara, organised an uprising against the Cuban armed forces, winning wide support among the people. The rebels began to enjoy ever greater military success, emerging victorious time and again from encounters with the regular army. Finally, on New Year's Eve, 1958, they captured the city of Santa Clara. Ché was the hero of this final set-piece battle. Just over two years after their disastrous landing, the revolutionaries entered the capital Havana, after the dictator Batista had fled to the Dominican Republic. A few days later, the city prepared a triumphant welcome for Fidel Castro.

Despite his asthma, the young Guevara was a keen athlete and a sports fan throughout his life. He excelled in strenuous sports such as rugby. Here he (left) and Fidel Castro are playing a game of baseball.

A REVOLUTIONARY BECOMES A LEGEND

On February 7, 1959, the government proclaimed Guevara 'a Cuban citizen by birth'. He was appointed chief of the National Institute for Land Reform and then President of the National Bank, signing Cuba's new banknotes with the three letters 'CHE.' Despite his official government posts, his principal role was as the leading ideologue of the new regime. As early as 1959, Guevara helped organise revolutionary expeditions in Panama and the Dominican Republic, all of which failed. On June 2, 1959, he married again, to his comrade-in-arms Aleida March.

Ché's present-day fame was sealed by a particular incident in 1960. The French freighter *La Coubre*, laden with 70 tonnes of weapons, exploded in Havana harbour on March 4, killing 75 and injuring more than 200 people. As Guevara stood with Castro at a memorial service for the victims, he approached the edge of the podium. The photographer Alberto Korda captured the now world-famous shot showing Ché Guevara with a pensive expression under a beret adorned with a red star.

On February 23,1961 Ché Guevara was appointed Cuba's Minister for Industry. But he was increasingly unhappy with the day-to-day business of government. As Minister, he negotiated with the Soviet Union about arms supplies, a situation that triggered the dangerous Cuban Missile Crisis of 1962. In the aftermath, fierce criticism was directed at the Soviet advisors, while the Russians were loath to support Guevara's plans to industrialise Cuba, preferring instead to revive the traditional monoculture of sugar-cane.

To escape the intractable political situation in Cuba, Guevara travelled to Africa, where he planned to establish a guerrilla network that could operate simultaneously in Africa, Asia and South America. His attempt to instigate a revolution in the Congo based on the guerrilla tactics used in Cuba was a

Travels of a revolutionary

Disillusioned with political developments in his own country, Ché Guevara took several trips to promote the revolutionary cause on a global scale.

1964 to 66
Guevara travelled around a number of African states and set up a guerrilla group in the Congo.

April to June 1966
Guevara established similar revolutionary cells in South America, in Brazil, Paraguay, Argentina and Bolivia.'

December 1966
He returned once more to Bolivia, where he was executed on October 9, 1967.

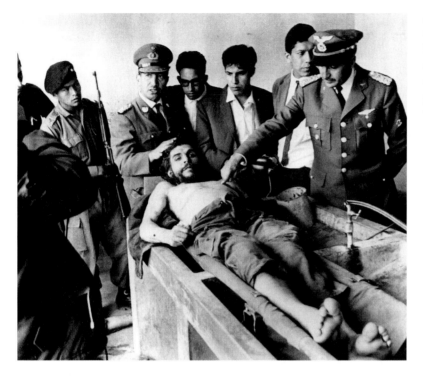

At 1.10 pm on October 9 Guevara was executed by NCO Mario Teran and his corpse placed on a stretcher and photographed as proof that he was dead.

failure. He spent the next six months in Africa and eastern Europe, putting together a memoir of the experience.

In October 1965 Castro publicly read out a letter of resignation from Ché Guevara. Even today, it is not clear who was the author of the document. Shortly after Guevara returned to Cuba he embarked on his final revolutionary enterprise – to spark revolution in Bolivia. Guevara and his guerrilla group clashed with the Bolivian army in March 1967. After seeing proof of his presence in the country, Bolivian president René Barrientes apparently called for Guevara's head to be displayed on a pike in La Paz. On October 8, 1967, the surviving members of his force walked into an ambush in the Quebrada del Churo gorge.

Guevara himself was forced to surrender after a bullet hit his leg. He was held prisoner in the schoolhouse in the jungle village of La Higuera, where his captors carried out orders from Barrientes that he was to be executed. But instead of disposing of a dangerous guerrilla fighter, the Bolivian government created a legend, whose picture has been carried ever since as an icon of revolution by demonstrators around the world.

How
Ivan became
terrible

Ivan IV was one of the most
bloodthirsty tyrants in history.
He more than merits his nickname:
'the Terrible'. But early in his reign
it seemed that he was going to
be a benevolent and enlightened
tsar. So what made Ivan into
the monster that he was,
and how did it all go
so dreadfully wrong
for Russia?

On November 19th, 1581,
Ivan beat his son's wife
because he felt that she
was wearing the wrong
clothes. The son – also
named Ivan – went to
his father to remonstrate.
The tsar lost his temper
and struck his son with
the iron-tipped staff he
always carried. One blow
made a deep hole in the
prince's temple, and he
died a few days later.

The character of Ivan the Terrible was as complex as it was cruel. His bouts of unrestrained bloodlust alternated with periods of equally extreme public repentance. He was deeply religious, but thought nothing of butchering priests who displeased him or ransacking churches for their gold. He was perhaps the most erudite and intelligent man in all Russia, but his political and personal judgment was disastrously flawed. One need not look far to uncover the first source of his ills: it was his appallingly violent and unhappy childhood.

A CHILDHOOD OF MISERY

It was Ivan's great misfortune to come to the throne when he was just three years old. His father's death in 1533 caused a three-way power struggle between his forceful mother and the two leading families of the boyars (noblemen), the Belskys and the Shuiskys. The tussle for control of Muscovy was played out murderously in the corridors of the Kremlin. Ivan regularly witnessed beatings and assassinations as one or other faction set out to destroy its enemies. One night, the metropolitan of the Orthodox Church was chased into the room where Ivan slept. As he was beaten and dragged away, the priest begged the boy to protect him.

When Ivan was eight, his mother was poisoned by the boyars, and her lover Obolensky was walled up in a dungeon and left to starve. Obolensky's sister was Ivan's nurse, and the boy loved her dearly. When the soldiers came to take her away, he had to be prised weeping from her neck. He never saw her again. And so the boy grew up horribly neglected. 'My brother Yuri and I were orphans in the absolute sense of the word,' he later wrote. The boyars who ruled in Ivan's name abused or ignored him: 'They treated us like foreigners or beggars. How many privations we endured! We often lacked both food and clothing. We were not brought up as children should be.'

Ivan was keenly aware that the suffering he endured was all due to men who were supposed to be his subjects. The injustice of it ate into his soul like acid. At the same time, he was daily afraid that he would be the next to be poisoned or hacked or cudgelled to death. One historian has remarked that long before he became Ivan the Terrible, he was Ivan the Terrified.

VIOLENCE AS THE KEY TO SURVIVAL

Everything that Ivan witnessed as a boy taught him that mercilessness was the key to survival, and now he began to teach himself the rudiments of cruelty. At the age of nine or ten, his greatest pleasure (apart from reading works of theology) was torturing birds. He would hurl cats and dogs from the battlements of the Kremlin, and then run down after them and watch their death throes. He became fascinated by the effects of pain. As a young teenager he and his gang would ride out like bandits to terrorise peasants in the surrounding countryside. By the age of 13 he was a practised thug and an experienced rapist.

At the same age Ivan finally felt strong enough to challenge the boyars. During a banquet in the Kremlin he stood up and accused Andrei Shuisky, the head of the Shuisky clan, of usurping his royal powers. It was an eloquent denunciation that stunned the boyars into silence. Shuisky was dragged from the hall by Ivan's bodyguards and thrown to his ravenous hunting dogs. They tore him apart in the street.

THE FIRST TSAR OF RUSSIA

Three years later, in 1547, Ivan had himself crowned. His predecessors had styled themselves Grand Dukes of Muscovy, but Ivan insisted on the title 'tsar', a contraction of the Latin *caesar*. He believed that he was descended from Caesar Augustus, and that autocratic power was his imperial birthright. The term tsar also had religious connotations. In the Russian translation of the Bible it is the word used for anointed kings: David, the builder of the holy city of Jerusalem, is Tsar David in Russian. Jesus, King of the Jews, is the tsar *iudeisky* – the 'Jewish Tsar'. To Ivan, both the glory of Rome and the mystery of the Kingdom of God were represented in the concept of 'tsar', with him as its earthly embodiment.

Despite Ivan's cruel streak and growing megalomania, the first decade or so of his reign was peaceful and progressive. In these years he codified Russia's laws; he created a standing army of musketeers; he clamped down on the ungodly behaviour of the priesthood, and drew attention to the many copying errors in the holy texts being produced in the monasteries – usually the fault of drunken monks. To combat the debasement of the Holy Writ he introduced the printing press to Russia. He gathered around himself some good advisers, not least his devout and kindly wife Anastasia, whom he chose from a family of minor Russian nobles. He also established the *zemsky sobor*, a 'Council of Nobles' which, in another land, might have developed into something like a parliament. If Ivan had died at this point he would be remembered as one of Russia's better rulers.

THE REIGN OF TERROR BEGINS

Ivan did in fact fall gravely ill in 1553. As he lay close to death, the boyars plotted the succession. They were certain he would not survive, and had no intention of allowing Ivan's son to take the throne. But they were reckless enough to speak of their plans within hearing of the delirious tsar. When, to their horror, Ivan recovered, the vengeful, suspicious side of his character came to the fore. From this point on his character began to deteriorate in the most alarming way. This degeneration was possibly due in part to mental damage caused by his illness, which may have been a form of encephalitis, a swelling of the brain.

St Basil's Cathedral was commemmorate the capture by Russia of the Khanate of Kazan. Built between 1555 and 1561, it has nine chapels built on a single foundation. According to legend, Ivan had the architect, Postnik Lakovlev, blinded so that he would not be able to create a more magnificent building for anyone else.

Ivan's first victims were the boyars who had hoped for his death. They were arrested one by one and brutally tortured. The bloodletting might have ended with that, but for another misfortune. In 1560 Ivan's beloved wife died suddenly. He was distraught, and he naturally suspected murder by poison. Another crop of suspects was harvested from among the ranks of the nobles, then yet another from the names they provided under agonies of torture. The killings took on a momentum of their own, and continued long after their original pretext, the search for Anastasia's assassins, was forgotten. This purge swallowed up the last of Ivan's gifted counsellors: he killed them all.

AN ABSOLUTE RULER

Anastasia had probably been the only person who ever loved Ivan; she was certainly the only one who could calm his rages and his paranoia. Now that she was gone, he began to plummet towards insanity. In 1564 Ivan did the most extraordinary thing. Without a word of warning, he left the Kremlin in a cavalcade of sleighs laden with treasure. He did not say where he was going, or when he was coming back. It looked like a wordless, aimless abdication, and it horrified the Russian people: what would happen if there were no tsar? Who would protect them? A harsh father is surely better than no father at all! A delegation of boyars was sent to find Ivan and beg him to return. They caught up with him at the monastery of Alexandrovsk, about 60 miles from Moscow. After a month of pleading, Ivan agreed to return – but on one condition: from now on his every word would be absolute law. No-one – not the Church, not the nobility – would have any right to criticise him or disobey his commands. The boyars gratefully agreed to Ivan's demands.

IVAN'S MOUNTED POLICE – THE *OPRICHNIKI*

Back in Moscow, Ivan created a novel instrument of government to enforce this new deal. It was a mounted police force made up of ruthless and ambitious young men whose job was to root out Ivan's enemies. The *oprichniki*, as they were called, were fanatical Ivan-worshippers, a kind of cross between a monastic order and a Gestapo unit. Each man carried a broom and a dog's head on his saddle to symbolise their cleansing mission and their faithfulness to the tsar. They patrolled the countryside, and wrought indiscriminate terror and death wherever they went.

The worst episode in the nightmare that descended on Russia was the sack of Novgorod. Ivan decided that the entire town was plotting against him, and he went with his *oprichniki* to punish it. An orgy of murder and torture lasted days, and outdid

anything inflicted on Russia by the Mongol horde. So many
were butchered that the river was clogged with mutilated bodies.
Ivan's personal sadism reached new heights. The torments
seemed to give him a sexual thrill – and to bring on a spiritual
ecstasy too. He often went straight from the bloodsoaked
dungeons to his harem, or to prayer in the nearest church.

From Novgorod Ivan went to Pskov. On arrival, he visited
the cell of a renowned hermit named Nikolai. Nikolai turned out
to be a wildman, naked except for the chains he draped around
himself. The hermit looked at the tsar and offered him a piece of
raw meat. 'I am a Christian,' said Ivan. 'I do not eat meat during
Lent.' 'You do worse,' said Nikolai. 'You feed on human flesh
and blood.' Ivan left the monk in peace, and left Pskov too,
leaving the people convinced they had been spared by a miracle.

A TERRIFYING FORCE OF NATURE

By now, Ivan was known among his people by the soubriquet
grozny. This word, usually translated as 'terrible', contains no
moral judgment in Russian. A closer rendering would be
'fearsome' or 'awe-inspiring'. The word is related to the Russian
for 'thunderstorm', and perhaps this provides a clue to the
meaning of Ivan's reign. To the people, his behaviour was as
elemental and unpredictable as lightning. The tsar's wrath came
directly from God, and it was not for any mortal to question His
blessing or His curse. Ivan certainly saw himself as a divine force.
The torments he inflicted on his enemies were the judgment of
God, they were the torments of hell that awaited his victims in
even fuller measure the moment they were dead.

Ivan felt genuine remorse for one death only – that of his
first-born son – caused by one of his terrible rages. Ivan wept for
his son, but also for himself. He had destroyed his own bloodline.
His royal house became extinct when he died in 1584. There
followed an interregnum so chaotic and homicidal that even by
comparison with Ivan's reign it is called 'The Time of Troubles'.
This period ended when the boyars elected a new tsar, a relative
of Ivan's wife Anastasia. The new ruler was Mikhail Romanov.
His dynasty ruled Russia, for good or ill, for more than 300 years
– until the Russian Revolution put an end to tsardom altogether.

Journalist
or warmonger?

William Randolph Hearst built up the first media empire of the 20th century. He seemed prepared to go to any lengths to scoop his rivals – even as far as encouraging the government to go to war.

Orson Welles and Joseph Cotten in *Citizen Kane*. The central character, the ruthless newspaper magnate Charles Foster Kane, was widely believed to have been inspired in part by Hearst.

William Randolph Hearst acquired his first newspaper in 1887, when his father George Hearst accepted the *San Francisco Examiner* in payment for a gambling debt. He gave the business to his son, then 23 and having been expelled from Harvard University, in search of a profession. Abandoning his studies, Hearst quickly began to mould the paper to his own design. Grandly known as 'The Monarch of the Dailies', it had huge dramatic headlines and was liberally illustrated. A raft of talented journalists were hired to concentrate on sensational stories with a straightforward style. A new newspaper audience was born and the paper's circulation figures vindicated Hearst's approach.

THE BIRTH OF THE 'GUTTER PRESS'

In 1895 Hearst bought the *New York Morning Journal*. At the time New York already had 14 newspapers, including the *New York World*, which was owned by Hearst's former mentor at Harvard, Joseph Pulitzer. Hearst immediately engaged in a bitter circulation war with Pulitzer. He increased the number of pages in the *Morning Journal* while reducing the price to one cent. He imitated Pulitzer's bold editorial style but used larger, more eyecatching headlines throughout the paper, and had no qualms about recruiting several of his rival's star reporters.

In the battle for circulation, Hearst and Pulitzer pounced on the revolt that had broken out in Cuba against Spanish colonial rule. Both papers ran exaggerated reports of the uprising and ran previously unseen pictures of the abuse of the Cuban people by the Spanish authorities. Hearst even declared that only the rebels could be trusted to supply reliable information. Conservative papers were outraged by this biased approach, but the public appetite for Hearst's sensationalism grew. Reports written exclusively from the rebels' viewpoint, with stories of Spanish rogues and Cuban heroes, were exactly what they wanted to read. The *Morning Journal*'s circulation rose from 77,000 copies daily to over a million.

THE 'YELLOW PRESS'

During the period of intense competition between Hearst and Pulitzer, Pulitzer's *World* ran a regular comic strip known as 'The Yellow Kid' after the colour of the title character's clothes. At the beginning of 1896, Hearst wooed the artist who drew the cartoon over to the *Journal*. So Pulitzer took on a new artist and continued to print the same comic strip. Both papers now had a comic strip printed in yellow with the same title – and the term 'yellow press' came to be generally applied to the downmarket 'gutter' newspapers.

'YOU FURNISH PICTURES. I'LL FURNISH WAR'

In reporting of the Cuban revolution, Hearst made it clear that he considered war to be the only solution of the conflict. It has even been claimed that he was actually responsible for the outbreak of the Spanish–American War, which ended with the cession of Cuba to the USA. It is hard to dispute that conduct of the Spanish-American War was heavily influenced by the reports in the yellow press. In 1897, illustrator Frederick Remington was sent to Cuba to be on the spot when the war broke out. When Remington wired that there was no war as yet, Hearst is said to have telegraphed back 'You furnish pictures. I'll furnish war'.

As a young newspaper editor, Hearst published exposés of city and financial corruption. He was even prepared to attack companies in which his own family held a stake.

When the war broke out, Hearst travelled to Cuba himself to report directly from the war zone. One of his reporters took part in an attack on a Spanish blockhouse, during which he was wounded. Hearst apparently said to him, 'I'm sorry you've been wounded. But wasn't it a great battle? We'll scoop every other paper in the world with this!' Circulation figures were his ultimate prize, not least because of the political influence associated with them.

THE WOULD-BE POLITICIAN

In his pursuit of his ambitions, Hearst overstepped the mark on a number of occasions. He published negative articles on the US president William McKinley and even called for his assassination. When the President was indeed assassinated in 1901, public opinion was outraged. But the furore did not have any lasting impact on Hearst's success. He continued to buy up newspapers across the United States and to found new ones. He served in Congress between 1902 and 1907; but his candidacy for Mayor of New York failed, as did his bid for the office of Governor of New York State. Although he was keen to be the Democrats Presidential candidate, Hearst failed to get a nomination. An opponent of the British Empire, Hearst opposed United States involvement in the First World War and attacked the formation of the League of Nations.

Though he was unable to make a serious impact as a politician, Hearst continued to influence political life through his media empire. In the end he owned more than two dozen publications, among them *The Los Angeles Examiner, The Boston American, The Chicago Examiner, The Washington Times* and *Washington Herald,* radio stations, film companies and a press agency. At the peak of the Hearst news empire in 1928, 20-30 per cent of Americans read one of his newspapers.

AT ODDS WITH HIS READERSHIP

But Hearst's politics were increasingly at odds with those of his readers. His papers had been initially supportive of working people and trade unions, but they soon adopted the opposite standpoint. As he grew older, Hearst became a staunch conservative who in the mid-1930s published a series of articles in favour of the Nazi regime. In the 1940s his papers campaigned against communism, minorities and the use of marijuana.

The late 1920s were the heyday of Hearst's media empire but the Wall Street Crash of 1929 dealt a devastating blow to the company and he gradually lost control of his newspaper holdings. It is unlikely that this part of the business was ever profitable – it was propped up by profits from other parts of the Hearst Corporation – including mining and forestry. The Crash, the subsequent depression and a court mandated reorganisation in 1936, when the Hearst Corporation was unable to service its debts, forced Hearst to relinquish overall control, although he retained a personal fortune of more than $200 million.

THE BATTLE OVER *CITIZEN KANE*

In 1941, actor and director Orson Welles filmed *Citizen Kane* – about the meteoric rise of a media magnate and his moral decline. The film was clearly influenced by Hearst's life and he tried to prevent its distribution. He was particularly incensed about the negative portrayal of his mistress, actress Marion Davies. He failed to stop the film being shown, but ordered his newspapers and magazines not to print any articles about or advertising for the film which had received good reviews elsewhere. He also spread rumours that Welles was a communist. On its release *Citizen Kane* was a commercial flop, although today it is celebrated as a masterpiece of cinematic history.

Although most of the
Templars were arrested
in 1307, the trials against
them lasted for the next
seven years. In March
1314, the last Grand
Master of the order was
burnt at the stake.

Death on Friday the thirteenth

In destroying the powerful Order of the Knights
Templar and seizing their assets, Philip the Fair of
France was able to solve his debt crisis at a stroke.
The date of their downfall has been regarded as an
omen of bad luck ever since.

On Friday, October 13, 1307, agents of Philip IV simultaneously arrested all the members of the order of the Knights Templars in France. They were tortured into admitting heresy and hundreds were condemned to death and executed in show trials. The order was completely destroyed.

The Templars had long been victims of vicious rumours in France – including heresy and various depraved acts – but with the protection of the Pope, as well as their immense wealth, they must have considered themselves untouchable. A combination of public ill-will and a debt-ridden but powerful king, were to prove their undoing.

THE TEMPLARS COME INTO BEING

Following the capture of Jerusalem in 1099 during the First Crusade, pilgrims could travel to the Holy Land for the first time in years. Many never made it as far as Jerusalem, victims of bandits and brigands along the pilgrimage routes. In 1118 nine knights founded a new order in the city. In addition to the traditional vows of poverty, chastity and obedience its members were obliged to protect pilgrims. When Baldwin II of Jerusalem bequeathed them his former palace in the city, built on the site of the ancient Temple of Solomon, they immediately became known as the 'Knights Templar' or 'Templars'.

Philip IV ruled France from 1285 to 1314. Dubbed 'Le Bel' because of his handsome appearance, he was a corrupt and ruthless king with ambitions to be head of a European empire. Before destroying the Templars he had already persecuted the Jews and the Lombards.

POOR KNIGHTS, BUT A WEALTHY ORDER

On joining the Templars, a knight would take a vow of poverty and bequeath his worldly goods to the community. In this way and also through donations from rulers and other wealthy individuals, the Templars amassed an enormous fortune. In around 1135, the Templars began to make loans from their holdings. Sixty years later, the interest on such loans had become their main source of income – an enterprise expressly sanctioned by the Pope even though ordinary Christians were not allowed under any circumstances to act as usurers. The Templars proved canny bankers. At the height of their power the 15,000 members were managing more than 9000 estates throughout Europe.

When the Templars withdrew from the Holy Land in 1291, their commitment to protect pilgrims and pilgrimage routes became superfluous. The moneylending business continued unabated and the order's great wealth ensured that its members could lead a comfortable life in Europe. But unlike the Knights Hospitallers, who had taken control of the island of Malta, or the Teutonic Order which had established the state of Prussia, the Templars still relied on the power of their wealth alone.

A KING IN NEED OF CASH

In the 80 years since the foundation of the order, states had become far more consolidated entities. Kings and emperors began to resent the power of the Church. And one of them, the ambitious Philip IV of France was in desperate need of money and was willing to do anything to get hold of it. In 1305, there had been a plan to unite the religious fighting orders into a single order known as the Knights of Jerusalem. Philip was keen to be the supreme ruler and control the revenues of the proposed order and even made this suggestion to Rome, although the plan eventually came to nothing.

At the start of the 14th century, the Templars' wealth in France was so great that Philip feared them as potential political rivals. When it was suggested to him that he could eradicate the order and use its wealth to clear the state's mountain of debt, he found the idea irresistible.

Initially, the king tried to get Pope Boniface VIII to excommunicate the Templars. When he refused, Philip had him kidnapped and so ill-treated that he died shortly afterward. Boniface IX, who replaced him, was reputed to have been poisoned by the king's agent. Pope Clement V agreed to Philip's demands and later moved the papacy to Avignon. Once he had papal approval, Philip's operation against the order quickly swung into

The Templars

Foundation
The order of the Knights Templar was founded in Jerusalem in 1119. It took as its uniform a white tunic emblazoned with a red Maltese cross.

Dissolution
Pope Clement V dissolved the Templars on March 22, 1312.

Reformation
The Templars reformed in Scotland, Portugal and Northern Italy. They were even readmitted to France under Napoleon.

The Templars today
The headquarters of the charitable order, which is still not recognised by the Pope, is Jerusalem. It has around 5000 members.

action. First, he undermined their reputation with propaganda. It was claimed that on their initiation to the order the Templars were expected to spit three times on the Cross, deny Christ's resurrection and enter into homosexual relationships.

TORTURE AND SHOW TRIALS

Then the king really went onto the offensive; almost all the Templars were thrown into jail. Torture was used to extract confessions, many of which were later retracted.

The trials were a sham, at which the verdict was a foregone conclusion: death by burning at the stake. On March 22, 1312, Pope Clement V dissolved the Templars. Their possessions were impounded and transferred to the Knights Hospitallers, but not before the state had stripped out the exorbitant cost of the trials. And even the Hospitallers were not granted the possessions of the Templars for free, but instead had to pay large sums of money to the king. By the time the last Grand Master of the Knights Templar, Jacob de Molay, was burnt at the stake in Paris on March 18, 1314, and invoked the wrath of heaven on the king and Pope, Philip had managed to completely clear his debts.

He did not have long to savour his success; both he and Clement V died later that year – Jacob de Molnay's curse apparently having wrought its revenge on both of them.

The Templars had four categories of brothers: knights, with heavy cavalry; sergeants, with light cavalry and of a lower social order; farmers, who administered the property; and chaplains, who were ordained priests.

Stealing Lenin's crown

Lenin held no formal position within the Bolshevik Party or the new state. He was leader of the Bolsheviks just because he always had been, solely by dint of his own personal authority. There was no specific job that a pretender to Lenin's mantle could aspire to.

Lenin was the mastermind of the Russian Revolution, and his successor Stalin transformed the Soviet Union into a socialist superpower. Stalin portrayed himself as Lenin's most loyal disciple and as his natural heir. But the truth is that the dying Lenin tried desperately to remove Stalin from office.

On 30 August, 1918, Vladimir Lenin, the leader of Soviet Russia, gave a speech to workers at the Mikhelson factory in Moscow. As he was walking back to his car a young woman named Fanny Kaplan shot him three times in the neck. While his life hung in the balance, the delicate question of the succession arose. Who would lead the country if Lenin died? And how would a leader be chosen?

THE PROBLEM OF THE SUCCESSION

In the event Lenin recovered and returned to work. Over the next three years, as the Bolsheviks fought and won a bitter civil war with the enemies of the Revolution, an obvious candidate for the post-Lenin leadership emerged. Leon Trotsky, architect of the Red Army, was the only man in the Bolshevik elite who could argue with Lenin on equal intellectual terms. One of the lesser lights in the inner circle was the brooding Joseph Stalin, whose only obvious skill was his talent for organisation. He held the unglamorous post of general secretary, a role which involved appointing all the lower-level party functionaries. He fulfilled this function well, but also used it to his own ends. Party members understood that it was to Stalin alone that they owed their living.

Lenin's fragile health grew worse while he was in power, and in 1922 he suffered two strokes. After the second stroke, he decided to name an heir. But he saw no-one worthy to wear his crown. So instead he wrote a critique of all of his senior comrades, including Trotsky, hoping that the chastened Bolshevik leaders would respond by instituting some form of collective leadership. The harshest words in 'Lenin's Testament' were reserved for Stalin.

Lenin instructed his secretary to hide the document until it could be read out at the next Party Congress. But Lenin's secretaries were reporting everything he did or said directly to Stalin (one of them was Stalin's own wife). Stalin knew that if Lenin's assessment of him became widely known, his political career would be over. In March 1923, Lenin had a blazing row with Stalin. He learned that during his illness Stalin had called Lenin's wife and subjected her to a torrent of abuse for allowing Lenin to dictate a few letters. Stalin claimed his only motivation

Lenin wrote: 'Stalin is too crude, and this defect, which is entirely acceptable in relationships among us as Communists, becomes intolerable in a general secretary. I therefore propose to comrades that they find a way of removing him from this job, and appointing someone who is more tolerant, more loyal, more considerate to comrades, less capricious…'

was a comradely concern for Lenin's health, but he knew that any pronouncement from Lenin now was liable to be damaging to his own interests. Lenin was outraged and dashed off a note demanding that Stalin apologise or relations between them would be at an end.

Stalin was appalled. 'This isn't Lenin speaking, it's his illness', he said, though he must have feared that the game was up. But to Stalin's immense good fortune, Lenin's seething rage brought on a crippling third stroke. It left him barely able to move, and he could not speak at all except in unconnected words: 'Look… congress…Oh hell! Oh hell!' It was Lenin's political life, not Stalin's, that came to an abrupt end.

When the Twelfth Party Congress took place in April 1923, Lenin's closest comrades decided not to make public the leader's criticisms of them. Lenin himself was too ill to insist. So Stalin's authority and powerbase remained intact. He waited impatiently for Lenin to die, and even took to reading medical books to find out how long the old man might hang on. When Lenin eventually expired in January 1924, he launched his bid for power. He mobilised the party faithful to outmanoeuvre Trotsky and other rivals, and by 1928 he was the undisputed leader of the Soviet Union. In the 1930s he unleashed the Great Terror, in which millions of innocent people perished.

Could the Terror have been avoided if Stalin had been removed, according to Lenin's last wishes? Probably not. Political violence was always a Bolshevik method, and the slaughter of rivals was a Russian tradition going back to Ivan the Terrible and beyond. Lenin himself had no qualms about liquidating his enemies, and had used the attempt on his life as a pretext for a bloody purge of political opponents: 'Hang them a hundred to a batch,' he said. With hindsight, this 'Red Terror' looks like a dress rehearsal for Stalin's campaign of state-sponsored mass murder. In this respect at least, Stalin was Lenin's truest disciple.

Lies
and
deception

3

Potemkin
and his
villages

Grigory Potemkin is today barely remembered outside Russia. Most people have heard that he erected pasteboard cottages in the countryside to fool Catherine the Great into believing that the peasants were living happy, rustic lives. But that story is a myth, and it diminishes the achievements of a truly extraordinary man.

The Winter Palace at St Petersburg was completed in 1762. It was designed as the winter residence of the tsars and Catherine the Great was its first occupant. The immense baroque palace has 1057 halls and rooms and 1945 windows.

'Potemkin village' is one of those phrases that has taken on a
life of its own because it conjures up such a useful image. We
can all see how someone might put a huge effort into tricking us
for a short moment in order to create a falsely pleasing long-term
impression. In politics, the expression 'Potemkin village' has
become a cliché for expensive, headline-grabbing policies which
fail to address the real problems behind society's painted facade.
Politicians as different as Soviet leader Mikhail Gorbachev and
British prime minister Tony Blair have been accused of
constructing Potemkin villages. US president George W. Bush
has been described as 'the Potemkin village idiot'.

There are some intriguing variations on the theme. 'Potemkin
parliaments' are institutions which, in dictatorships, rubber-
stamp the despot's decisions in order to lend a democratic gloss
to an authoritarian process. 'Potemkin courts' are a judicial
sham, a way of paying lip service to justice when the real aim is
to eliminate opponents of the government. Other adaptations of
the phrase include 'Potemkin economy', 'Potemkin society',

'Potemkin science' and 'Potemkin education reform'. In every case, the use of the word Potemkin suggests cynical deceit – a pretence made all the worse for being so flimsy and transparent. Potemkin's name has become a synonym for tawdry, deliberate falsehood.

THE AMBITIOUS COURTIER

Grigory Potemkin was the adviser and consort of Catherine the Great, and a fine Russian statesman in his own right. He hitched his star to Catherine's from the very start of his career. In 1762, as a 23-year-old army officer in the Preobrazhensky Guards, he took part in the palace coup that brought her to power. On the night that the German-born Catherine snatched the throne from her feeble husband, Peter III, she rode out at the head of the Preobrazhensky regiment. She was 33 years old, and she was dressed in the striking green uniform of a cavalry captain. As the mounted column set off to arrest the tsar, it was suddenly noticed that Catherine had forgotten her *dragonne*, the decorative loop of braid that officers wore on the hilt of their swords. The young Potemkin galloped over to Catherine, tore off his own *dragonne*, and offered it to her. This chivalrous gesture, made by a youthful and good-looking cavalryman, pleased Catherine immensely. It was Potemkin's only contribution to the coup, but, once the drama was over, Catherine made sure that he received a promotion along with generous gifts of money and serfs.

After that first encounter, Potemkin was never far from Catherine's thoughts. He was often invited to her soirées, as a

lively and entertaining guest. He had a special gift for mimicry, and on one occasion he dared to imitate the Empress's speaking voice, making much of her marked German accent. The assembled courtiers were horrified by Potemkin's impudence, and it could easily have cost him everything. But Potemkin had judged his gamble well: Catherine roared with laughter.

Potemkin became a courtier. He rose swiftly through the ranks, all the while growing closer to Catherine. He was certainly in love with her, or at least with an idealised regal image of her, and she was becoming increasingly fond of him. By 1768, when war broke out between Russia and the Ottoman Empire, he was a *Kammerherr*, a chamberlain of the court, as well as a captain in the Guards. In this latter role he requested permission to leave St Petersburg to fight the Turks. Catherine granted the request, but missed him while he was gone. When he returned in 1771 he was greeted by Catherine as a hero. Absence had made the queen's heart grow fonder, as Potemkin had calculated that it would. It was a short time after this that they became lovers.

Their affair was passion-filled and all-consuming. They could not bear to leave each other's side, and when they had to be apart they constantly scribbled little *billets doux*, which were carried to and fro through the corridors of the palace by trotting footmen. Many of these are as intimate as they are brief. 'I am going to bed,' wrote the Tsaritsa of All the Russias at the end of one evening. 'The doors will be open. Darling, I will do whatever you command. Shall I come to you or will you come to me?' Potemkin's apartments were connected to Catherine's by a secret

In the depths of the Russian winter, Empress Catherine, ensconced in her great travelling sleigh, made her way through her Empire accompanied by foreign guests including the ambassadors of several major European nations. She aimed to impress them with evidence of Russia's modernisation.

staircase – so secret that everybody in the court knew about it. One of them made the short walk to the other's bed every night. In the daytime, they often met in the *banya* – the Russian bathhouse – where, wreathed in steam, they made love and talked politics by turns.

THE SOUTHERN TSAR

Potemkin's ascendancy to the pinnacle of Catherine's affections brought him wealth and power too. The gifts that she showered upon him made him fabulously rich, and the titles and responsibilities she bestowed gave him formal influence: in his mid-thirties he became a member of the State Council, Catherine's advisory cabinet. He was given command of Russia's Cossack cavalry, and was made Governor-General of 'New Russia', the lands that Russia had wrested from the Ottoman Empire in the recent war. But the true source of his power was his closeness to Catherine. For years to come, he was her dearest friend and counsellor, the person who understood her intuitively and utterly. The spiritual connection remained long after the fire went out of their affair and both of them had found other, younger lovers. To the court and to foreign diplomats and spies, Potemkin was the 'demi-tsar'.

In New Russia, a vast swathe of territory on the northern shores of the Black Sea, Potemkin was to all intents and purposes a full-fledged emperor. He was resolved to consolidate Catherine's political and territorial gains in the south, and this became his life's work. It was a task worthy of his huge ambition and energy, and he set to it with great gusto. In this phase of his life he most resembles Peter the Great, who by the force of his own will founded a new Russian capital on the Baltic coast, built a navy, dragged Russia out of its medieval somnolence and turned it into a great European

Potemkin's influence on Catherine lasted long after their love affair had ended. They corresponded regularly and he was party to the most important state documents. His energy was astonishing; as well as his military exploits, his colonising efforts in the south of the empire led to the creation of several major cities – a long way from the 'cardboard villages' that bear his name.

power. Potemkin, for his part, conquered the Crimea and established a fleet on the Black Sea (so that Russia would have a port in the south as well as the north). He reformed the army, abolishing sadistic punishments, redesigning the uniforms for comfort and practicability, and doing away with the ridiculous powdered wigs that were the bane of an infantryman's life. He ruled his domain as a benevolent despot, always ready to dispense mercy and munificence to the pitiful Russian villeins who looked on him as a distant father.

And like Peter, Potemkin was a builder. The tsar has the eponymous St Petersburg to his credit, but Potemkin has many cities to his. Among them are Odessa, the naval port of Sevastopol, Nikolayev, Kherson and Ekaterinoslav – 'Catherine's Glory' – known since Soviet times as Dniepropetrovsk. These cities were surrounded with new plantations and populated with adventurous colonists. Like America in the 19th century, New Russia attracted 'the poor, the tired, the huddled masses yearning to be free'. Renegade cossacks, Greek and Albanian peasants, heretical Old Believers,

To the court and to foreign diplomats and spies, Potemkin was the 'demi-tsar'.

Corsicans, German farmers, persecuted Jews – Potemkin made them all welcome in the virgin southern lands. He took a lively interest in the progress and problems of these foreign immigrants, and was always looking for new sources of colonists. At one point he even considered inviting British convicts to settle in his brave new world.

THE GRAND TOUR OF 'NEW RUSSIA'

But even while this great work was going on, there were rumours in St Petersburg that all the stories about new cities, mighty warships, vines weighed down with fat grapes and so forth, were just fabrications put about by Potemkin himself. He had plenty of enemies at court who were happy to pass on such tittle-tattle.

Some of the stories reached Catherine's ears, and perhaps this helped her to make up her mind to go and see it all for herself. Both Catherine and Potemkin had much to gain from a royal tour of New Russia. Potemkin wanted to show to his sovereign all that he had achieved in the new lands, in particular the diamond-shaped jewel of the Crimea with its brand-new navy. Catherine wanted to satisfy her own curiosity, and to show it all off to the foreign ambassadors who were to accompany her. Peter the Great had called Petersburg his 'window on the west'; New Russia would be Catherine's shop window, her imperial showcase.

The Empress and her entourage set off from her palace in Tsarskoye Selo, south of St Petersburg, in the winter of 1787. The snowy procession consisted of 14 carriages and more than 150 sledges. Catherine's carriage was a horse-drawn fur-lined house on skis. She shared this little mobile home with her latest lover, a pretty young dunce named Mamonov. They were joined in her carriage from time to time by the ambassadors who had been invited on the trip – the envoys of Austria, France and England – and by other courtiers, hand-picked for their ability to amuse the Empress on the long journey. It took the best part of a month to reach the golden-headed city of Kiev. Here the party met with Potemkin, and waited for the frozen river Dniepr to melt, so that they could continue their journey south by boat.

OBSERVATIONS ON THE TOUR OF THE SOUTH

That day came on April 22, 1787. Catherine and her court embarked on specially-built barges no less luxurious than her winter carriage. Bands played on the foreshore and cannons fired the royal salute. During the past weeks, Potemkin had worked hard to ensure that the riverbanks were clean and tidy for miles downriver, and that the buildings on the foreshore were pleasing to the eye. Perhaps this last-minute spring-clean, magnified a hundredfold in the telling, helped to foster the rumour that all the buildings on the riverside were merely pasteboard facades, that they were only meant to be seen by the Empress for a short moment as she passed down the middle of the broad river.

The French ambassador, count Louis-Philippe de Ségur, may even have been alluding mischievously to these stories when he wrote in his diary: 'Towns, villages, country houses and sometimes rustic huts were so wonderfully adorned and disguised with garlands of flowers and splendid architectural decorations that they seemed to be transformed before our eyes into superb cities. Palaces suddenly sprang up and magically created gardens.'

Another member of the party, Charles-Joseph de Ligne, an Austrian prince, set out to see the New Russia for himself, and to disprove the rumours if they were false. At one of the frequent riverside stops he left his barge and went for a walk. He was a friend of Potemkin's, and so is not an impartial witness, but his testimony has the ring of truth. 'I know very well what legerdemain tricks are,' he wrote. 'But I made several excursions without the Empress. I discovered many things with which even Russians are unacquainted. Superb establishments in their infancy; growing manufactories; villages with regular streets surrounded with trees and irrigated with little rivers.'

Catherine II the Great was Empress of Russia from 1762 until her death in 1796. German by birth, her marriage to Peter III was partly the result of some diplomatic manoevring by Frederick the Great of Prussia and the Count Lestocq – who had great influence at the Russian court – to draw Russia and Prussia closer together. As a ruler she wanted to be perceived by Europe as a civilised and enlightened monarch, although her behaviour to her subjects was often tyrannical.

Catherine herself joined in the rumour-scotching by writing a parody of the stories being told 'in the cities of Moscow and Petersburg, and in the foreign newspapers'. Here is her rather leaden spoof: 'I saw the mountains walking towards us with a heavy gait, and bowing down to us with a languid expression. Let those who do not believe it go and look at the new roads that have been built. They will see that everywhere steep descents have been turned into comfortable slopes. In a story, however, the heavy gait and the bowing sound better.'

THE CARDBOARD LIBEL

On May 1st, Catherine wrote to Count Nikolai Saltykov, a known opponent of Potemkin at court. 'Yesterday I saw with my own eyes the regiments of light cavalry, of which it was said to me by many old fishwives [she was referring to government ministers in Petersburg] that they exist only on paper. These regiments are not cardboard at all; in fact they are very beautiful'.

That, surely, should have put paid once and for all to the accusations against Potemkin. So how come the lie became so deeply entrenched, and has persisted to this day? The answer lies with a shadowy enemy of Potemkin's, a Saxon diplomat named Georg von Helbig. He was, in essence, a foreign spy at Catherine's court, and it was part of his job to collect court gossip. He knew that, in a country like Russia, the content of palace rumours told at least as much as facts and hard statistics about the true state of affairs.

Helbig did not accompany the imperial party on the tour of the south, but he wrote down everything he heard about it. His despatches all revolve around the same idea: that the entire New Russia project was nothing but a stage-set. 'Only the closest buildings are real,' he wrote of the city of Kherson. 'The rest are drawn on pasteboard, then nailed together and brightly painted.' He also claimed that the great fleet which was inspected by Catherine at Sevastopol 'was made up of merchants' boats and old barges, which were brought here from all around and paraded as martial ships'.

According to Helbig, the same herd of cattle and band of peasants were ferried overnight from place to place and put on display like toys in a doll's house. When they arrived exhausted, after journeys of a hundred miles or more, the peasants were given colourful suits of clothes and made to dance on the riverbank. Catherine was unwittingly gazing on the same people day after day. Helbig gave this rather comical scenario a sinister twist by claiming that other peasants were starving in their thousands while all this was going on.

The coinage *Potemkinsche Dörfer* – Potemkin villages – is Helbig's own dubious contribution to history. He used it in his despatches, but the expression took flight when he wrote into a biography of Potemkin that he published on his return to Germany. Helbig's book of 'anecdotes' was translated into French and English, and widely read throughout Europe in the first decades of the 19th century. This little volume is the seed of the Potemkin-village legend. But it is nothing but a malicious fairytale, what we would now call an urban myth.

20TH-CENTURY POTEMKIN VILLAGES

Grigory Potemkin did not build any cardboard villages; only real, solid cities. But the concept of the Potemkin village lived on in his native land, and found a literal embodiment 200 years after Catherine's grand tour. In the later years of the Soviet Union, curious westerners who went to the USSR were routinely chaperoned around model schools, kindergartens, factories and hospitals, and told that they were typical of the country as a whole. This was the Potemkin principle in operation, and it was so much a standard propaganda manoeuvre that the Soviets thought everybody did it. When Soviet premier Nikita Khrushchev visited America in the 1960s, he was taken to visit an industrial plant. On the way in, he noted that the car park was full of automobiles – and he took this to be a deliberate trick on the part of his hosts. He thought that the car park had been stuffed to make him think that all American workers were so well-paid that they could buy their own cars. The truth was: the cars did indeed belong to the workers. But Khrushchev could not credit it; he was sure that he was looking at a Potemkin factory.

The Soviet espousal of the Potemkin principle reached a high-point in 1980, with the Olympic Games in Moscow. Just before the athletes and the world's media arrived in the Soviet capital, bright kiosks selling all manner of undreamed-off luxuries were installed throughout the city. Muscovites were astonished: it was suddenly possible for anybody to buy Czech beer, American cola, tinned caviar, bananas... The kiosks closed as soon as the Games were over. Moscow was 'depotemkinised', and reverted to its usual regime of endless queues and chronic shortages.

Grigory Potemkin would have thought such a sham unworthy of a great nation. Everything about him was larger than life. His enormous physique, his immense energy and appetites, his profound but rumbustious love for Catherine, his lordly personality, his military conquests and empire-building – all of these bear the mark of genuine feeling, tangible success, substantial achievement. Potemkin was overpoweringly real, a flesh-and-blood titan. It is hard to imagine a person less likely to resort to the empty pretence that is now forever associated with his name.

Emperor
of the USA

In the second half of the 19th century, an
eccentric, impoverished Englishman – who
proclaimed himself 'Emperor of these United
States and Protector of Mexico' – won the
hearts of the people of San Francisco.

Joshua Abraham Norton was born in Shropshire in about
1815. In 1820, his parents John and Sarah emigrated from
England to South Africa, where they built up a small fortune.
This allowed Joshua Norton to emigrate to the United
States, and in 1849 he arrived in San Francisco with
$40,000 to invest.

He set up several successful property businesses before moving into commodities – specifically rice. There were a large number of Chinese immigrants in San Francisco, and consequently a huge and consistent demand for rice. Even better for Norton, China had just embargoed rice exports because of famine. As a result, the price of rice in San Francisco had rocketed from 9 to 79 cents a kilo. Norton decided to gamble his fortune in 91 tonnes of rice from Peru. But he had not reckoned on other people having the same idea. The Japanese business community had also organised rice shipments and, before long, the market was saturated – and prices plummeted. By 1858, Norton was bankrupt.

HIS IMPERIAL MAJESTY DECREES...

This financial disaster seems to have disturbed Norton's mental equilibrium. Until then, he had not been noted for his eccentricity, but his bankruptcy led to a bizarre proclamation. On September 17, 1859, Joshua Norton appointed himself 'Emperor of these United States and Protector of Mexico'.

Norton sent his investiture speech in a letter to various newspapers – but no one published it. Nevertheless, the emperor took his new role very seriously, regularly inundating the

Emperor Norton proposed many ambitious projects including the building of a bridge across San Francisco Bay. The Bay Bridge eventually opened in 1936, more than half a century after Norton's death.

newspapers with decrees, some of which were published. As time went on, Norton's 'imperial directives' sold papers – people enjoyed reading the latest edicts from his eccentric majesty.

In one, Norton reorganised the political system of the United States, announcing on October 12, 1859, that the US Congress had been dissolved. 'It has come to Our attention,' he wrote, 'that the principle of universal suffrage has been abused, and that deceit and corruption are preventing the fair and legitimate expression of the will of the people...'

When Congress continued to function as normal, Norton was livid. In July 1860, he dissolved the Republic and declared that the country would henceforth be governed by a monarchy. Finally, in August 1869, in view of the continued defiance of the politicians, he decreed that both the Democratic and the Republican Parties were to be abolished.

Although Norton had no political power, and his influence extended only so far as his deferential treatment in San Francisco, the people around him humoured him, referring to him as His Imperial Majesty and even honouring the worthless currency he had issued in his name.

Not everyone treated Norton with tolerant indulgence. Armand Barbier, a policeman recently arrived in San Francisco, had little time for the self-appointed ruler. He believed that anyone who thought that he was emperor of the United States needed his head examining and should be detained. Norton's arrest caused a public outcry, and before long a judge and the local police chief had arrived at the police station, made a formal apology and released the emperor. From then on, Norton was greeted by every police officer in the city with a military salute.

AHEAD OF HIS TIME

Not all his decrees dealt with national politics. In 1872, Norton announced that he was sick of the corrupted, abbreviated names that many people used for San Francisco, his adopted home. 'Whoever uses the dreadful term "Frisco"... is guilty of a serious misdemeanour,' he wrote, 'and liable to a fine of $25, payable to the Imperial Treasury department.' This type of pronouncement simply caused amusement. Others were more visionary: Norton advocated the formation of a kind of United Nations and condemned religious sectarian conflict.

Some of his more practical suggestions were years ahead of his time. On several occasions, he ordered the building of a bridge to link Oakland and San Francisco, but to his great annoyance, the instruction was ignored.

One particular act of courage earned Norton the respect of his fellow citizens. During the 1860s and 1870s, there were frequent attacks on Chinese immigrants in San Francisco. On one occasion, a gang was making its way to Chinatown, spoiling for a fight. All of a sudden, the men were confronted by a lone figure. Joshua Norton said nothing and did nothing. He simply stood there wearing an old blue army uniform, decorated with gold buttons and epaulettes. He bowed his head, as if he was praying. The gang came to a standstill, said nothing and then dispersed.

ONE MAN AND HIS DOGS

The emperor's daily life was, by and large, pretty uneventful. Accompanied by his two dogs Lazarus and Brummer, he walked

Thousands of Chinese migrated to California during the gold rush of the 1850s. At first they mostly lived in rural areas where they worked in mines or on farms but within a few years a Chinese neighbourhood had sprung up in San Francisco. During the economic slump in the 1870s, the Chinese – who had been the victims of prejudice since the days of the gold rush – became a scapegoat for thousands of unemployed whites.

the streets, inspecting the state of pavements and public utilities, listening to people's troubles and making philosophical speeches.

Sometimes he ate in good restaurants and was always served politely – although the proprietors knew that they would be paid in Norton's own worthless currency. Indeed many shops and restaurants found that if they displayed signs in their windows proclaiming 'By Appointment to His Imperial Majesty, Emperor Norton I of the United States', their trade improved.

Norton was also given complementary tickets to every theatre production – not only for himself but also for his two dogs.

In an official census, Joshua Norton is listed with his title of 'Emperor'.

When there was nothing showing in the theatres, the trio attended lectures given in the Academy of Sciences. On January 8, 1880, Norton was on his way to one of these lectures when he collapsed in the street. The next day, the *San Francisco Chronicle's* front page headline read: 'Le Roi est Mort'.

Norton's legacy was $10 in cash, a collection of walking sticks, his correspondence with Queen Victoria – to whom he had offered his hand in marriage – and shares in a worthless goldmine. But the citizens of San Francisco dug into their own pockets to pay for a proper funeral. On the day, the shops closed, a long procession of mourners filed to the cemetery and a crowd of more than 10,000 people paid their last respects. The next day, a newspaper leader article stated that the world would be a far better place if all rulers were as philanthropically minded and honourable as Joshua Norton.

Forefathers or fantasy

In the 1970s, the harrowing
story of Kunta Kinte – an African
stolen in the 18th century from
his tribe in the Gambia to
become a slave in the New
World – became a world-wide
bestseller. But the book's author,
Alex Haley, was not telling the
whole truth.

In 1976 alone, 1.6 million
copies of a 700-page
blockbuster were sold in
the USA. It went on to be
translated into 37
languages. Alex Haley's
book told the history of his
family, which he had traced
back seven generations to 1750.
During his childhood, Haley had
listened avidly to his maternal
grandmother's tales of the family's
ancestors in the Gambia and their
fate as slaves in the USA. In the
mid-1960s, he began to delve into
the history of his forebears.

At last in paperback!

ROOT

by Alex Haley

Dell   MONTVILLE WAREHOUSING COMPANY, INC.
Change Bridge Road · Pine Brook, New Jersey 07058
1P-40-17464-3 $2.75

At last in paper

ROO

Eventually, his research took him to the Gambia and the village of Juffure, where he met an oral historian, an old man who told him the story of Kunta Kinte.

In 1767, 16-year-old Kunta Kinte had been gathering firewood when he was captured by slave traders who shipped him to America. Haley thought he remembered hearing the name Kinte many times in his grandmother's tales. He believed he had discovered the African roots of his own family.

SPELLBOUND BY THE SMALL SCREEN

The book was such a runaway success that the American television network ABC decided to make it into a film series. The series was a huge hit, drawing 130 milion viewers and sparking a new interest in genealogy, particularly among African-Americans. In 1977 *Roots* won the National Book Award and a special Pulitzer Prize. It had challenged the prevailing view of black history, showing that slaves did not give up all their ties to African culture but valued their heritage, keeping words and stories, songs and folk beliefs alive.

The book brought success, but also controversy. In 1977 Haley was accused by two other authors of plagiarism and the cases went to court. Margaret Walker claimed that Haley had

Roots was broadcast early in 1977 in eight episodes, screened on eight successive evenings. It broke every ratings record, with more than 130 million tuning into the gripping story.

lifted entire scenes from her novel *Jubilee*, but the action was dismissed. Harold Courlander accused Haley of having lifted 80 passages from his novel *The African*, published in 1967. Haley denied ever having read the novel and maintained that *Roots* was based on oral testimonies and his own research. But there were so many parallels with *The African* that Haley was forced to settle out of court, paying Courlander $650,000. The judge who presided over the case, swore Courlander to silence about the settlement. He felt that Haley was such an important figure for African-Americans that his image should not be tarnished.

A NOVEL, NOT HISTORICAL FACT

In 1993, a year after Haley's death, journalist Philip Nobile unearthed evidence in Haley's papers indicating that much of his family's 'history' was invention. The notes Haley made during his early research had no mention of Kunta Kinte, while in later papers, the family name Kante appeared. A tape-recording of Haley's conversation in the Gambia with the oral historian who knew of Kunta Kinte, suggested that Haley had pressed the old man to tell a story that fitted one he had already thought up.

Nobile wrote an article for *The Village Voice* about his discovery. As a result, several historians examined the facts in *Roots*, and concluded that there were discrepancies in Haley's family tree, particularly before the American Civil War (1861–65). The ancestors who were supposed to have lived on a slave plantation had simply never existed, which implied that at least 182 pages of the book had no factual basis.

The BBC made a documentary about Nobile's findings but it was never shown in the USA. Instead, the NBC network broadcast a special programme in 2002 to mark the 25th anniversary of the first screening of *Roots*. The programme failed to mention that parts of Haley's book were either invented or copied. Today, the book is still being reprinted by its publisher, Doubleday, with no foreword to this effect. Commentators suggest that no publisher with such a long-running bestseller on its backlist would wish to debunk it. Meanwhile, for the Gambia, the book attracted, and continues to draw large numbers of African-Americans searching for their roots.

A conquistador mistaken for a god

Hernán Cortés conquered the mighty Aztecs with just a tiny force of men, guns and horses – and a huge stroke of luck.

In about 950 AD, an early Mesoamerican king who was a priest of Quetzalcoatl, become known by the god's name. The king, described as bearded and fair-skinned, was exiled by his enemies – but vowed to return in a 'one reed' year of the Aztec 52-year calendar cycle. So when a bearded, fair-skinned stranger landed on the east coast of Mexico in 1519 during a 'one reed' year, the Aztecs believed him to be the returning Quetzalcoatl.

The arrival of Hernán Cortés was also preceded by several unsettling omens. An enormous comet had been seen in the night sky, a fire had destroyed an important temple, a bolt of lightning had been sent by the god of fire

Landing on the Mexican coast, Cortés sank 10 of his 11 ships. The surviving vessel was offered to any of his 100 or so compatriots who would rather go back to Cuba – thereby admitting that they had no stomach for the task ahead. No one took him up on the offer.

Xiuhtecuhtli and, according to scouts posted in neighbouring Mayan territory, 'mountains' had been seen moving on the ocean. These 'mountains' were in fact Cortés' flotilla of 11 ships.

A BOUNTY-HUNTING CONQUISTADOR

During the 1500s, Spain and Portugal undertook a military and political conquest of large parts of the newly discovered Americas. European influence was spread through language, the imposition of government and taxes, the introduction of Christianity as well as further exploration and mapping of the continent. The Spanish conquistador Hernán Cortés aimed to exploit the situation and make his fortune.

Cortés was born in 1485 in southwestern Spain. At the age of 18, he left Spain for Hispaniola, an important island base for the Spanish in the West Indies. There, he worked as a farmer and trained as a soldier before sailing, under Diego Velázquez, in 1511 to conquer Cuba. By 1518, Velázquez was governor of Cuba and Cortés one of his most trusted friends, and he decided to commission Cortés to explore the Mexican coast. But something made Velázquez suspicious of Cortés' motives and, at the last minute, he changed his mind. Perhaps he wanted to prevent Cortés from taking all the glory or assuming governorship on the mainland for himself.

In January 1519 Cortés was about to embark when Velázquez arrived at the dock, determined to revoke his commission. But Cortés put to sea against orders. He was making himself technically a mutineer. A warrant was issued for his arrest but Cortés was not unduly worried. He had control of a fleet of 11 ships, carrying some 600 men, 16 horses and about 20 guns of various sizes, including a bronze cannon. They were headed for Mexico and the legendarily wealthy Aztec empire.

Cortés landed on the Yucatan Peninsula, a long way from the major Aztec centres. His troops stormed the Mayan town of Tabasco and freed Jéronimo de Aguilar, a Spanish priest who had been shipwrecked several years earlier. Aguilar had learned to speak Mayan during his captivity and could now act as the force's interpreter. This allowed Cortés to glean valuable information about the customs and practices of the local Indian populations.

A stone *stele* stands guard at the temple of Quetzalcoatl. The temple was a round building, a shape believed to please the god of fertility, the arts and the wind, because it presented no sharp obstacles.

THE POWER OF SUPERSTITION

Cortés and his men then sailed up the Grijalba River where they came face to face with a large native army. They fought back ferociously, and won. The decisive victory owed much to the effect of horses and guns – neither of which the Amerindians had encountered before. They thought the cavalry was a kind of centaur, not understanding that the armour-plated horses and riders were actually two separate entities. They also feared that the invaders could control the weather, mistaking deafening discharges from the Spanish cannon for thunder. All of these misconceptions helped to bolster the widespread fear that Cortés was an avenging god.

To appease him, the Indians sent gifts including 20 Indian women. One of them, Malintzín, was Cortés's second stroke of luck. Malitzín spoke Mayan as well as Aztec and was able to translate from Aztec into Mayan – from which Jéronimo de Aguilar could then translate into Spanish. Malintzín also became Cortés' mistress and later bore him a son. (Some of Malintzín's own people used the Spanish term 'La Malinche' when referring to her. Later, this became a word meaning 'traitor to one's people'. Today, Mexicans dismiss as 'malinchista' anyone mimicking the language and customs of another country.)

For a while, the Spanish remained on the coast but in mid 1519 the army advanced into the Mexican interior.

The next battles were with the Tlaxcala people. Despite initial stiff resistance, the Tlaxcaltecs were eventually defeated – a victory that would prove hugely significant to Cortés's success. The Tlaxcaltecs and the Aztecs were in a state of permanent conflict and, as far as the Tlaxcaltecs were concerned, any enemy of their hated neighbours was a friend of theirs. They willingly joined the Spanish cause – bolstering Cortés's small force with about 1000 of their own men.

Once news of this allegiance reached the Aztec king, Montezuma, he realised that the Spanish invaders would be formidable adversaries, so rather than engaging them in battle he welcomed Cortés to Tenochtitlán (present-day Mexico City) as his guest. But Cortés did not return or respect Montezuma's

hospitality – within a week he had put the Aztec ruler under
house arrest, much to the fury of the king's subjects.

Cortés was not able to enjoy his triumph over Montezuma
for long – in 1520 word reached him that a Spanish expedition
had arrived from Cuba with a contract to capture him and relieve
him of his riches. So Cortés and his troops marched back to the
coast, leaving just 80 men behind to guard Tenochtitlán. Once he
reached the coast, Cortés managed to defeat the rival expedition
– after which most of the men who had been ordered to take him
prisoner switched allegiance, swelling his ranks to 1300.

THE END OF THE AZTECS

Cortés headed back to Tenochtitlán at the head of this army –
straight into the middle of an uprising. In his absence the
garrison he had left in charge of Tenochtitlán had lost control of
the city; they and King Montezuma were under seige. Cortés was
acutely aware of the danger of the situation – the Spanish were
vastly outnumbered – and he cajoled Montezuma into addressing
the furious mob outside from a tower. But the attempt was futile
– the crowd threw anything they could get
their hands on at their king, and fatally
wounded him.

Cortés's army was not strong enough to
combat the furious Aztec rebellion and on
July 10, 1520, under cover of darkness,
the Spanish withdrew from Tenochtitlán.
With a surviving force of only 440, most
of whom were wounded, Cortés reached
the coast once more.

But the Spaniards had unwittingly left
behind them in Tenochtitlán an invisible
and deadly ally – smallpox – against which
the indigenous population had no
immunity. The disease spread like wildfire,
killing huge numbers and significantly
weakening the Aztec army. Montezuma's
successor Cuitláhuac died of the disease
after a reign lasting just 80 days.

Amerindian civilisations

The Maya
Based on the Yucatan Peninsula, they were
led by a priest-king. They had a calendrical
system, extensive knowledge of astronomy
and mathematics and a well-developed
system of writing.

The Incas
The Incas lived on the west coast of South
America. Their ruler was venerated as the
son of the Sun God. They had a highly
advanced network of roads.

The Aztecs
The Aztecs lived in the south of modern
Mexico. They were ruled by a warrior king.
In 1500, there were around 250,000 people
living in the capital city, Tenochtitlán.

Aztec rulers accumulated vast wealth. By the time Cortés arrived, the king, Montezuma, lived in a splendid palace. His crown was made from precious stones and feathers from a tropical bird, the *quetzal*. No one was allowed to look the king in the face, and even nobles had to go barefoot before him.

Cuitláhuac's successor, Cuauhtémoc, was to be the last Aztec ruler. On April 28, 1521 Cortés returned to Tenochtitlán. His army had been swelled by Cuban mercenaries and Tlaxcaltec volunteers. For more than three months, the Spanish and their allies besieged Tenochtitlán, the city's inhabitants, both men and women, defending it to their deaths. Eventually, the Spanish were forced to take the city house by house, and Cuauhtémoc gave up. He tried to flee but was captured on August 13, 1521. The last Aztec king's name translates as the apt 'descending eagle' or 'setting sun'.

'All the walls are spattered with blood, and the water flows red as if someone had dyed it.'

FROM AN AZTEC LAMENT.

The Spanish settlers built Mexico City on the ruins of Tenochtitlán. The presidential palace now stands on the site of the palace of Montezuma, while the city's cathedral towers over the ruins of an Aztec temple.

Lost
and found

4

The **curse** of **gold**

In 1848, gold was discovered in the tailrace of a sawmill in California. The mill was owned by John Sutter, a wealthy businessman. Once the news broke, hordes of fortune hunters invaded Sutter's estate, driving him to the brink of ruin.

The discovery of gold nuggets in the American River meant dreams of untold wealth from a lucky strike for hundreds of thousands of prospectors. For John Sutter, owner of the land through which the river ran, it spelt disaster. Through a combination of hard work and good luck, Sutter, a Swiss emigré, had enjoyed a successful career in the New World and had established a small empire based on ranching and lumber. His vast estate centred on the American River, a tributary not far from San

Francisco. Sutter's vast estate and enormous wealth had even earned him the nickname the 'Emperor of California'.

A NEW LIFE IN THE NEW WORLD

John Sutter was born on February 15, 1803. His ancestors had founded paper mills and printing presses in the towns of Alsace and Baden, and Sutter followed in the family tradition. But his firm went bankrupt and a warrant was issued for his arrest on charges of irregular financial dealings. So Sutter packed his bags and fled where Swiss law could not touch him – the west coast of North America.

California was very inaccessible in the early 19th century – almost 3000 miles of prairie and mountains separated it from the rest of the United States. The overland route was fraught with danger, as the trail passed through the territory of Indian tribes who were hostile to passing settlers, so anyone wanting to get to California had to go by sea. The voyage was long and risky – the Panama Canal had not yet been built – and many ships foundered off Cape Horn. But Sutter was fortunate, arriving safely in California in 1839.

California comprised a long, narrow coastal strip, inhabited mostly by Spanish-speaking settlers. In 1821, Mexico had gained its independence and California became a province of the new state. The area immediately inland from the coastal strip was Indian territory, and it was there that Sutter went. With the permission of the Mexican governor, he bought a plot of land in the Sacramento Valley, about 60 miles east of modern San Francisco. The native Indians were expelled from the estate by force.

To begin with, Sutter's daily life involved cattle ranching, setting traps and trading in furs. Woodland was cleared to

Major gold strikes of the 19th century

Gold on three continents

Gold was discovered in Australia in 1851, in Rhodesia in 1881, and in Siberia at the end of the 19th century.

The Black Hills of Dakota

In 1875–76, in the wake of a military expedition led by General George Custer, the Black Hills of South Dakota in the USA witnessed a huge influx of gold hunters. This provoked conflicts with the indigenous Sioux Indian population – including the ferocious battle at Little Bighorn in 1876.

Alaska

In Alaska, major gold strikes were found on the Yukon River in 1886 and on the Klondike River in 1896! The American writer Jack London gave a vivid account of the lure of gold and the frustrations of the gold hunter in his novel *The Call of the Wild* (1903).

make way for grazing and the business grew. By 1845, Sutter's 'New Switzerland' covered 230 square miles and was grazed by 12,000 head of cattle, 2000 horses and 10,000 sheep.

THE DISCOVERY OF GOLD

In 1847, Sutter decided to build a sawmill on the river that ran through his land and hired a carpenter, James Marshall. On January 24, 1848, Marshall climbed down into the American River to clear an object that had jammed in the mechanism of the mill. He saw something shining brightly in the water of the drainage culvert – gold.

Sutter immediately foresaw the effect that word of the discovery would have – hordes of gold hunters invading his land – so he did his utmost to stop the news from leaking. But some of the estate labourers couldn't resist having a go at panning for gold themselves, and they bartered the nuggets they found with Sam Brannan, a tradesman in Coloma, a settlement nearby.

Brannan had the same premonition as Sutter. He too envisaged gold diggers arriving in droves – but unlike Sutter he could see the potential to profit from the prospectors. The diggers would need equipment – and he would supply it. He put all the nuggets that the labourers had exchanged with him in a bottle, travelled to San Francisco and spread the word that sensational gold strikes had been made on the American River. As proof, he displayed the bottle of nuggets. This marketing exercise resulted in a mass exodus of many of San Francisco's residents – an exodus that had a serious impact on the city. Shops were forced to close because their employees failed to turn up for work; schools suddenly experienced a chronic lack of teachers, and sailors abandoned ships and hastened alongside deserting soldiers to the river of gold.

SUTTER'S PREDICTIONS COME TRUE

Things turned out just as Sam Brannan had planned. His business boomed and he became California's first millionaire. But John Sutter was not so lucky. His pastures were devastated and his cattle slaughtered by the incoming hoardes. People in the grip of gold fever were indifferent to one man's property rights. Ever

more fanciful stories spread enticing more speculators to Sacramento. One gold hunter claimed that with just one thrust of his spade he had lifted 30lb of gold nuggets; another claimed he had found gold inside a fish that he was cooking.

Despite the rumours, most people unearthed nothing and many of those who did simply gambled it away. The obsession with digging for gold caused other jobs to be neglected, and the prices of basic provisions rocketed. An egg cost $1, old newspapers were sold for $10 each and moneylenders charged 5 per cent interest on loans – every week.

The discovery of gold at Sutter's Mill led to a population explosion in the previously remote valley. According to some estimates, the population of California increased by 86,000 in two years.

THE FORTY-NINERS

Gold fever reached a peak on December 5, 1848, when President James Polk told Congress about the discovery of gold in California. The President's address opened the floodgates to a new deluge of fortune-seekers who became known as the Forty-

Niners, named after the year they arrived in California.The overland trek, on foot or in or wagons, could take up to nine months. For those who came by sea, San Francisco was the most popular port of call, and its population exploded from about 800 in 1848 to over 50,000 in 1849. Only a handful of this new influx hit the jackpot, though, largely because few had the start-up capital needed to mine gold efficiently.

Violent crime was rampant, and most prospectors' living conditions were so insanitary that there were frequent outbreaks of cholera – estimates suggest that one in every five miners who came to California in 1849 was dead within six months.

The businesses that sprang up to meet the needs of the gold diggers boomed. Shopkeepers, bar owners and prostitutes did well, and several entrepreneurs laid

'California, here I come.'

SLOGAN OF THE FORTY-NINERS

the foundations for successful business empires. Some of these businesses are still around today including Levi Strauss – whose rugged, hard-wearing trousers could stand up to the rigours of a gold digger's work – and John Stetson, who manufactured a broad-brimmed hat to protect heads from the blistering Californian sun.

John Sutter lost most of his fortune, but he was not prepared simply to accept the loss of his property. He spent the rest of his life instituting legal proceedings to try and recover his land, but his claims for compensation were repeatedly dismissed. He died in 1880, still fighting.

The stone of ill fortune

A vast yellow diamond has been linked to bad luck since 1477 – implicated in the downfall of kings, queens and empires.

On a November day in 1981, Christie's held a jewellery auction in an exclusive Geneva hotel. One of the items for sale, Lot 710, was listed as an 'unnamed yellow diamond of precisely 81.56 carats, framed with 15 small brilliants'. It is rare to see a stone of this size with no name or provenance and some wondered whether it may have been none other than the legendary Florentine stone, once part of the Habsburg diamond collection that disappeared more than 60 years earlier.

Stories of the large, yellow diamond date from 1477 when

Once considered the most beautiful woman in the world, Sisi (Elisabeth), Empress of Austria, was famed for her fashion sense and her diet and exercise regimes. But she was doomed to meet a violent end.

Charles the Bold of Burgundy is said to have been wearing it when he fell in battle. The first clearly documented mention dates from 1657 when it was owned by the Medici family of Florence. An Antwerp diamond merchant, Jean-Baptiste Tavernier, who was compiling a catalogue of the world's most valuable precious stones, came across the gem in the Medici treasure chamber. It was known as the Grand Duke of Tuscany after its owner. Tavernier was entranced by the great diamond which had 126 facets enhancing its golden glow.

In 1736, when Francis, Duke of Lorraine, married the Austrian princess Maria Theresa of Habsburg, he inherited the title and property of the Grand Duke of Tuscany, including the 137-carat diamond. Maria Theresa nicknamed the diamond the 'Florentine' after its Medici origins. The Florentine made its first public appearance in 1745, when the Duke of Lorraine was crowned Holy Roman Emperor. For this occasion, the stone had been set into the Habsburg family crown.

When, in 1770, Francis's 14-year-old daughter Marie Antoinette married the Dauphin, later to become King Louis XVI of France, she wore the priceless showpiece around her neck as a wedding present from her father. But the diamond did not bring its new owners much luck – the French Revolution resulted in their execution on the guillotine in 1793, and the Florentine vanished without trace.

AN UNLUCKY LOVE TOKEN

The diamond resurfaced when Napoleon I, who had crowned himself French Emperor, married into the Habsburg family in April 1810. His marriage to Josephine had failed to produce heirs, so he married 'a womb' to try and ensure his succession. Archduchess Marie Louise was the 19-year-old daughter of Emperor

Diamond facts

Grading
Diamonds are graded for quality according to the four 'c's: colour, clarity, cut and carat.

Colour
The best diamonds are colourless and transparent with a very high refractive index. Traces of nitrogen give a yellow tint.

Clarity
A diamond's clarity is lowered by the presence of fine 'inclusions' of minerals in the stone. Clarity is graded on a scale ranging from 'flawless' to 'imperfect'.

Cuts of diamond
The commonest diamond cuts are the brilliant, the Dutch rose, the marquise, pendeloque, and the emerald cut.

Carats
One carat is the equivalent of 200 milligrams. Thus the Florentine weighs (or weighed) 27.454 grams.

Francis I of Austria – who wanted the union to bring peace to Austria. Napoleon gave his new wife a wedding present on an imperial scale – the Florentine. A year later she bore him a son, but neither their child nor Napoleon's wedding gift led to a lasting union. When Napoleon abdicated in 1814, the Habsburg Archduchess returned to her family – with the diamond which was then set into the Habsburg crown.

When her marriage to Napoleon failed, Marie Louise took the Florentine diamond home to her father, Emperor Francis I of Austria, had the stone reset into the Habsburg crown, now also crown of the Austrian Empire

The diamond remained in the crown until 1888, when the Austro-Hungarian Emperor Franz Josef had it incorporated into a necklace for his popular wife Sisi. This, too, was inauspicious – ten years later, at the age of 60, Sisi was assassinated by a young anarchist wielding a needle file. She died from a puncture wound to the heart. From then on, no Habsburg wanted to wear the jewel and it went on permanent display as part of the Austrian crown jewels in Vienna.

THE LOSS OF AN EMPIRE

In the aftermath of the First World War, when political turmoil threatened to sweep away the Austrian monarchy, the Habsburgs deposited the Florentine and other jewellery in a Swiss bank. When the Austrian public got wind of what they regarded as a 'towering act of betrayal' there was a groundswell of indignation in what was already a volatile atmosphere of revolutionary upheaval. In November 1918 the emperor, Charles I, was forced to sign a document in which he renounced 'any further part in the business of government'.

'Then along came this Steiner fellow, who made off with everything. He left us completely destitute.'

OTTO VON HABSBURG

A few months later the family fled to Switzerland in exile; all they possessed were the jewels. But the Austrian government had passed laws stating that all Habsburg property belonged to the state, which implied that the Habsburgs could not offer the jewellery for public sale.

THE TRAIL GOES COLD

The family was obliged to use a middleman, Bruno Steiner, to dispose of the jewellery – including the Florentine which was by then thought to be worth more than 10 million Swiss francs (at least £4 million). The Habsburgs made a poor choice of agent and the stone, along with the rest of the crown jewels, was stolen. This spelt financial ruin – the theft could not be reported as the jewellery did not officially belong to them. It is rumoured that everything was taken to South America and that the Florentine was taken to be recut in the United States in the 1920s. Perhaps part of it resurfaced, briefly, as the nameless jewel in the auction in 1981. Or perhaps it still lies intact in a strongroom somewhere.

The inglorious end of the Hun king

Known to the Romans as the 'Scourge of God', Attila devastated much of Europe between AD 433 and AD 453. He created one of the most formidable armies Asia had ever seen but died not on the battlefield but in his nuptial bed.

Probably the only person who ever knew the truth about Attila the Hun's mysterious death was Ildico, his new wife. On the morning after their wedding, Attila was discovered lying dead in his bed in a pool of blood. Ildico, whom he had almost certainly married for political reasons, became a widow

Attila, once the terror of Asia and Europe, died in the marital bed.

Attila (top left) took a great delight in music and entertainment at his court. It was one such celebration that probably led to his mysterious death.

on the first day of what otherwise would have been her honeymoon.

RUMOURS AND SUSPICIONS

On the face of it, the great king's sudden death was decidedly suspicious and rumours swiftly spread. Could Ildico herself have had a hand in the affair? She had made no attempt to call for help during the night. She also came from a tribe Attila had conquered and he may even have personally ordered that her close relatives be put to death.

Or was it an assassination? Attila had many enemies, both at home and further afield. More than a few of them were capable of organising his murder. If they did, it was probably by bribing one of his bodyguards, possibly one bearing a grudge against his master. But key questions defied answer. If Attila had been murdered, how had this been managed without leaving a single mark on his body? Or what mysterious poison could have produced such results?

A TRAGIC ACCIDENT

In the heated debates that followed, calmer heads raised the possibility that Attila might simply have died of natural causes. He had already celebrated his 50th birthday – a ripe old age for the time. But following a reconstruction of Attila's final hours and intensive questioning of the bride, the conclusion was that Attila's death was an accident. The evening before, the king had been celebrating his wedding. He was not known as a heavy drinker but, on this occasion, he had been drinking heavily before he went to bed. It was the last time he was seen alive.

What followed necessarily remained conjecture. Attila's doctors agreed that his death was caused by a haemorrhage. After retiring, he had suffered one of his frequent heavy nosebleeds. In his drunken stupor, Attila fell asleep on his back. When his nose started to bleed, the king did not awaken. Instead, he breathed in the blood, which blocked his windpipe and suffocated him. Attila literally drowned in his own blood.

The news of Attila's unexpected and sudden death shocked the known world. There was disbelief that such a tempestuous figure should have died in bed rather than on the battlefield. Feelings of relief soon tempered astonishment for, over the preceding decades, Attila and his ferocious Huns had terrorised peoples across Asia and Europe.

A PEOPLE ON THE MOVE

The Huns originally lived as nomads on the steppes of Central Asia. Around AD 1, they began to drift west – perhaps in search of new pastures – eventually settling in the area between the Rivers Volga and Don. Then, around AD 375, they made their presence felt again. It was almost certainly economic forces that forced the Huns to migrate further to the west, displacing other peoples, such as the Visigoths, who were driven across the River Danube and into the Roman Empire. The migration sparked off what might be described as a migratory chain-reaction.

Their victims' readiness to take flight was doubtless due to the fearsome reputation the Huns had already acquired. Ammiannus Marcellinus, a Roman historian, noted: 'This people, who are well versed in the arts of war, are impelled by a burning desire for plunder.' As the panic spread, few thought to ascertain the truth of the rumours. There is no doubt that some of the most blood-curdling accounts of their deeds were greatly exaggerated. Archaeologists have demonstrated that the Huns were far from being the uncivilised barbarians of popular legend.

ACCOMMODATION WITH THE ROMANS

Undoubtedly, the land-hungry Huns showed no mercy to anyone who opposed them. After reaching the Lower Danube region in around AD 400, they stood at the threshold of the Roman Empire itself. At this point Rome's days of glory were past. The empire had been split in two. The Byzantine Emperor reigned over the eastern half of the Empire from Constantinople, while another ruled the Western Empire, having abandoned Rome as its capital in favour of Ravenna. Faced with the overwhelming might of the Huns, the Roman rulers decided to pay them off and agreed to give them substantial amounts of gold in annual tribute. They received assurances that they would be left alone. The citizens of both parts of the empire were able to continue living in peace, while the Huns could consolidate their rule over the Hungarian lowland plain east of the River Tisza without fear of attack.

But this lasted only until Attila became sole ruler of the Huns. He and his brother Bleda had jointly succeeded to the throne in 433 after the death of their uncle. Bleda died in 445, and it is widely assumed that Attila had a hand in his death. In any event, Attila now had a free rein. He used the increased Roman tributes to establish a highly organised empire, which stretched as far as the Ukraine in the east to – for a while at least – the Rhine in the west. At the same time, the king regularly dispatched his horse archers across the Danube to add military weight to the repeated financial demands that he was making on the Romans.

As a result of their victories in many devastating battles – here the Huns are seen triumphing over the Alans in 372 – this warrior race steadily extended its dominion across much of Europe.

DEFEAT IN GAUL

In late 450, Marcian, on his succession to the imperial throne
in Constantinople, ordered the tribute payments to stop. Attila's
response was to turn west, rather than east. Probably this was
because he had fallen out with Flavius Aetius, the chief military
commander of the Western Empire, over which of the two rival
claimants to the Frankish throne to support. Attila backed the
elder son of the dead king and Flavius the younger. So Attila
launched an attack on Gaul in AD 451 with a 500,000-strong
force, his ambition now being to extend his kingdom across Gaul
to the Atlantic coast. The threat he posed led Theodoric I, the
ruler of the Visigoths, to ally himself with the Romans. Their
combined forces defeated Attila at Châlons-sur-Marne, though
Theodoric and many others perished on the field.

Despite this crushing blow, the following year Attila led his
army into northern Italy. Much of the Po Valley, including Milan,
Verona and Padua, was laid waste and depopulated, while
Aquileia, on the tip of the Adriatic, was wiped off the face of the
Earth. Its survivors are believed to have fled into the lagoons of
the Adriatic, where they were to build a new city – Venice. Rome
itself soon came under threat as well.

According to legend, Pope Leo the Great tried to persuade
Attila to spare Rome and leave Italy. The saints St Peter and St
Paul appeared in support of the Pope's plea. They told the
superstitious Attila that he would die at once if he ignored the
Pope's urgings. Attila withdrew. A more prosaic explanation is
that, as a result of famine, Attila's men were short of supplies,
while they were also threatened by an outbreak of plague. Attila
also had to deal with Marcian, who had sent his army across the
Danube unopposed to strike into the heartland of his domains.
Before he embarked on this new adventure, he was determined
to marry a new, young wife. Which is where his story ends.

The kingdom Attila had created did not long survive his
death. In 454, the Ostrogoths and other Germanic tribes revolted
against the Huns' domination and Attila's sons proved incapable
of dealing with the resulting crisis. The Huns were scattered to
the winds. Their great empire came to an end even more swiftly
than it had arisen.

Eaten by dragons

The Komodo dragon, which lives only on the island of Komodo and a few neighbouring islands in the Lesser Sunda chain of Indonesia, often reaches 2.75m in length. A male can weigh up to 250kg after a large meal.

The Komodo dragon has been blamed for many unexplained human deaths or disappearances. Baron Rudolf Reding von Biberegg is thought to be the first European victim of the dragons. He disappeared in July 1974 on the Indonesian island of Komodo – only his broken camera and glasses were ever found.

Early in the morning of July 18, 1974, a small group of adventure tourists set sail from the Indonesian island of Flores. They were on their way to spot dragons on the remote island of Komodo. Among their number was a Swiss baron, 74-year-old Rudolf Reding von Biberegg. The itinerary for the day was to find and watch the Komodo dragon, a large, potentially dangerous reptile, in its natural habitat.

The group was well prepared, having brought goat's meat to entice the voracious lizards, and a picnic for themselves. They landed on a flat stretch of beach and made their way inland across the hot, dry, barren landscape in search of the animals. It did not take long to find them. Hardly had they laid out the goat's meat before the enormous lizards put on a positively prehistoric spectacle for the tourists – who had retired to a safe distance.

From all directions, the animals rushed to the meat and fell upon it, tearing at it with sharp claws and rows of sharply-pointed teeth. Baron Reding was spellbound. Long

These enormous lizards strip their prey of almost every last scrap of meat and will eat bones, hooves and hide.

after the creatures had withdrawn, hissing and flicking their tongues, he and his astonished companions stood silently rooted to the spot.

Lunch was next on the agenda and the tourists and boat crew unpacked food and drink and set it out. Reding was not in the mood for lunch or making conversation and told the group that he wanted to spend a few hours by himself back at the boat. He set off alone – a decision that cost him his life.

THE BARON DISAPPEARS

What happened next remains a mystery. No one knows if Reding really intended to go back to the boat, or whether, perhaps, he had decided to take another look at the dragons. Whatever his reason, he was not with the boat when the group returned to the beach a few hours later.

Everyone in the party was worried and they made a thorough search of the area around the anchorage, but found nothing. Although they were now seriously anxious for Reding's safety, they had no choice but to leave the island, having brought too little water and not enough food for an overnight stay. They sailed back to Flores in the almost certain knowledge that something dreadful had happened.

The Komodo dragon

Favourite foods
This carnivore prefers carrion, but will also hunt larger animals such as wild pigs.

Favourite foods
Komodo dragons are cannibals – some 10 per cent of their food comes from young or the weak members of their own species.

Massive appetites
They can consume vast quantities of food incredibly quickly: one individual weighing 50 kilograms was seen to devour an entire 31-kilogram pig in 17 minutes.

Behaviour
Komodos are solitary, but will gather in groups to consume large prey or to breed.

Hundreds of teeth
Komodo dragons have mouths full of flat, serrated teeth, highly adapted for cutting flesh. The teeth break off easily and are replaced frequently; a dragon may grow as many as 200 new teeth each year.

THE SEARCH FOR CLUES

The group reported the incident to the authorities as soon as they returned, and a search party was organised. The next day more than a hundred people travelled to Komodo and combed the island for signs of the missing man. Eventually, high up in the island's hills and miles off the beaten track, they found an ominous clue – Reding's glasses and his smashed camera. There was no other trace of the missing man or his body, which suggested only one thing. He had been completely devoured.

No one will ever know for sure what happened. What is known is that Komodo dragons are predators and actively hunt their prey, roaming their territory in search of food. They can also sprint for short distances at speeds of 15 miles per hour – about as fast as a dog – and could probably outrun a hot, tired 74 year old. They can eat up to 80 per cent of their body weight at one meal, using their sharp teeth to carve out huge chunks of flesh and tissue. Reding might have been hunted and killed, or had an accident or suffered a stroke in the humid tropical climate, becoming easy prey. A few years later, he was officially declared dead.

Today, the home of the Komodo dragons is a National Park covering 669 square miles of land and marine area. It is a major tourist attraction, with more than 15,000 visitors a year coming to view the 'world's last surviving dragons'.

Under the spell of the dark continent

A missionary, doctor, explorer, scientist and anti-slavery activist, David Livingstone spent 30 years in Africa, exploring almost a third of the continent from its southern tip almost as far north as the equator.

On the border between Zimbabwe and Zambia, the River Zambesi – a mile wide at this point – plunges into a narrow slot-like chasm lying at right-angles to the river's original course. This is the Victoria Falls – named by the Scottish missionary and explorer David Livingstone after his Queen. On his return to Britain in 1856, Livingstone was greeted as a national hero. His book *Missionary Travels and Researches in South Africa*, was published the following year and became a bestseller. But instead of retiring on the proceeds, Livingstone was irresistibly drawn back, time and again, to the 'dark continent' – so named by the Victorians as vast areas were unmapped and its peoples were considered to be uncivilised.

MILLWORKER TO MISSIONARY

David Livingstone was born on March 19, 1813, in Blantyre near Glasgow. His father, a tea merchant, did not earn enough to provide for his large family so, at the age of ten, David, like most other children in his village, went to work in a cotton mill. Work started at six in the morning and ended at 8 pm – when the children were expected to go to night school. They often fell asleep at their desks but David worked hard. He loved reading, especially books about travel and science. He was also drawn to nature and explored the area around his home in Scotland collecting flowers and shells. At 20 the young man became an earnest Christian, and when a missionary society opened in Blantyre, Livingstone became deeply interested in its work.

In 1833, Livingstone, who had studied theology and qualified as a doctor, read an article by Karl Gützlaff, a missionary to China, which described his work in the Far East. It captured his imagination and he set his sights on going to China as a medical missionary. In 1838, he was accepted as a member of the London Missionary Society. But the first Anglo-Chinese war, better known as the Opium War (1839–42), put paid to any likelihood of Livingstone going to the Far East at that time.

Then a fellow Scot, Dr Robert Moffat, came home on leave from an African mission station at Kuruman. The base, 500 miles north of Cape Town, was as far inland as missionaries had penetrated into Africa. Listening to Moffat's plea for Africa's unexplored interior and how he had 'sometimes seen in the

Livingstone travelled 29,000 miles in Africa, adding about 1 million square miles to the known area of the globe. The provincial capital of the region of Zambia immediately to the north of the Victoria Falls, still bears his name.

morning sun the smoke of a thousand villages' where the gospel had never been preached, Livingstone decided to apply for a posting to Africa instead of China. The London Missionary Society agreed and in 1840, Livingstone set sail.

CONSIDERATION AND RESPECT

On July 31, 1840, Livingstone reached the mission station at Kuruman in the modern Northern Cape Province of South Africa. In order to assimilate the language and understand the lifestyle of the local people, Livingstone spent several months in a native village miles away from Kuruman. He treated the people's illnesses and, later, did what he could to fight the slave traders.

He worked alone for four years before meeting, working with and then marrying Robert Moffat's daughter, Mary. Together they had six children, one of whom died in infancy. Their first home was in a settlement north of Kuruman, where Livingstone

'I shall either open up a path into the interior or perish in the attempt.'

DAVID LIVINGSTONE

had already opened a mission station. It was here that Livingstone was attacked by a lion, which injured his shoulder so badly that his left arm never fully recovered.

His missionary work involved venturing ever further into the wilderness. But it also allowed him to collate a wealth of geographical data: in his first phase of exploration, between 1841 and 1856, he discovered Lake Ngami in the middle of the Kalahari Desert, charted the middle and upper reaches of the Zambezi and discovered the Victoria Falls.

But life in Africa was not easy for a young family, and malaria was an ever-present threat. Livingstone grew increasingly worried about the welfare of his family and his children's education, and eventually he decided that he must continue his work alone and they must go to Britain. In April 1852 the family travelled to Cape Town where Mary and the children boarded ship. After 16 years in Africa, Livingstone made his first visit to England, in December 1856. He found himself thrust into a limelight which he did not enjoy. Societies and colleges vied with each other to honour him – the universities of Cambridge, Oxford and Glasgow all gave him honorary degrees – but the London Missionary Society, which had sent him to Africa, felt that it was inappropriate for him to spend so much time exploring the country when he was there as a missionary. Livingstone was shocked, as he believed himself to be as sincere a missionary as ever. He withdrew from the society and joined the Royal Geographical Society, representing them as the Queen's consul.

A DISASTROUS EXPEDITION

The Zambesi Expedition, from 1858 to 1863, was the low point in Livingstone's career. In March 1858, with his wife and a team including his brother Charles, he sailed for the Cape. They were dogged by misfortune. The boat on which he had hoped to sail up the Zambesi proved useless; he called it 'an asthmatic tin can'. Livingstone could command and organise Africans but his management of colleagues and a large expedition was disastrous. Six years of disharmony and frustration followed. Team members were unhappy to be told what to do without consultation and his younger brother was not well suited to the work.

Mary Livingstone had become ill on the voyage from England. She was forced to stay in Cape Town while the expedition went on to the mouth of the Zambesi. She did not see her husband again for more than three years. When they were finally reunited, they had just three months together when, in April 1862, Mary died. She was buried under a great baobab tree at Shupange on the lower Zambesi. It was a terrible loss for Livingstone; the couple had been extremely close despite long periods of separation – in 18 years of marriage, they had spent fewer than nine years together.

For all its problems, the trip had yielded some important geographical findings, such as tributaries that led to the Zambesi from as far away as Lake Chilwa and Lake Malawi. Livingstone returned to Britain in July 1864 and stayed for a year during which he wrote his second book – *The Zambesi and its Tributaries* – and spent as much time as he could with his children. But he was eager to return to Africa and, in August 1865, he sailed for the third time.

LIVINGSTONE'S FINAL JOURNEY

This last journey, which lasted for seven years, was commissioned by the Royal Geographical Society. They wanted Livingstone to explore the great African watersheds – and, in particular, to locate the source of the Nile. But he did not want to be a mere geographer; he wanted his improved geographical knowledge to result in the spreading of Christianity. His horror of the slave trade – which he described as 'that open sore of Africa' – had grown but it appeared that the governments of Christian nations actually wished to maintain it. Portugal protected the slavers; Britain talked but did nothing. Worst of all was the awareness that his own explorations had simply opened new avenues for slave traders. His own overland journey involved crossing country devastated by the slave trade, and Livingstone, being European, was often viewed with suspicion and hostility; it took grit and determination to keep going.

Livingstone's own physical health was also deteriorating. His damaged left arm caused him great pain; he also suffered from frequent bouts of malaria, dysentery and pneumonia. He was becoming deaf, and was plagued by piles that often bled profusely, leaving him weakened by the constant loss of blood. His poor health obliged Livingstone to rest for long periods at a time, usually in the small settlement of Ujiji on the shore of Lake Tanganyika. He was obsessed with the idea of finding the source of the Nile but, though often convinced that he was almost there, the mystery eluded him. During one

On Henry Stanley's expedition to find Livingstone, he took with him such superfluous items as an enamel bath, an oriental carpet, silver goblets and bottles of champagne, which, so the story goes, he and Livingstone opened and drank together to celebrate their meeting.

expedition, some of his followers deserted him taking with them provisions and, worse, the chest of medical supplies. To save their own skins, the deserters concocted the story that Livingstone had been killed – a story that made headline news in the *Times* on December 5, 1867. Despite rumours of his death, the explorer pressed on for four more years, eventually returning to Ujiji on October 23, 1871, utterly exhausted.

'DR LIVINGSTONE, I PRESUME?'

Henry Stanley was born in 1841 in Denbigh, North Wales. Illegitimate and unwanted, the baby was entered on the birth register of St Hilary's Church as 'John Rowlands, bastard'. At first, the young boy was looked after by relatives, but when he was six his grandfather died and he was consigned to a life in the workhouse.

At 17, Rowlands ran away to sea, working his passage to New Orleans as a cabin steward. There, he gave himself a new name – Henry Morton Stanley – after a cotton broker for whom he had worked. With the outbreak of the American Civil War in 1861, Stanley enlisted, spending several years as a soldier and at sea. He then led a roving life in the United States, working as a freelance journalist.

On his final expedition, Livingstone was racked with pain. His dysentery attacks were almost continuous but he kept crossing the swamps and reached the southern side of Lake Tanganyika, still mapping to within a day of his death. When he became too ill to walk, he was carried on a litter.

In 1867, Stanley met James Gordon Bennett, publisher of the *New York Herald*, who gave him a job. He became Bennett's ace reporter, travelling to battlefields around the world. In 1869, Bennett got wind of a new story. The British explorer David Livingstone had been missing in Africa since 1866. In 1867, the British government had sent out a search party, which, although failing to find their man, did hear that he was still alive. Now the *New York Herald* decided to follow up the story, and sent Stanley – with no expense spared – to track down the elusive Livingstone.

The search was arduous – the terrain was difficult, the rainy season was just beginning and local tribes attacked the expedition. On November 10, 1871, the party arrived at Ujiji. It did not take Stanley long to find Livingstone. Coming face to face with a European whose body had become so emaciated that he resembled a skeleton, he uttered the legendary words, 'Dr Livingstone, I presume?'

Stanley's arrival was very welcome; he had brought medicines and provisions, and news and letters from home. Although Stanley was a good deal younger than Livingstone, the two men got on well and became good friends during the four months Stanley stayed at Ujiji. Stanley tried to persuade his friend to go back to Britain with him but Livingstone would not give up on his quest, having convinced himself that none of his friends would want to see him home before he had located the source of the Nile. He never did.

On May 1, 1873, he was found dead in an African native hut, kneeling beside his bed as if in prayer. His heart was buried under a tree in Africa. His corpse was embalmed and carried 1500 miles – a nine-month march – across Africa to be shipped home for a hero's funeral at Westminster Abbey, at which Stanley was one of the pall-bearers.

Exploring Africa

The Phoenicians
In c.600 BC, the Phoenicians were the first people to sail around Africa.

Ibn Battuta
From 1325 onwards, the Arabian traveller travelled throughout north and east Africa.

Bartholomew Diaz
From 1416, the Portuguese explored the West coast. In 1488 Diaz rounded the Cape of Good Hope.

Vasco da Gama
In 1497 Vasco da Gama discovered the sea route to India.

Leo Africanus
His famous account *A Description of Africa* appeared in 1550.

The
final message
from the Stardust

In 1947 a British passenger plane with
11 people on board disappeared.
Despite a massive search of the
Andes no trace of the plane was
ever found. For 53 years the
families of those on board had
no idea what had happened
to their loved ones. But in
2000 the plane reappeared
in a glacier, more than
30 miles from where it had
last been reported.

The Argentinian team that
discovered the remains of
the *Stardust* recovered a
number of items including
a propeller, a piece of a
wing and an oxygen
canister as well as clothes,
cans of food and some
human remains. The metal
of the plane's shattered
fuselage had turned
completely white.

As Captain Reginald James Cook made his final approach towards Santiago on August 2, 1947, what he saw was not the lights of the Chilean capital but a sheer rock face of ice and snow. It was a 6800 metre Andean mountain called Tupungato. Six passengers and four crew died with him, including radio operator Dennis Harmer. The flight from Buenos Aires in Argentina to Santiago had gone without a hitch, largely because the Stardust, a British civilian version of the wartime Lancaster bomber, had been flying above the stormy weather front at 7300 metres. In 1947 few types of aircraft were capable of flying so high.

As Harmer radioed the tower at Santiago in Morse code, four minutes prior to their scheduled arrival time, there was no hint of imminent disaster. Nevertheless, his transmission – 'ETA Santiago 17.45 STENDEC' – contained a confusing element. The first part was clear – estimated time of arrival in Santiago 17.45 – but what did STENDEC mean? The Chilean radio operator in the control tower requested confirmation of the message, and in response Harmer twice more transmitted the phrase STENDEC. Then contact was broken.

A search and rescue mission immediately got under way. When no wreckage was found near the airport, the search area was widened. Even so, it appeared that the Stardust had vanished into thin air. It was not long before a raft of conspiracy theories began to circulate, largely to do with the passengers on board the flight: a Swiss, a Palestinian, a German and three British nationals, one of whom was a diplomat carrying secret papers. Were anti-British espionage agents behind the disappearance of the Stardust? Maybe a bomb had been brought on board. Some people even thought that the mysterious final radio transmission STENDEC meant that the plane had been abducted by aliens.

WRECKAGE IS FOUND IN THE ICE
Half a century later, mountaineers 5000 metres up the icy slopes of Tupungato found a Rolls-Royce aircraft engine and a propeller. In February 2000, an expedition found more bits of wreckage, on one of which the name Stardust could be made out.

From the layout of the wreckage, it was clear that the plane had not been brought down by a bomb; the propellers had still been turning normally when the *Stardust* collided with the side of the mountain. Neither was there any evidence of extraterrestrial involvement in the crash. The only feasible explanation was human error – the pilot had begun his approach to Santiago far too early, well before the aircraft had cleared the Andes. But the question remained as to how an experienced flight crew could have made such a disastrous mistake.

THE JETSTREAM EFFECT

Strangely, the explanation lay in the high technical specification of the *Stardust*. At 7300 metres, the plane was flying in a level of the atmosphere about which very little was understood at that time. We now know that this is the height at which the jetstream, a high-altitude wind, blows from the west at speeds of more than a hundred miles an hour. The *Stardust* was heading directly into it, which slowed down the aircraft's speed considerably, though the pilot would have had no inkling of this. The crew's calculations showed they had crossed the Andes, but the jetstream's powerful wind meant they were still on the wrong side of the mountains. Speed indicators to take account of phenomenon had not yet been invented. The thick cloud cover prevented the cockpit crew from seeing the ground so they had no visual clues to guide them. When *Stardust* began its descent, it was not above Santiago airport, but was on a collision course with Mount Tupangato.

The impact may have triggered an avalanche that buried the wreckage. There was even a possible interpretation for STENDEC. An error in taking down the message sent by the plane could have been transcribed as 'STENDEC' rather than 'STR DEC' – the two sequences of letters are almost identical in Morse code. 'STR DEC' was a common abbreviation for 'starting descent'.

Mountain air crashes

1972, the High Andes
On October 12, 1972, a Fokker Friendship aircraft crashed in the High Andes. All attempts to locate the plane were unsuccessful. The survivors stayed alive by eating those who had died. Finally, two of them managed to trek to safety and organise a rescue party. In all, 16 of the 45 passengers and crew were rescued.

1985, Japan
On August 12, 1985, 520 people on a Japanese Boeing 747 died when it flew into Mount Osutaka near Tokyo.

2005, Afghanistan
On February 4, 2005, a Boeing 737 crashed into a mountain, killing all 104 passengers and crew on board.

Women
of the world

5

The revenge of the bandit queen

An outlaw who kicked against the oppression of women, Phoolan Devi was implicated in one of the largest gang massacres in modern Indian history. But, in 1996 after 11 years in prison, the 'Bandit Queen' found a new way to champion women's rights – as an MP.

The peace of the Indian village of Behmai was shattered by shots and screams. When the uproar died down, 22 men lay dead on the riverbank. It was February 14, 1981, and Phoolan Devi had taken bloody revenge for her rape and for the murder of her lover, Vikram Mallah. She was now at the top of the Indian police's Most Wanted list. But among the poor and oppressed, the 'Bandit Queen' enjoyed an almost mythical reputation as a modern day Robin Hood.

BORN AN 'UNTOUCHABLE'

Phoolan Devi was born in August 1963 in Ghura Ka Purwa, a village of mud huts on the Yamuna river in the Indian state of Uttar Pradesh. She faced a bleak future as both a female and an 'untouchable'. In Indian society, anyone born into a low caste – and Phoolan's, a sub-caste of boatmen called mallahs, was the lowest – had virtually no chance of escape. The women were there to satisfy the sexual demands of their masters and worked in the fields for a meal and the equivalent of a few pennies a day. They remained illiterate and their best hope was to marry at 14 and bear sons. Villagers gossiped that Phoolan's father, who worked for a landowning family of the thakur caste, must be cursed – his wife had borne only one son but four daughters.

Even as a young girl, Phoolan had a sense of pride and justice; she railed against the traditional role of Indian women. She stood up in public against her bullying cousin Mayadin on several occasions – who took his revenge by arranging the 11-year-old's marriage to a man three times her age, who then moved her miles from her village and her family. Child marriages had been illegal in India since 1927 but were still widespread among rural communities. Phoolan was beaten, abused and treated as a slave by her husband. He eventually abandoned her and sent her home, where she was now considered tainted. The shame was so great that her mother wanted Phoolan to commit suicide, suggesting that her daughter jump down the village well.

Ignoring her mother's advice, Phoolan quickly earned a reputation for being a troublemaker. She wrote in her autobiography, 'I was discovering piece by piece how my world was put together: the power of men, the power of privileged castes, the power of might. I didn't think of what I was doing as rebellion; it was the only means I had of getting justice'. Whether sticking up for herself or for her family, Phoolan was always punished by the thakurs. In a legal dispute over a piece of land, she represented her father's interests to the village council and found herself confronting her wealthy uncle and, once again, her cousin Mayadin. Mayadin not only spread slanderous rumours about her but also, in 1979, accused her of theft. The 16-year-old girl was arrested, gang-raped and beaten by the police – but there was no evidence against her and after a month of sexual abuse and torture she was released. Phoolan now harboured an obsessive hatred for any man who abused women.

A CAREER AS A BANDIT

Phoolan Devi had never known love or respect until she met Vikram Mallah. She swore never to rest until she had avenged his murder.

Shortly after her release, Phoolan vanished from the village – possibly having been abducted by dacoits – armed gangs that still exist in remote areas of northern India. They survive by looting entire villages, kidnapping and hijacking. Buses still travel in armed caravans to fight off likely raids. Considered to be criminals by the police and upper castes, dacoits are often regarded as heroes by the lower castes, who comprise most of their members.

Phoolan moved with her new companions to the labyrinthine Chambal ravines, home for centuries to India's most notorious dacoits. There were two factions in the 30-strong gang – the thakurs, led by the oafish Babu Gujar and the mallahs, led by a man named Vikram. Phoolan, against her wishes, was taken by Babu Gujar as his mistress. But deep tension between Gujar and Vikram, his deputy, led Vikram to shoot the leader and assume his role. In Vikram, Phoolan encountered something she had never found in a man before – respect for others, including women. He taught her his tricks of the trade and the two became partners in crime –

and lovers. Soon Phoolan was a crack shot and a gang leader herself and the duo had become a sort of Indian Bonnie and Clyde. But unlike many bandits, Phoolan Devi did not steal purely for her own benefit. Like a latter day Robin Hood, she stole from the rich and gave to the poor, particularly poor women. Her inspirations were Durga, the Hindu goddess of strength and power, and Mahatma Gandhi, the Indian statesman who had fought for equality. After each crime – whether the ransacking of a high-caste village or the hijack of a bus – Phoolan would insist on the gang giving thanks to Durga for protecting them.

> *'It was an odd feeling… For the first time, a man had touched me tenderly, and I felt that I could trust him.'*
>
> PHOOLAN DEVI ON VIKRAM MALLAH.

DISSENT IN THE RANKS

But not everyone was happy with the new leadership. The gang included several higher caste members who loathed being ordered about a couple whom they regarded as social climbers. Two brothers from the thakur caste, Sri Ram and Lala Ram, shunned Phoolan and Vikram and formed their own gang. Then during a robbery in spring 1980, a rich relation of the Ram brothers was murdered by Phoolan and Vikram's gang. Sri Ram had had enough. It was time to wipe out the mallahs.

One night Phoolan was woken by a deafening explosion. Next to her, she heard Vikram muttering something about a 'bastard' shooting at him. When she opened her eyes she saw Sri Ram holding a gun – there was no mistaking his distinctive red hair and beard. Vikram was dead. Sri Ram's accomplices dragged Phoolan from her tent and carried her down to the river. She was bundled into a boat and taken to Behmai, the Rams' home village, where she was locked up, beaten, tortured and repeatedly raped, night after night, by Sri Ram and his men.

After three weeks she was helped to escape and she set about forming her own gang. She took to wearing a red bandana around her forehead – the sign of revenge – and focused on pursuing the Ram brothers.

The Indian caste system

Four castes
Hinduism originally specified four castes: priests, warriors, peasants and artisans, and farm labourers. The distinctions have become far more detailed over time and today there are around 3000 castes.

A career defined by birth
Membership of a caste is hereditary and linked to the job that a person may be permitted to do.

The caste system in modern India
The modern Indian constitution does not permit people to enjoy any privilege or to be discriminated against on the basis of the caste to which they belong.

The caste system in rural areas
In rural areas the caste system is still intact. Hindu fundamentalists are still calling for it to be revived.

The attacks launched by her gang were targeted mainly at thakurs – the Rams' caste. At the same time, she appointed herself avenger for all women. Whenever she heard of a rape, a forced abortion or a woman being made to commit suicide for bringing shame on her family, she exacted bloody vengeance against the perpetrators. She wrote, 'I would crush them. Otherwise there was no justice for girls like me. The only thing to do with men like that was to crush their serpents, so that they could never use them again'.

FROM PRISONER TO POLITICIAN
Seventeen months after escaping from Behmai, she returned to take her revenge. Although she could not find the Ram brothers, she is said to have recognised two of their gang. She ordered 22 thakur men to be dragged from their homes and shot. She was 18. The press described it as the largest massacre by bandits in Indian history. A huge manhunt was launched, but Phoolan Devi's legendary reputation among the poor was only enhanced as she evaded capture. She was mobbed wherever she went and flowers were placed in the bandits' rifle muzzles.

After months on the run, Phoolan Devi learned that her parents had been arrested, so she agreed to negotiate terms of surrender with the police chief of the Bhind district of Madhya Pradesh. Several demands would have to be met before she would turn herelf in. She was not to be extradited to Uttar Pradesh, where Behmai is located; no-one from her gang was to be hanged, or locked up for more than eight years; she was to be held in a 'first-class' jail; and at her arrest, pictures of the goddess Durga and Mahatma Gandhi were to be displayed. On February 13, 1983, the Bandit Queen laid down her weapons in Bhind. A crowd of 10,000 cheered as music blasted from

loudspeakers and the slight khaki-clad figure bowed to the portraits of Durga and Gandhi.

The authorities did not keep their side of the bargain. Phoolan Devi was detained for 11 years without trial. On her release in February 1994, illiterate and devoid of formal schooling, she decided to enter politics, as a 'mouthpiece for women and the poor'. She entered parliament in 1996 as a member of the socialist Samajwadi Party, and won re-election in 1999. The former Bandit Queen, whose main concern was now women's rights, became a media star and a much sought-after interviewee.

Phoolan Devi's past eventually caught up with her. On July 25, 2001, she was shot dead in front of her house in New Delhi. When asked why she hadn't been given adequate protection, a policeman said, 'We spent years chasing Phoolan Devi through the Ravines. Now she's a candidate and we're supposed to give her protection?' Speculation about her murderers' motives ranged from conspiracy theories in the run-up to the regional elections to the involvement of Phoolan's last husband, whom she married in July 1994 and who allegedly feared that she was about to disinherit him. But the man arrested for Phoolan's murder had a personal rather than political motive: he said he had killed her to avenge the massacre of thakurs at Behmai 20 years earlier.

A Devi doll was even manufactured, clad in khaki with a bandolier of bullets strapped across its chest.

The rebel convict Mary Bryant

Between 1788 and 1850 the British authorities transported more than 162,000 prisoners to Australia. Mary Bryant, a Cornish teenager, was on one of the first 11 of these ships – now known as the First Fleet – to New South Wales. In 1791 she made an audacious bid for freedom.

Prison ships were were first established on the Thames, but others – such as the one where Mary was held – were soon moored in Portsmouth harbour. Conditions on board were overcrowded and airless – not helped by the fact that portholes on the landward side were all boarded over as a deterrent against escape.

Mary Bryant was born as Mary Broad on May 1, 1765, in Fowey, a Cornish fishing village. She was the second child of a fisherman, William Broad, and his wife Grace. Eighteenth-century Cornwall was a poverty-stricken area and many people were literally starving. The desperate situation led people to look outside the law merely to survive. The government tried to contain the situation with draconian punishments – sometimes even minor offences could result in the death sentence.

Mary became involved in petty crime, collaborating with two other young women who were also on the breadline. They repeatedly ambushed, robbed and beat wealthy ladies in their neighbourhood – and got away with it for several years. But one of Mary's victims, Agnes Lakeman, who had been assaulted and robbed of some coins and two pieces of clothing – a silk bonnet and a coat – recognised her during an identity parade in January 1786. Two months later, on March 20, 1786, Mary was tried at Exeter on charges of highway robbery to a value of 32 shillings, and condemned to death by hanging. She was taken back to prison to await execution, but her sentence was then commuted to deportation 'beyond the seas' for a period of seven years. There was a practical motive for commuting the death sentence for young women to one of deportation – there was a chronic shortage of women in the penal colonies.

TRANSPORTS TO BOTANY BAY

North America had long been the main destination for convict transports, but this was no longer an option after American independence in 1783. Britain's prisons overflowed with convicts awaiting deportation. Many prisoners were housed on decommissioned warships, where they were segregated by sex, clapped in heavy irons and herded together in unsanitary and cramped conditions. Mary was confined to a cell on board the hulk *Dunkirk*. In order to gain better treatment, she began a relationship with one of the prison officers.

To help solve the prison crisis, the British government had decided to set up a new penal colony in Australia. The first convicts to be deported – 568 men and 191 women – were transferred to the so-called 'First Fleet'. Mary was one of more

It took a 252-day voyage across 15,000 miles of open sea, for the First Fleet to reach Botany Bay on January 19-20 1788. The 759 prisoners were chained up for the entire eight-month journey and the men selected for hard labour almost immediately they disembarked. The women stayed on board for another two weeks while tents and huts were put up to house them.

than 100 deportees put on board a cargo ship, the *Charlotte*, and on May 13, 1787, they embarked. Soon after the ship set sail for Botany Bay – close to the present-day city of Sydney – Mary realised that she was pregnant. If she had still been on board the *Dunkirk*, she might have been able to rely on the support of her lover; now she had only her own resources.

Conditions on this ship were even worse than on the *Dunkirk*. The hatches could not be opened, so it was dark and airless below deck. Rats, bedbugs, lice, cockroaches and fleas plagued both prisoners and crew and many died on the voyage. Despite these adversities, on September 8, 1787, Mary gave birth to a healthy baby girl, whom she called Charlotte Spence.

Mary knew that life in her new home would be difficult – it had been made clear to the women that they were there to act as sexual playthings for the men. Perhaps to protect herself from the likelihood of rape once they landed, Mary married a fellow convict called William Bryant while she was still on board ship.

Life in the new colony was punishing. The work involved in building the settlement that was later to become Sydney was backbreaking, food was in short supply and disease was rife among the prisoners.

A DARING ESCAPE PLAN

In March 1790, Mary gave birth to a son, Emmanuel. She began to dream of escape: in contrast to the men, no return passage to England was provided for women convicts who had served their time. Although she had only two years of her sentence remaining, and William just a few months of his, Mary and her husband planned a daring mission.

Mary gathered provisions, muskets and nautical equipment, and with William, her two children and a small band of rebel companions, made off with the Governor's 30-foot cutter. They sailed for ten weeks, covering 3254 nautical miles to reach the island of Timor in Indonesia, a trip that involved navigating the then uncharted Great Barrier Reef and the Torres Straits.

On reaching the Dutch colony, they persuaded the authorities that they were shipwreck survivors and were, at first, welcomed. But their good fortune did not last – they were found out, apparently after William confessed, and were put on a ship back to England to face execution.

During the voyage home, William Bryant and the children died of fever – the younger child, Emmanuel and his father in late 1791 and Charlotte in May 1792. Mary herself expected to be hanged or returned to Australia. Instead she was imprisoned in Newgate jail, during which time there was a public outcry as well as a press campaign by the famous writer and lawyer James Boswell. As a result, Mary was pardoned in May 1793, as were the four surviving men of her crew. At the age of 28, she became a free woman and returned to her native Cornwall.

Female outlaws

Anne Bonney
At the beginning of the 18th century, the Irishwoman terrorised the Caribbean with acts of piracy. She was captured at the age of 20 and sentenced to death.

Calamity Jane
Born Martha Jane Canary in the state of Missouri, USA, in 1852, she lived the life of an adventurer and gunslinger in the gold rush cities of the American West, but settled down to a bourgeois existence in 1885.

Barbara Krämer
In the latter half of the 18th century, the robber Barbara Krämer led a notorious band of brigands in the south of Germany. After many years living as an outlaw, she was captured and hanged herself in prison.

The lady
of the
camellias

Marie Duplessis, fêted in the 1840s as the most beautiful courtesan in Paris, died of tuberculosis at the age of 23. Her story inspired Alexandre Dumas the younger to write his most successful novel, *La Dame aux Camélias*, and Verdi to compose his most beloved opera, *La Traviata*.

In the 19th century, young girls would starve themselves in order to mimic the alluring pallor and feverish bright eyes that characterised consumption – the disease that killed Marie Duplessis.

In the autumn of 1844 the writer Alexandre Dumas met a young Parisian prostitute. But Marie Duplessis was no street girl; she was a 'kept woman' with all the trappings of wealth – an apartment, a carriage, even a box at the opera – and only one lover at a time. Dumas (known as 'the younger', the illegitimate son of the author of *The Three Musketeers*) was 20 years old and completely besotted. He and Marie became lovers. But one evening when Dumas was at the theatre, he bumped into Marie on the arm of a much older man – Count Gustav Stackelberg, a former Russian envoy. Although Dumas knew that Marie earned her living through her liaisons with other men, he must have found it hard to accept when presented with evidence of her profession. Later that night he ended their relationship.

A NORMANDY PEASANT GIRL

Alphonsine Plessis was born on January 15, 1824, in the hamlet of Nonnant in Normandy. Her home life, with her drunken father, Marin, was miserable and brutal. By the time Alphonsine was ten years old she was begging on the street for food. But within a couple of years, she learnt that there were easier ways for a pretty girl to earn money – her father had noticed the effect his daughter's beauty had on men and had begun offering her to his friends in return for payment.

When she was 15 Alphonsine escaped to Paris. There she learnt to dance, to read and write, to ride and, perhaps most important of all, to appreciate the arts. This allowed her to hold her own in educated company. The final stage in her metamorphosis came with a change of name. Adding Du to Plessis lent an aristocratic air, and she dropped Alphonsine in favour of Marie; she also took to wearing a corsage of camellias – the most expensive flowers available in Paris.

Before long, Marie presided over a salon renowned throughout the city. The men who flocked to her gatherings were very respectable – often older married men sidling out to meet their mistresses, or wealthy youths enjoying a night on the town. Tickets for such evenings were much in demand – a soirée at the salon of Marie Duplessis did not come cheap. But behind the exclusive façade and hectic lifestyle, Marie knew that she was not well. She suffered from a troublesome and persistent cough. In 1844 she consulted the leading doctors in Paris who suggested a variety of sometimes improbable cures and advised her to take a break from city life. To recuperate, she toured the health spas of Germany – where she met Count Gustav Stackelberg who had, himself, recently lost a daughter to tuberculosis, and who would became her final patron.

AN AFFAIR TO REMEMBER

Alexandre Dumas' books and plays opposed adultery, prostitution and upheld the sanctity of the family. Under certain circumstances, though, he believed a man could be forgiven his adultery; a woman, never.

Perhaps the young Alexandre Dumas was over-sensitive to his beloved's profession but his own family background was not overly respectable to say the least. His mother was a dressmaker who gave birth to him out of wedlock in 1824. His father, the renowned writer Alexandre Dumas, did not legally recognise the boy until he was seven years old, at which point he gave him his name. He also decided that his son needed a good education which necessitated removing him from his mother. The separation hit young Alexandre hard. The pain felt by his mother also made a deep impression, inspiring later tragic 'mother' characters in Dumas' novels and plays. His boarding school education was tough, too – other schoolboys made his life a misery, taunting him about his illegitimacy. But at least he had a share of his father's wealth and fame. And it was through these connections that he gained entry to the illustrious circle that gathered around Marie Duplessis. Although the ending of his affair with Marie broke the young writer's heart, his story, rewritten as a novel, also brought him worldwide fame. The trigger was Marie's early death, just 18 months after the unfortunate theatre evening. He elaborated on the circumstances of her death, and his fictional heroine, dumped by her rich patrons, dies in abject poverty, giving Dumas the opportunity to write about the double standards of high society in an extraordinarily candid way.

In his novel *La Dame aux Camélias*, he casts himself as Armand Duval (his initials) – a young man of good family – and Marie Duplessis as Marguerite Gautier, a prostitute. Marguerite is dying of consumption, when Armand's father persuades her to relinquish her young lover – and the only man she has ever loved – for the sake of the family's, and by inference, Armand's, reputation. Marguerite's sacrifice kills her.

Dumas had an interesting explanation for 'The Lady of the Camellias', the sobriquet he created for Duplessis: 'For 25 days in every month the camellias were white, and for five they were red. No one ever knew the reason for this variation in colour which I mention but cannot explain.' The colours of the camellias obviously corresponded to Marguerite's menstrual cycle, so perhaps Dumas wrote this passage to illustrate the innocence of his narrator.

CAMILLE – AN ACTRESS'S DREAM ROLE

The story of the exquisite and warm-hearted courtesan who died young, alone and destitute touched people's hearts. It has been frequently reworked, Dumas' novel being just the first in a line of different versions. The stage play, *Camille*, was a huge success with tragic actresses in the 19th century queueing up to play Marguerite. The great French actress, Sarah Bernhardt, having made the role her own on stage, became the living embodiment of 'Camille' – so much so that, when the play was filmed in 1912, not even the fact that she was 68 years old prevented her from being cast as the twenty-something heroine.

Father and son, or père et fils

Dumas père
Alexandre Dumas père (1802-70) was one of the most famous French writers of the 19th century, best known for his historical novels *The Three Musketeers* and *The Count of Monte Cristo*, both written in the period 1844-45.

Dumas fils
Alexandre Dumas fils (1824-95) was Alexandre Dumas' illegitimate son. His romantic novel, and later, play, *La Dame aux Camélias* was a huge success. Other novels include *A Prodigal Father* (1859), based on his own father and *L'Affaire Clémenceau*. His plays include *Denise* (1885) and *Francillon* (1887).

144

As early as 1853, Giuseppe Verdi used the drama as the basis of *La Traviata* or 'the wayward woman'. The opera keeps Dumas' Parsian setting but the heroine is given an Italian name, Violetta. Italian conservatism necessitated the removal of many of the more risqué scenes from the play. Violetta is utterly reliant on the goodwill of her friends – which is swiftly shown to be shallow.

> '*Poor girl… her death was especially sad, because in her world one only has fair-weather friends.*'
>
> FROM ALEXANDRE DUMAS: *LA DAME AUX CAMÉLIAS*

She believes that to return the love of a young man such as Alfredo would only lead to her impoverishment and disappointment, a belief which turns out to be tragically correct.

In 1937, the Swedish film star Garbo gave one of her greatest performances as the eponymous *Camille* in George Cukor's version of the story. The director recalled, 'While we were doing *Camille*, Garbo didn't talk much to Robert Taylor. She was polite, but distant. She had to tell herself that he was the ideal young man, and she knew if they became friendly, she'd learn he was just another nice kid'. She was nominated for an Oscar for her performance.

In 2001, Baz Luhrmann's film *Moulin Rouge* transposed the story to the Paris of the Roaring Nineties, in and around the eponymous nightclub. Against a chaotic all-singing, all-dancing backdrop, Nicole Kidman's nightclub singer Satine discreetly coughed blood into a white handkerchief while her hopelessly smitten love, Christian, a young poet and composer played by Ewan McGregor, vied with a wealthy rival for her attention.

Alphonsine may not have taken her last consumptive breath in the tender embrace of a lover, but the poor girl from the French countryside, sold into prostitution by her abusive father, has achieved a sort of immortality – and to this day visitors leave flowers on her grave in Paris's Montmartre cemetery.

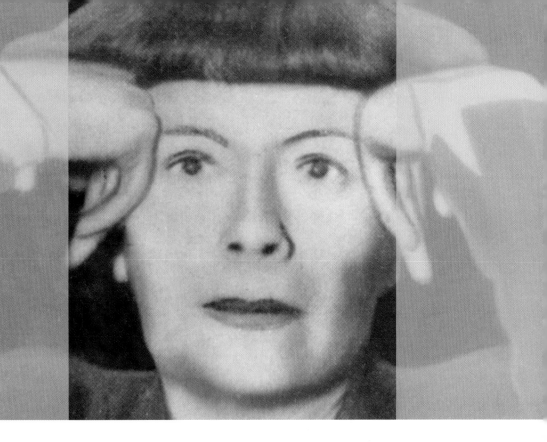

A ruthless **female double agent**

As a French Resistance agent, Mathilde Carré's stealth, feline looks and duplicity earned her the nickname *la chatte* (the cat). Arrested by the Germans, she turned double agent and betrayed many of her colleagues.

'On a cold rainy day last week, curious Parisians packed a dingy courtroom in the Palais de Justice to hear a red-robed judge pronounce sentence on Mathilde Carré... The French thought they understood Mathilde, though they could not forgive her.' So began a report in *Time* magazine on January 17, 1949. Although widely reported, the trial

'A pert, petite woman with bangs – the very picture of a Parisian gamine', is how *Time* magazine described Mathilde Carré (above) in its report on her trial.

of Mathilde Carré raised few eyebrows. By 1949, the world was reeling with shock at the evidence of Nazi inhumanity that had emerged from the Nuremberg War Crimes trials – and by comparison the intrigues of a French double agent paled into insignificance. But as far as Carré was concerned, the trial was a matter of life and death – four years after the end of the Second World War, being found guilty of spying for an enemy power could still warrant the death penalty.

THE HEROIC RESISTANCE FIGHTER

Born in France in 1910, Mathilde Carré was educated at the Sorbonne and became a teacher. On her marriage to an army officer she moved to Algeria but, not long after the outbreak of war, her husband was killed and the widowed Carré volunteered to return to Paris and train as a nurse.

In June 1940, the German army occupied the French capital and Carré's unit moved out, eventually settling in Toulon – a major port on the Mediterranean coast. She ran a reception centre for French troops who had become separated from their units. Here, her path crossed with that of a charismatic young Pole, Roman Czerniawski, who, disguised as a Frenchman, was working undercover against the German occupation.

Carré was both impressed and attracted by Czerniawski – codenamed 'Walenty' to the Poles and 'Armand' or 'Victor' to the French – and she joined his Paris-based espionage network, Interallié. Her codename was 'Victoire' – all the staff in her section had cryptonyms beginning with V. (Interallié named its agents and their sectors using christian names grouped by letters of the alphabet.) Travelling all over the country, Carré gathered information about German troop movements, including identifying and pinpointing *Luftwaffe* and SS Panzer

Female agents during the Second World War

Yvonne Corneau
Under the codename 'Annette', she conducted secret operations in occupied France, barely escaping arrest by Germans.

Odette Sansom
At the end of the war, she was awarded the George Cross for her work as a secret agent in the service of the British, as well as the French order of the Legion d'Honneur, and was fêted as a national heroine.

Ruth Weiner
As Ursula Beurton, she was one of the most successful spies of the 20th century. From 1930 onwards, she worked under the codename Sonja as an agent for the military intelligence division of the Soviet Red Army.

divisions near Bordeaux, and ascertaining that the German attack on Gibraltar had been abandoned. Her stealthiness soon earned 'Victoire' a second codename, *la chatte*.

LOYALTY VERSUS LIFE

When Carré's resistance cell was betrayed by a double agent, German counterintelligence – the Abwehr – began making arrests of French agents. Carré was detained by Hugo Bleicher in November 1941 and given an ultimatum – either become a double agent or die. Carré chose to live.

To save her own skin she revealed the names of more than 30 comrades. But she went a step further: continuing to use her codename 'Victoire', she successfully set traps for them all, one after the other. Even her former lover Roman Czerniawski and his new girlfriend were among her victims.

Carré may have become Bleicher's mistress; whether she did or not, under his control she maintained radio contact with London, giving the Allies one false scent after another. She was certain of one thing – she would remain alive only while she was of use to the Germans.

Meanwhile, Carré continued to enjoy French and British trust as a loyal member of the Interallié. Now that the group's communications network had been all but destroyed, Carré was called to London along with a resistance leader, Pierre De Vomecourt. The Abwehr, thrilled to be infiltrating the British Special Operations Executive (SOE), had no hesitation in letting Carré and Vomecourt leave France.

> *'A spy in the right place is worth 20,000 men at the front.'*
>
> NAPOLEON BONAPARTE

THE CAT LOSES A LIFE

It didn't work out quite as planned. Once she was in London, British counter intelligence, MI5, quickly discovered Carré's dual allegiance and she was arrested in 1942 and taken to Holloway prison. Later she was moved to a detention centre near Aylesbury, where it was noted that she also acted as an informant against her fellow prisoners. Carré remained in Britain for the rest of the war when she was extradited to face trial in France.

Mathilde Carré pictured at her trial. During Carré's time in Britain, an MI5 informer called Mrs Barton reported on a party at Claridges where Carré met Lord Selbourne (Minister for the Special Operations Executive), with whom she got on extremely well. Barton said that 'even if only half of what she told me is true it seems to me that he is behaving exceedingly foolishly. . . [she] is an exceedingly dangerous woman'.

During the years she spent in prison before appearing in court, Carré wrote her memoirs, *J'ai été la Chatte* (I was the she-cat). During her trial she refused to admit her guilt and, despite the glowing testimony of Paul Archard, one of her wartime resistance commanders, few others spoke in her defence. She had betrayed too many. Carré was dumbfounded when she was sentenced to death by hanging. But within a few months, her sentence was commuted to one of life imprisonment. She eventually died in 1970. It seemed that this cat did indeed have nine lives.

Truth and legend

6

How the
USA tried to steal a
Russian submarine

In 1974, when the CIA embarked on a
clandestine operation to recover a Soviet
nuclear submarine from the depths of the
Pacific Ocean, they enlisted the help of
the eccentric billionaire Howard Hughes

On July 4, 1974, ships sailing the choppy waters of the northern Pacific Ocean, 1700 miles northwest of Hawaii, were confronted by a baffling sight. A huge ship, surmounted by a towering superstructure that resembled a drilling derrick, lay almost motionless at anchor. Captains of passing ships sent incredulous radio messages to the ship, asking how it was possible to drill for oil in this location, where the seafloor plummets to a depth of 5000 metres. They were informed that the ship, the *Glomar Explorer*, belonged to the legendary billionaire, pilot, inventor and engineering genius, Howard Hughes. It was collecting manganese, a vital component in the production of steel, from the seabed.

TREASURE ON THE OCEAN FLOOR

Most of the manganese mined – with considerable difficulty in Russia, China, South Africa, Brazil and Australia – was used in the production of steel. A chance discovery had recently revealed that the Pacific ocean bed was littered with curious mineral lumps resembling pieces of horse dung and measuring up to 25 centimetres across. They were found to have a manganese content of up to 40 per cent and the Pacific deposits alone were estimated at over 10 billion tonnes. It is still not clear how the manganese lumps were formed or how they came to be on the ocean floor.

It was likely that an entrepreneur such as Howard Hughes would try to raise this mineral wealth from the seabed and so make the USA less dependent on imports. But this seemingly plausible explanation was a cover story, hiding a much more bizarre Cold War reality. The crew of the *Glomar Explorer* was on a mission that would yield even greater riches – Soviet nuclear secrets. They were intending to raise a sunken Soviet submarine, armed with intercontinental ballistic nuclear missiles and which contained the potential to wipe out millions of people. They were participants in 'Project Jennifer.'

Howard Hughes (1905–76) was a legendary hypochondriac, movie-producer and aviator, who made a vast fortune building military aircraft for the US Government. A consummate political lobbyist, he had built close links with the CIA who commissioned his company to build the *Glomar Explorer.*

THE SINKING OF K-129

By the time 'Operation Jennifer' got under way, submarine K-129 had been lying on the seabed for six years. In February 1968, the vessel had set out on a routine voyage from Vladivostok, setting course for the strait that lies between Sakhalin Island and the northernmost tip of Japan. On April 11, according to the official account of the incident, the submarine was rocked by an explosion. The blast ripped a hole in the hull and water surged in under extreme pressure. The crew of 86 Soviet submariners must have perished instantly – they had no time to send out a distress call. Other theories have been advanced to explain the sudden disappearance of K-129. It is possible that the Soviet vessel was involved in an underwater collision with the US submarine Swordfish, which was known to be patrolling the same area as the K-129. A few days after the accident, Swordfish had limped into dock at the US base at Yokosuka with major damage.

Whatever the case, the Americans, unlike the Soviets, knew exactly where the vessel had sunk. They had heard the explosion on the listening devices of their underwater sonar surveillance array known as SOSUS ('Sound Surveillance System'). They were able to plot the precise location, some 750 nautical miles northeast of Hawaii, at a depth of around 5000 metres. The Russians, on the other hand, were completely in the dark about the dramatic events that had taken place. Soviet submarines patrolling the northern Pacific broke radio silence to send frantic transmissions to one another in a desperate attempt to locate their missing submarine.

COLD WAR SECRETS

The K-129 was a vessel of the Golf II class, which was powered by conventional diesel-electric engines and had already been superseded by nuclear-powered submarines. Its main distinguishing feature was an enormous conning tower, the largest ever seen on a submarine, which housed three SS-N-5 intercontinental ballistic missiles along with their firing mechanisms. Why the CIA was so intent on recovering this obsolete submarine was never explained, but no doubt the tense political climate at the time played a part in this decision.

On the political stage, the first steps had already been taken towards détente, but the Cold War showed no signs of abating. Submarines of both superpowers regularly shadowed one another in the depths of the ocean. Both sides regularly undertook surveillance missions in each other's territorial waters. US submarines counted the number of naval ships that were under construction at Soviet shipyards, tapped into underwater telecommunications cables and listened in on telephone conversations. They took photographs, through their periscopes, of the dock installations at Soviet naval bases and followed almost every vessel of the Soviet Navy in order to draw up diagrams of the noise made by their engines and propellers, which could subsequently be used as sonic 'fingerprints' to identify individual ships.

Repeated sightings of actual or imagined periscopes of Soviet submarines off the coast of New York or Florida spread panic among American bathers. Many people insisted they had even seen periscopes in places where the water was only 1.5 metres deep. Against this background of fear and paranoia it is scarcely surprising that 'Project Jennifer' swung into operation at the CIA immediately after the sinking of the *K-129*.

Once the sunken submarine had been located in the spring of 1969, the CIA commissioned the building of the *Glomar Explorer* at one of the shipyards belonging to the Hughes Corporation. The salvage vessel had a displacement of 63,000 tonnes and was equipped with a gigantic loading platform amidships, popularly referred to as the 'Moon Pool,' which could be opened up below to allow enormous, grabbing arms to extend down into the depths. The salvage team were briefed to recover the Russian nuclear missiles and decoding devices from the stricken submarine in order to find out exactly how advanced Soviet technology was. If at all possible, they were instructed to raise the entire submarine for examination.

The CIA planned to lift the submarine up to just below the surface and then remove it from the scene underwater, ensuring that the operation remained clandestine. In fact, the Soviets were well aware of the operation although they did not attempt to thwart it.

A TECHNOLOGICAL MIRACLE

The Summa Corporation, the holding company that controlled all the concerns owned by Hughes, supervised construction of the alleged research vessel. Launched at Chester, Pennsylvania, in November 1972, the *Glomar Explorer* was a superlative piece of engineering. Even seasoned oilmen were awe-struck. The 'Moon Pool' alone, which occupied almost the entire width of the ship, was 61 metres long, 23 metres wide and just under 20 metres deep. Above it, towering into the sky, stood the derrick. It was designed to allow sections of pipe, each 20 metres in length, to be linked together to snake down to a depth of up to six miles. It wielded a grab mechanism with eight claws capable of lifting objects of up to 7000 tonnes. Tried-and-tested techniques used in building oil-drilling vessels ensured that the *Glomar Explorer* would remain completely stable while the submarine was being salvaged.

'Certain agencies are taking steps to raise a Soviet submarine that sank in the Pacific. From a well-wisher.'

TEXT OF AN ANONYMOUS MESSAGE SENT TO THE SOVIET EMBASSY IN WASHINGTON, DC

A top-secret underwater dock accompanied the *Glomar Explorer* on her mission. This vessel, the *Hughes Mining Barge I* (or *HMB-I* for short), was built specially for this task. She carried the grab mechanism out to the *Glomar Explorer* and, once the salvage operation was complete, it was planned that she would serve as a transportation platform for the *K-129*.

'PROJECT JENNIFER': INTO THE OCEAN DEPTHS

In July 1974 the *Glomar Explorer* arrived at its appointed destination in the northern Pacific, directly above the *K-129*. The salvage operation could only begin once the sea was completely calm. It was several days before the eight grabs on their connecting rods were lowered inch by inch down to the ocean floor 5000 metres below and several more days before the grabs were positioned directly over the submarine.

Progress in the ocean depths was tracked on monitor screens on board the *Glomar Explorer*. When the salvage crew could see that one of the grabs was touching the submarine's hull, they tried to manoeuvre all the other grabs nearer so that they could grip the submarine like giant claws. But the move was miscalculated and the grab mechanism slammed down violently into the seabed. It then had to be painstakingly pulled back up for a distance of about 100 metres. As the crew stared fixedly at their monitors they feared that they had damaged the apparatus irreparably, bringing an end to their mission. Yet in the dim underwater light, the grabs looked remarkably intact. A second attempt was made and this time the claws were successfully positioned around the submarine – 'Project Jennifer' was now in full swing.

Painfully slowly, the 5000-tonne Soviet submarine, completely waterlogged, was lifted off the ocean floor. Straining to lift this enormous weight, the *Glomar Explorer* sunk lower in the water and began to buck and roll under the strain. The crew stood by in strained silence, aware that it was possible that their ship might capsize. Down in the depths, the *K-129* hung suspended in the arms of the grab. In nine hours' lifting, the steel coffin with its cargo of nuclear missiles had risen just 1500 metres closer to the surface. If everything went smoothly, it would take 30 hours to bring the submarine to the surface.

A Soviet submarine of the same class as the *K-129*. Propelled by diesel power, the Golf II class of submarines were designed to dive to a maximum depth of 300 metres.

Suddenly, three of the grabs failed and released their grip, sending a violent shock reverberating through the *Glomar Explorer*. Although two grabs were still holding the front part of the submarine, the rest of the hull was suspended in mid-water without any support. Further disaster struck when the steel plating of the submarine tore apart along a line of rivets and the major section of the *K-129* broke free and sunk back down into the ocean depths. The men on the

Glomar Explorer were transfixed with horror, aware that intact nuclear warheads were about to hit the ocean floor. Nobody was sure how the warheads had been constructed or confident that they would withstand the impact. It was possible that the salvagers had just set a nuclear catastrophe in motion. The seconds ticked by agonisingly slowly. But when the impact came there was no explosion; the men on board could breathe again.

Only the section of the submarine that still remained in the grab could now be salvaged. Everything else, including the codebooks and all the radio, sonar and encoding equipment – which the CIA had particularly wanted to save – had been swallowed by the sea. The remains of the submarine that were eventually eased through the open hatches of the 'Moon Pool' were of little use to the CIA operatives. Their mission had failed.

The *Los Angeles Times* broke the story of the *Glomar Explorer* in 1975 and the United States announced that they had found the bodies of eight Soviet submariners in the recovered section of the submarine. They had been buried at sea with full military honours about 90 miles southwest of Hawaii. The ceremony was videotaped and presented to the Soviet Union.

THE LATER CAREER OF THE *GLOMAR EXPLORER*

The Cold War era of underwater surveillance and pursuit furnished ample material for novels and films. Even the CIA conceded that the underwater chase portrayed in the feature film *The Hunt for Red October*, was completely realistic. 'Project Jennifer' undoubtedly inspired the producers of the James Bond films. *The Spy Who Loved Me* has a sequence in which a converted supertanker swallows up a submarine – the ship having a similar grab device to that of the *Glomar Explorer*.

With the end of the Cold War the *Glomar Explorer*'s glory days were over. For many years the vessel was mothballed. In 1996 she was converted into what she had once purported to be. Nowadays, she is employed as a drilling vessel on the hunt for oil in the Gulf of Mexico. Even the *HMB-I* was deployed in other roles, first being used by the US environment agency as a floating underwater research platform and later, in the 1990s, serving with the US navy as a base for experimental stealth submarines.

A
king of many
facets

Revered for his learning and wisdom, King Solomon is seen as the epitome of a wise and just ruler. But is the biblical account of Solomon misleading? Was the king really an extravagant despot whose rule marked the end of a Jewish golden age?

The tenth of King David's many sons, Solomon came to power after his mother, Bathsheba – David's favourite wife – persuaded the king to keep a vow to grant the succession to Solomon instead of his brother, Adonijah, who had already been anointed in an earlier ceremony.

Solomon's history is recorded in Kings 1–11 and Chronicles 1–9. The name Solomon (Shlomo) means 'peaceful', or 'complete', from the Hebrew *Shelomoh* (Arabic *Sulaiman*).

A RUTHLESS KING

On his father's death in about 961 BC, Solomon swiftly and brutally established his authority. When the thwarted Adonijah seemed to be undermining royal authority over the palace harem, Solomon had him executed and his chief supporters banished or killed. The murder of one, Joab, the army commander, had repercussions for the rest of Solomon's reign, encouraging uprisings in Edom and Aramea. But Solomon never waged a serious military campaign against these or any other adversaries, despite an army of 12,000 horsemen and 1400 charioteers.

No warrior king, Solomon turned instead to domestic matters. Following systems developed in Egypt and Mesopotamia, he divided his kingdom into twelve administrative districts, cutting across tribal boundaries to enhance the power of central government. Each district was headed by a prefect who was responsible for providing the king with a month's worth of food and fodder, offerings for daily worship and workers for his construction projects.

AN ARCHITECT AND TRADER

Solomon's building projects were hugely ambitious, from defensive fortifications throughout the kingdom to the citadel of Zion – which included a new royal palace and the magnificent temple of the Jews. The latter took seven years to complete and housed the hallowed Ark of the Covenant, adorned with exquisite carvings by craftsmen from Syria and Phoenicia. Solomon's architectural endeavours were funded by heavy taxation and took workers away from other projects. Popular resentment was fuelled

The Queen of Sheba makes a fleeting appearance in biblical history, but she remains a mysterious and exotic figure who has intrigued successive generations of artists and writers. Her legendary appearance at the court of King Solomon has been the subject of numerous pictures, such as this 18th-century painting from the School of Tiepolo.

when Solomon extended the system of forced labour – formerly the preserve of prisoners and foreigners – to include 30,000 Israelites. To obtain the materials for his extravagant buildings, Solomon had to develop skills in both trading and diplomacy. He owned copper and iron mines and refining operations in southern Palestine. A treaty with King Hiram of Tyre gave Israel cypress and cedar trees, along with gold, in exchange for wheat and oil. Hiram and Solomon also made trading agreements centred on the Red Sea, including the creation of a fleet, built by the Phoenicians, financed by Israel and manned by mixed crews. On the African coast near Somaliland, they traded iron and copper for ivory, precious stones, silver, gold, peacocks and monkeys.

SOLOMON AND THE QUEEN OF SHEBA

Solomon also controlled caravan routes connecting Egypt with Syria and his trade in Anatolian horses and Egyptian chariots was a virtual monopoly. The proceeds were supplemented by tolls on caravan traffic. Merchants were required to pay him tribute in spices and precious metals, horses and fine clothing.

It seems to have been Solomon's increasing control of land routes and sea trade further south to Arabia that inspired the story of the legendary Queen of Sheba's visit to Jerusalem. Although the story focuses on her curiosity about Solomon's wisdom, the queen, who arrived 'with a very great retinue, with camels bearing spices, and very much gold, and precious stones' was more likely to have been on a trade mission. The Bible tells of her admiration for Solomon's wisdom and the splendour of his court. 'You possess even greater wisdom and goodness than I was led to believe', she said, giving the king 120 hundredweight of gold, jewels and precious spices. The two monarchs also concluded a mutually beneficial trade treaty. Ethiopian

Ancient Israel

Unification of the Hebrews
Saul unified the Hebrew-speaking tribes, becoming in the process the first King of Israel (c.1020–1004 BC).

Expansion into Palestine
His successor David (c.1004–965 BC) expanded the kingdom to cover all of Palestine up to the border with the lands ruled by the Phoenicians. The Bible claims that David's realm extended as far as the border with Egypt and the River Euphrates.

Loss and division of the kingdoms
During the reign of Solomon (965–926 BC), who succeeded David, several of the conquered territories were lost. On his death, the kingdom split into the two separate kingdoms of Israel and Judah.

Christianity also includes the story that they conceived a child who came to the throne in Ethiopia, founding a branch of the house of David in Africa.

The story draws both on Solomon's reputation as a lover of many women and his renown as the wisest ruler of his day. His royal harem may not have been as extravagant as the 700 wives and 300 concubines claimed by the Bible, but it was substantial. Many of the marriages were made for diplomatic reasons and his wives included Hittites, Moabites, Edomites, Sidonians and Ammonites. The marriages did sometimes cause problems in his own kingdom, mainly because the foreign wives brought their own customs and religions, in contravention of many of the strict regulations governing ritual matters in Israel.

A NEW KIND OF KING

Solomon changed the definition of kingship in ancient Israel. Unlike his warrior father, he offered sacrifices and blessed his people, taking over certain priestly functions. Rather than rely on prophets for divine messages, he communicated directly with God. Determined to weaken tribal society and affirm central control, he established a new bureaucracy that was dependent on his influence, while priests and village elders were also integrated into the government.

He was exceptionally tolerant of pagan religions; elements of style and ritual from other cults were introduced into services at the temple and there was an increase in marriage with foreigners among his people. It has been argued that Solomon's toleration of other religions led to the collapse of the kingdom after his death. When he died and the throne passed to his son Rehoboam, the kingdom split in two. Eventually, both the northern kingdom of Israel and the southern kingdom of Judah fell to foreign invaders.

A REPUTATION FOR WISDOM

Shortly after he became king, God said to Solomon in a dream, 'Ask what I shall give you'. He requested an 'understanding mind to govern the people, that I may discern between good and evil'. The reply reflects a particular aspect of his reputation, his ability to give judicious decisions. A famous example is the story of two

Artists are intrigued by the story of the Judgment of Solomon, and many have attempted to capture the arresting moment of crisis and moral choice. Nicolas Poussin (1594–1666), an artist who was inspired by classical and biblical history, depicted the dramatic scene in 1649.

harlots who gave birth to male children at the same time. When one child died, each woman claimed the living child as her own. Having heard their stories, Solomon asked for a sword. 'Divide the living child in two', he said, 'and give half to the one and half to the other.' One woman agreed, but the other offered to give up the baby rather than see it killed. It was she who was the real mother as she had showed a mother's compassion.

He is also celebrated for his use of proverbs, which drew on the lore of civilisations including Mesopotamia, Egypt and Canaan. He often used examples from the natural world and both in legend and in the Koran, Solomon was shown as having the ability to converse with birds and beasts. He was also a talented solver of riddles – a gift that entranced the Queen of Sheba.

Despite his power and reputation, Solomon continually sought to broaden his mind, seeking insights from all fields of knowledge and studying assiduously. He is said to have written the books of *Proverbs*, *Ecclesiastes*, the *Song of Solomon* and the *Wisdom of Solomon* in the Apocrypha.

Solomon created an organised, wealthy and visually magnificent nation-state and was prepared to be ruthless to attain his aims. But it is not his political and architectural achievments that have ultimately endured; it is his reputation as a judge and thinker that has continued in perpetuity.

The
captured
moment

Photographer Robert Capa sought to capture
the poignancy and horror of conflict as well as the
bravery and heroics. His extraordinary picture of a
dying soldier was a defining image of the Spanish
Civil War – but for many years there were doubts
about its authenticity.

On a hot, late summer's afternoon in 1936, a shot shattered the silence on the slopes of the Cerro Muriano mountains near the city of Córdoba. Civil war was raging throughout Spain and the apparently idyllic scene on the mountainside was deceptive. Mortally wounded, a soldier sank to the ground, his rifle falling from his hand. The final moments of the soldier's life were recorded for posterity by the news photographer, Robert Capa, in an iconic image that vividly captured the horrors of the events that were unfolding in Spain.

A RESTLESS SPIRIT

Capa was born Andrei Friedmann in 1913 in Budapest. At the age of 17, he took part in the student protests against the fascist government of Miklós Horthy and was forced to leave Hungary. In 1931, he moved to Berlin, where he enrolled at the German College of Politics. He soon became fascinated by photography, and began working as a film and photographic assistant at the publisher Ullstein and the photo agency Dephot.

He completed his first successful assignment on November 27, 1932, in Copenhagen, when he surreptitiously photographed Leon Trotsky giving an address to students. In different circumstances the publication of the pictures in the magazine *Welt-Spiegel*, a supplement to the daily newspaper the *Berliner Tageblatt*, would have guaranteed him a successful career. But he was a Hungarian Jew and was forced to flee Nazi Germany in September 1933.

He made his new home in Paris. There, in the Montparnasse district in the autumn of 1934, he met Gerda Pohorylle, a Polish emigré who became both his partner and his agent. The couple initially found it hard to sell their photographs. So they invented a rich American photographer whom they called 'Robert Capa'.

Robert Capa's photograph of the dying soldier appeared in the French magazine *Vu* in 1936, with the following words 'With lively step, breasting the wind, clenching their rifles, they ran down the slope covered with thick stubble. Suddenly their soaring was interrupted, a bullet whistled – a fratricidal bullet – and their blood was drunk by their native soil.'

He was apparently only interested in selling his pictures if the price was sufficiently high. The ruse paid off handsomely and Parisian publishers willingly paid the fees that they asked – in some cases three times the going rate. When the scam was unmasked, Friedmann adopted the fictitious photographer's name as his own and Gerda Pohorylle changed her name to Gerda Taro. The deception had given their careers a major boost and they were jointly commissioned to produce a photo-story on the Spanish Civil War for the magazine *Vu*.

Capa worked for *Life* magazine during the Second World War. In 1942 he joined the Allied invasion convoy, then followed the troops in Sicily during the grim Italian campaign in the winter of 1943–44. Soon after Anzio he left Italy for London and went on to produce his extraordinary pictures of the D-Day landings.

A WORLD-FAMOUS PHOTOGRAPH

In August 1936, a few weeks after the military revolt of July 17 that sparked the civil war in Spain, Robert Capa and Gerda Taro travelled to Barcelona. Over the next few months they documented the tragedy and violence of the war for a number of international newspapers. On September 5, 1936, Capa was just a few metres away from a young soldier as he was shot and killed. Capa sent the extraordinary photograph that resulted to a press agency in Paris. On September 23, the French magazine

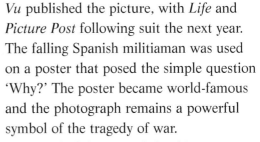

Vu published the picture, with *Life* and *Picture Post* following suit the next year. The falling Spanish militiaman was used on a poster that posed the simple question 'Why?' The poster became world-famous and the photograph remains a powerful symbol of the tragedy of war.

Capa had discovered that his true vocation was to portray war with an unflinching eye, to reveal its horrors, yet never lose sight of the human story. The international press honoured his work by acclaiming him the world's foremost war photographer in 1938.

A LIFE AND DEATH IN WAR

Depicting war became Capa's whole life – all the more so after Gerda Taro was killed in Spain in 1937. Just a couple of months later, Capa documented Chinese resistance to the Japanese occupation. In 1939, he emigrated to the United States, where he worked as a freelance photographer. From 1941 to 1945, he was commissioned by *Life* and *Collier's* magazines to cover the Second World War, producing dramatic images of the D-Day landings on June 6, 1944.

In 1948, Capa captured the first Arab-Israeli conflict on film, focusing not only on the battlefront, but also on the suffering of the civilian population. He took pictures of the wounded, those who had been bombed out of their homes, refugees, the traumatised and the grieving.

Capa's work became so popular that his name on a magazine was sufficient to guarantee a huge readership. He seemed to be able to express the horror of war and to shape people's collective consciousness of an event in a way that still holds true today. In 1947 he became involved in the foundation of the prestigious photographers' co-operative Magnum and travelled the world promoting, publicising and selling his own work and that of fellow photographers.

On May 25, 1954, while on an assignment in the Nam Dinh region of Indochina, Capa stepped on a landmine. He was killed instantly. If he had stayed safely behind the troops carrying the mine-detectors, he might have survived. But that just wasn't Capa's style – the immediacy of his pictures came from being at the heart of the action and he had spent his professional life trying to put himself in the place of those who were involved in the actual conflict.

Capa's body was returned to the USA, but his mother turned down the offer of a funeral at the American military cemetery at Arlington, on the grounds that her son had always detested war. A single word was inscribed in Hebrew script on the photographer's gravestone: 'Shalom' – Peace.

War photography

The Crimean War

In 1855, Roger Fenton produced 360 daguerrotypes of the Crimean War. The long exposure time needed explains the posed look of many of the images.

The First World War

Photography was first deployed for propaganda. Photographers were attached to military units and the pictures they took were subject to strict censorship.

Later wars

Disengaged from the military, war photographers developed into independent reporters of events. Robert Capa's photographs played a leading role in this development.

'This is going to be a beautiful story,' Capa declared as he set off on May 25, 1954, to cover his final story for *Life* magazine in Vietnam's Red River Delta. When he died, he was clutching his much-loved Nikon camera, which contained his final images.

FAKING HISTORY?

Many years after Capa's death, the authenticity of some of his images came under scrutiny, in particular his picture of the dying soldier. Critics focused on the fact that Capa had already used deception to advance his career. The opinion gained widespread currency in 1975 when the journalist and historian Phillip Knightley published a book in which he examined the various ways in which war correspondents distort the truth. For the next 20 years there were suspicions that Capa had staged the photo.

'If your pictures aren't good enough, you're not close enough.'

ROBERT CAPA

It was not until August 1996 that a contemporary eyewitness was able to scotch the rumour. Following an appraisal of the fallen soldier's clothing and equipment, Civil War veteran Mario Brotóns Jordá identified him as a member of a local citizens' militia from the village of Alcoy, the 'Columna Alcoyana', to which he himself had also belonged. Research in the state archives revealed that on September 5, 1936, the day Capa had shot his picture, only one member of the Columna Alcoyana had died in the battle at Cerro Muriano. The anonymous soldier finally had a name: Federico Borell García.

But even the identification of the dead man did not convince all the doubters. In response to an exhibition of Capa's photos in London, in July 1998, Knightley suggested that García might well have posed for the photographer before he was killed.

The search for the truth now entered a new phase. Richard Whelan, Capa's biographer and executor of his estate, solicited the help of the chief investigator of the homicide department in Memphis, Tennessee. His brief was to investigate the photo using forensic methods. The detective concluded that that the body position of the victim demonstrated incontrovertibly that the falling soldier was already dying when the photo was taken. Robert Capa had fortuitously clicked the shutter of his camera at the defining moment.

The **ugliest princess** of all?

A 1515 portrait by Quentin Massys has long been thought to show Margaret Maultasch. It is also said to have inspired John Tenniel's depiction of the Ugly Duchess in *Alice's Adventures in Wonderland*.

In 1342, Europe was rocked by a marriage scandal involving Countess Margaret of the Tyrol. The countess became legendary for her hideous appearance and appalling morals. But was she really the innocent victim of a smear campaign?

In 1282, the Tyrol, a mountainous region in the eastern Alps that straddles the present-day border between Italy and Austria, came under the control of Meinhard II. Four years later he acquired the neighbouring province of Carinthia. But it was not long before his new territories came under threat.

Meinhard's son, Duke Heinrich VI of the Tyrol and Carinthia, produced no male heir. His younger daughter Margaret was the only possible candidate to succeed him. But it was unheard of at that time to have a woman on the throne. The powerful ruling dynasties of the region – the Wittelsbach, Habsburg and Luxemburg families – already had their eyes on the Tyrol and eagerly sought an opportunity to seize the kingdom.

But in 1330 Heinrich concluded a treaty with the Holy Roman Emperor, Louis IV of Bavaria from the House of Wittelsbach, allowing female succession in his domain. The 13-year-old Margaret was then married to Prince Johann Heinrich of Bohemia from the House of Luxemburg who was five years her junior.

'Margaret Maultasch ... got her popular name from the fact that she had such a big mouth.'

JACOB GRIMM

When Heinrich died five years later, it was soon clear that the treaty was worthless. Louis IV had also secretly concluded an agreement with the Habsburgs whereby Tyrol-Carinthia was to be divided between him and Margaret's Habsburg cousins on Heinrich's death.

But Margaret was ready to defend her territory. With the help of her brother-in-law Charles (later Holy Roman Emperor Charles IV), she managed to safeguard the Tyrol from seizure. She was less successful with neighbouring Carinthia, which was lost to the Habsburgs.

At Runkelstein Castle, Bolzano, the 'castle of pictures' in the South Tyrol region, there is a renowned cycle of frescoes from the 14th century depicting myths, legends, games, jousting, giants and dwarves. This fresco of a lady with a golden plait is thought to depict the real Margaret.

Margaret grew increasingly discontent. The Tyrol was under the control of the Luxemburgs and her husband had barely reached puberty. In 1341, Margaret had the doors of the castle barred against him on the grounds that the marriage had not been consummated. A year later, in 1342, Margaret took a second husband and was excommunicated by the Pope. Her new spouse, the widower Louis of Brandenburg, was the son of that same Louis who had betrayed her father so shamefully. It was no love-match, but rather a ruthless and decisive checkmate move against the Luxemburg family.

A SMEAR CAMPAIGN

A full-blown scandal ensued. Margaret's first husband, Johann Heinrich, could not let the slur that he was impotent go unchallenged. The Luxemburg dynasty and the Pope started to spread tales about Margaret's dissolute lifestyle, including her sexual proclivities.

The propaganda spread by the Luxemburgs soon became fixed in popular imagination. As early as the 14th century, medieval writers claimed that she was hideous with a large, deformed mouth. A famous 16th-century portrait by Quentin Massys shows a very ugly woman who is alleged to be Margaret.

Margaret's supposed appearance is not the only derivation of the disparaging nickname 'Maultasch' or 'ugly old bag'. Both 'Maul' and 'Tasch' ('pocket') were slang terms for the vagina. So the nickname also branded her a prostitute, a slander that helped restore Johann Heinrich's reputation.

But the story has a happy ending. In 1347 the Luxemburgs renounced their claim on the Tyrol and in 1359 the Pope revoked Margaret's excommunication. She was free to marry Louis with the blessing of the Church. In 1363 the Habsburg Rudolf IV persuaded Margaret to cede Tyrol to his control. She retired to Vienna, where she died six years later on October 3, 1369 – very probably an ordinary looking woman who had nevertheless bequeathed to the world the term 'ugly old bag'.

The enduring Maultasch myth

In Margaret's lifetime
The historian Hugo Spechtsart compares the scandal of her marriage with the abduction of the beautiful Helen of Troy in classical mythology.

16th century
It is falsely claimed that she married Rudolf IV of Habsburg.

19th century
In 1816, Jacob Grimm published the story of Margaret Maultasch in his *German Sayings*.

20th century
In 1923, Margaret was the subject of Lion Feuchtwanger's novel *The Ugly Duchess*.

The hunt for the missing treasure

As the Allies closed in on Berlin in 1945, the Nazis raced against time to spirit away the spoils of war. Though a fortune in gold bullion, hidden deep in the Bavarian Alps, was recovered by the Americans in the immediate aftermath of the victory, what happened to the substantial hoard of stolen foreign currency?

Nazi invaders looted the central banks of ten occupied countries and seized hundreds of tonnes of gold to finance the German war machine. Nazis also stole gold from Jews and other victims of persecution, much of which was sent to the Reichsbank to be melted down. At the end of the war the Allies recovered huge quantities of bullion.

On April 14, 1945, the chief cashier of the main branch of
Berlin's Reichsbank, Georg Netzeband, was entrusted with
164 jute sacks containing 730 bars of gold. He was to take the
treasure to an abandoned potash mine near the town of Merkers
in Thuringia, central Germany, where the Nazis had hoarded
much of their war booty. It was assumed that the treasures would
be safer in Merkers than in Berlin, which was being subjected
to heavy aerial bombardment. But this proved to be a serious
miscalculation; six days earlier, the city, the potash mine and the
treasure hidden there had fallen into the hands of advancing
American forces.

A RACE AGAINST TIME

It was essential to the Nazi government that the Berlin hoard
should not be allowed to fall into enemy hands. Netzeband
instead headed south towards the Alps with a lorry containing
the gold. But as the German front collapsed, a safe hiding place
became increasingly elusive. Then, suddenly, a man became
involved who was to become the key figure in the whole affair.

Colonel Franz Pfeiffer, commander of the Alpine division,
had been tipped off about the gold by friends in Berlin. When
Netzeband arrived in the mountains, Pfeiffer seized the valuable
cargo. Netzeband had no choice but to submit – and he was not
even given a receipt. He later reported that it was not only the
sacks of gold that had disappeared into the mountains. There
were also great quantities of foreign currency, mainly US dollars
and pounds sterling, which had been loaded up with the gold
at Munich and other places where the lorry had stopped on its
journey south.

Under cover of darkness Pfeiffer dispatched a mule train to
an isolated forester's house at Einsiedl, high above Lake Walchen
near the Austrian border, but it was not long before he realised
that too many people knew about the hiding place. Villagers had
seen the lorry and the mules. The gold ingots were too bulky and
heavy to be carried further through the mountains so were left in
place. Accompanied by a few handpicked troops Pfeiffer set off
for the higher slopes with the paper money, which was divided
among three groups of men. Each group headed into the

darkness, unaware of the destination of their colleagues. Only Pfeiffer knew their ultimate goal.

THE AMERICAN 'GOLDRUSH TEAM'

The Americans learned that a substantial part of the Nazi gold hoard and other treasures were concealed in the Alps. A special unit, the 'Goldrush Team', was formed to track down the loot. German mountain troops, exhausted by the fighting, were defecting in droves. And they all told the same story: a SS unit had picked up the gold and taken it to an unknown location. This story, spread by Pfeiffer, was a smokescreen. Exhaustive inquiries finally led the Americans to the Berlin gold. A total of 728 ingots were dug up and taken to Frankfurt – the Germans had mislaid two ingots in the course of their frantic game of hide-and-seek. But where was the paper money?

SEEKING THE LOST FORTUNE

Englishman Ian Sayer and German Rudolf Elender dreamed of finding the Nazi treasure. For years, they pursued their quest independently. It was the discovery of a handwritten record kept by Georg Netzeband that set them on the right track. Statements made by witnesses and old maps and documents helped flesh out the picture. The two treasure-hunters then began to compare notes: the trail clearly led to the Alps. They had been seeking the

More than 500 top-ranking Nazis disappeared when Berlin fell. Wearing civilian clothes, they carried their passports to a new life – stolen money and treasure – some of it probably at first hidden in the mountain fastness of the Alps.

treasure for 26 years when, in the autumn of 2000, they travelled to a location 1600 metres above Lake Walchen in the Bavarian Alps. Determined to try and solve the mystery once and for all, they were equipped with a treasure chart recently recovered from the estate of a mountain infantryman and accompanied by geophysicists with equipment for pinpointing buried objects.

THE TREASURE PROVES ELUSIVE AGAIN

The two men had prepared meticulously. Sayer had even met Franz Pfeiffer, the key player in this game of hide-and-seek, shortly before his death. Pfeiffer's testimony had merely muddied the waters, but their investigations had uncovered a receipt signed by Pfeiffer, made out not to chief cashier Netzeband, but to the Americans. Dated August 24, 1945, it recorded the sum of $404,840 and £405, money that appeared nowhere in the Allied records. Was it possible that the currency had been misappropriated by the Americans?

Shortly after the end of the war Pfeiffer emigrated to Argentina, where he evidently had ample funds at his disposal. A transaction that was profitable for both the escaped Nazi and the American liberators appears to have taken place.

In the end, Sayer and Elender came away from their mountain quest empty-handed. They had hoped that at least part of the money would still be buried at the site. Yet their painstaking search did provide professional historians with compelling evidence that the treasure had ultimately been spirited away overseas.

Legendary gold

The Nibelungenlied
The Song of the Nibelungs describes the legendary treasure trove of the Nibelungs. Hagen von Tronje, the murderer of Siegfried, is supposed to have sunk this treasure in the River Rhine.

The gold of the Templars
In 1314, when the last three leaders of the Order of the Knights Templar were burnt at the stake, they took to the grave the secret of the treasure hoard of the Templars, the richest of the Christian knightly orders.

Thracian treasure,
Dazzling gold wreaths and intricate, jewellery made for the Kings of Ancient Thrace some 4000 years ago have been discovered in Bulgaria in the past few years.

'Our informer was a personal friend of the commander of the mountain troops.'

RUDOLF ELENDER

Death
in the harbour

A struggle for life is depicted in a dramatic relief on a Roman sarcophagus. As a young man drowns in the turbulent waters of the harbour at Ostia, rescuers rush to the scene and attempt to grasp his flailing arms – a tragic death commemorated for eternity.

This relief of the drowning man not only records his moment of death, but reflects the desire of his family to ensure the survival of his soul in the afterworld.

It was a day like any other, when a tragic accident took place in the waters of the crowded harbour at Ostia, the Roman Empire's most important port. A young man fell overboard and thrashed about in the choppy water. He could not swim and although several other boats tried desperately to rescue him, it was ultimately to no avail. His strength faded rapidly and a small boat was lowered in a last attempt to save him. But before the boat could reach the young man he had drowned.

A MYSTERIOUS SARCOPHAGUS

No writer described the fate of the young man, no historian deemed it worthy of mention and no poet made it the subject of a lament. Only a relief on a sarcophagus in Ostia's necropolis, or cemetery, bears silent witness to the tragedy. The young man's lavishly decorated coffin suggests that he came from a wealthy family. Their prime concern would have been to create an enduring memorial, whatever its cost, to their son's life. In doing so they might also have hoped to admonish the gods who had allowed such a disaster to take place.

The carved sarcophagus recalls the incident with great precision. The buildings on the fringes of the relief clearly indicate that ancient Ostia was the site of the accident. The alarm on the faces of the crews of the other ships is clear, as is the desperation of their abortive rescue attempt. It is a snapshot of a tragic moment, but also a lasting reminder of the incident, which must have taken place at some point in the 3rd century AD. No more details are known, nor is anything likely to come to light in future. How the young man fell unnoticed into the water or whether someone else was to blame for his death are questions which will never be answered.

The sarcophagus

The 'flesh eater'
The Greek word *sarkophágos* literally means 'flesh eater'. They were originally made from a type of limestone containing chemicals that hastened decomposition.

Sarcophagi in ancient Greece
Sarcophagi were in common use in Greece after the 6th century AD. Though most were made of wood, surviving examples are of stone and terracotta. Many are in the shape of a couch, on which the deceased reclined.

Sarcophagi in the Roman Empire
As burial became more common than cremation in the Roman Empire, sarcophagi decorated with relief carvings were found throughout the areas they had lived. The scenes portrayed were intended to commemorate the virtues of the deceased person, while at the same time depicting the afterlife. Mythological scenes were frequently used as allusions to the life of the deceased.

The German High Command, aware that their troop numbers were substantially less than those of the Allied forces, embarked on the Western offensive with reluctance. Even the German tank divisions, although trumpeted by many as the new miracle weapon, had fewer vehicles than the French. But the innovative German approach to tank warfare had given them a significant initial advantage.

PUTTING FAITH IN TANK WARFARE

Fascinated by tank warfare, Adolf Hitler charged General Heinz Guderian with the task of establishing a separate tank unit within the German Army. Guderian decided to concentrate the tanks into just a few divisions, giving them immense firepower as a result. In contrast, the French spread their tanks across the entire army to provide protection for each individual unit. German tank divisions also carried enough fuel with them to travel 100-140 miles before they required new supplies – which were dropped by the air force in fuel containers. Their independence from the rest of the army enabled the tank units to penetrate far beyond enemy lines and cut off their supply lines.

The idea of a lightning war, or *blitzkrieg*, involving concentrated tank units was in fact a British innovation, devised in the aftermath of the First World War. But the revolutionary tactic was later rejected by both the British and French armies because it was unproven in actual warfare. Even General Guderian found himself faced with many obstacles.

TACTICAL INNOVATIONS

To beat France, Lieutenant-General Erich von Manstein and his colleague Major Henning von Tresckow had devised an extremely sophisticated battle plan. Following French experiences in the

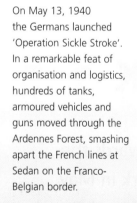

On May 13, 1940 the Germans launched 'Operation Sickle Stroke'. In a remarkable feat of organisation and logistics, hundreds of tanks, armoured vehicles and guns moved through the Ardennes Forest, smashing apart the French lines at Sedan on the Franco-Belgian border.

First World War, the French army had dug itself in behind
the 80-mile-long Maginot Line. To the south, neutral but well-
defended Switzerland provided a natural bulwark against
Germany, while to the north lay the hilly Ardennes. The French
believed that the tank units would find it impossible to operate
in such difficult terrain and so the natural frontier was ignored in
all defensive planning. It was this strategically weak point in the
French defences that the Germans exploited to their advantage.

CONFUSING THE FRENCH

At first, von Manstein confused the French with a quite different
approach. On May 10, 1940, the Luftwaffe launched an attack
on the airfields of neutral Luxembourg, Belgium and the
Netherlands, establishing immediate air superiority. On the first
day of the assault, 78 German paratroops landed in gliders on the
roof of the Belgian fort of Eben-Emael. They overpowered the
troops, who had been expecting an aerial attack, and blew open
fortified doors that protected the heavy artillery. For 24 hours,
they kept 1200 soldiers pinned down, until land forces arrived
and the fort fell completely into German hands. This allowed
the Germans to cross the Albert Canal. They then overran the
defensive lines behind the canal, forcing the Belgians to flee,
despite the arrival of British and French reinforcements. Further
north, the German advance into the Netherlands was similarly
successful, although there was fierce Dutch resistance, especially
around Rotterdam. But on May 15 the Dutch surrendered.

AN UNSTOPPABLE ADVANCE

In response to the German assault, crack units of the French
and British armies pressed north to support Belgium and the
Netherlands and prevent German troops from advancing further

south towards France. The Allied command was unaware that the largest tank squadron ever assembled was already rolling through the Eifel Mountains and the Ardennes and making for the River Meuse. Masked by dense forest, 1500 German tanks reached the river on May 12, encountering hardly any resistance on the way.

On the other side of the river, French defensive forces waited. They soon found themselves under attack from 12 dive-bomber formations. With bombs raining down, the French artillery were forced to take to their dug-outs. General Guderian seized the opportunity to concentrate his tanks along a one-mile wide section of the Meuse west of the French city of Sedan. A tank guards regiment was transported across on inflatable boats, while ferries carried light vehicles to the far side of the river. The French defensive line was overrun. After just eight hours, the bridgehead established by the Germans stretched five miles into enemy territory and pioneer units had constructed a temporary bridge, which the German tanks now crossed.

THE ALLIED COLLAPSE
Faced with this unexpected situation, France and Britain were in a state of shock and confusion, unable to decide where they should deploy their troops. The road to

On the night of May 10–11, the Germans launched an attack on the Belgian fortress Eben Emael, believed to be the most powerful fort in Europe. Glider-borne paratroops managed to subdue the entire fortress and its garrison, opening up access to the strategic Albert Canal.

Paris now lay open to the German forces, as did a possible assault route from the rear against the French defenders manning the Maginot Line. Realising that they risked being cut off and encircled, Allied troops began to withdraw from Belgium on May 16. At this point the German High Command, concerned that the Panzer divisions were becoming over-extended, ordered the advance to halt. This pause was to give their infantry time to link up with the tank units. In the meantime General Guderian was ordered to reconnoitre the area. He interpreted this order freely, allowing his tank units to advance 50 miles to the west. With the unexpected appearance of German tanks French resistance crumbled. They had assumed that the Germans would wait for reinforcements before continuing their advance. On 20 May, only ten days after the initial invasion of France, General Guderian reached the English Channel at the town of Abbéville. He had encircled the elite of the French and British forces and forced them into a desperate situation. To the north, the Netherlands had capitulated, Luxembourg was overrun and Belgian resistance was on the point of collapse.

The German Western offensive

10 May, 1940
Germany invaded the Netherlands, Belgium and Luxembourg, which soon surrendered.

3 June, 1940
338,000 British and French troops were rescued from Dunkirk.

14 June, 1940
By June 1940, the Germans occupied three-fifths of France. On 14 June, Paris fell.

The German assault on Britain
In August 1940 the Germans launched 'Operation Sealion', the invasion of Britain. An essential precondition was to secure air control over the English Channel. The Battle of Britain began. A succession of air battles were fought over southern Britain in the late summer of 1940 and in September the London Blitz began. The German assault on major English cities lasted until May 1941.

DRAMA ON THE CHANNEL COAST

On May 22, the German tank divisions advanced rapidly north, heading for the ports of Boulogne and Calais. Only one port remained open for the evacuation of the Allied armies: Dunkirk. The Allies appeared to be in a desperate race against time when, quite suddenly, the miracle happened. The wheels ground to a halt, and a deathly silence descended over the combatants. German tanks advancing to the coast were ordered to halt on May 23 by Field Marshal von Rundstedt, commander of Army Group A, who was concerned about the wear and tear his Panzer divisions were suffering. A day later, on May 24, 1940, Adolf Hitler personally approved the halting of the armoured advance. A day later Boulogne succumbed to Army group B, and Calais fell on May 26. Dunkirk remained in French hands and British and French troops began to congregate there.

But why did Hitler stop the successful advance? Historians have suggested a number of reasons for his decision. Hitler and his General Staff were afraid that the tanks would become bogged down in the marshy terrain inland of Dunkirk. They were needed for the forthcoming attack on Paris. Power struggles within the General Staff undoubtedly had an impact: Hermann Goering was keen to give his Air Force exclusive rights to annihilate the encircled Allied forces and prevent their evacuation. At this stage Hitler still envisaged a peace treaty with Britain so was not keen to risk British humiliation.

Yet the decision that he took in May 1940 was a key marker on the road to German surrender five years later. Ultimately, Hitler's order allowed Britain to continue to fight – its military strength weakened but intact.

OPERATION DYNAMO

The British and French command seized the opportunity that had been granted them and embarked at once on the improvised 'Operation Dynamo'. Using all the vessels that they could lay their hands on, they began to evacuate the encircled and desperate troops on the night of May 28.

Aware of the desperate urgency of the situation, a motley flotilla of torpedo boats and destroyers, yachts and fishing boats, set off from British waters to Dunkirk, where they ferried the exhausted soldiers from the beaches to larger transport ships waiting offshore. For over a week, soldiers huddled on the beach, with Luftwaffe bombs exploding all around, as they waited for rescue. By the time the swastika was hoisted over Dunkirk on June 4, 1940, almost all the equipment of the British expeditionary force had been destroyed or had fallen into German hands, but 338,000 Allied troops had been rescued.

Solving
the
mystery

7

Early
conquerors
of the **sea**

Polynesians, sailing in simple double-hulled canoes and
navigating with the help of wind direction, stars and
cloud formations, had explored and settled the Pacific
region from as early as 1500 BC.

In November 1520 the Portuguese seafarer Ferdinand Magellan rounded Cape Horn and entered the Pacific Ocean, where he set a northwesterly course towards the Equator, which he reached on February 13, 1521. It was a nightmare voyage. The provisions were swiftly exhausted. The crew's hunger became unbearable, with the men devouring anything that appeared remotely edible: strips of leather, wood

'It is possible that their civilisation may be traced back, island by island, to the East Indies.'

CAPTAIN JAMES COOK ON THE ORIGINS OF THE POLYNESIANS

shavings boiled up into a soup, and – as a special delicacy – rats. At least 19 sailors died of scurvy. The voyage to the nearest large group of islands, the Marianas, was 10,000 miles and lasted several months. On this journey, they traversed an area of the Pacific known from its numerous islands as 'Polynesia'.

PACIFIC ODYSSEY

The area of the western Pacific was aptly named. Present-day French Polynesia alone comprises more than 1500 small islands scattered over a huge area of 60,000 square miles. As Magellan and his men passed through the region, they sighted only two islands, both of them uninhabited. As the islands were surrounded by coral reefs the sailors were unable to make a landfall, and their hopes of obtaining desperately needed provisions were dashed.

On March 6, 1521, two larger islands, Guam and Rota, lying almost 2000 miles from mainland Asia, finally came into view. The islanders greeted the foreigners, who were weak with hunger, with a hail of spears. Magellan replenished his food supplies, burnt the islanders' villages and lost no time in weighing anchor and resuming his voyage, but not before he had caught a brief glimpse of the boats that were drawn up on the beach. He was so impressed that he called the islands Las Islas de Velas Latinas ('The Islands of the Lateen Sails'), after the triangular sails used on the boats. He had no inkling that the seamanship of the inhabitants and the efficiency of their vessels were more than a match for him, the great European explorer.

In 1830, many Europeans refused to believe that the vast spaces of the Pacific Ocean could have been navigated without even the most basic equipment. It was thought that Polynesia had been colonised from the Americas, because the primitive boats must have relied on the easterly direction of the prevailing trade winds.

AT ONE WITH NATURE

Long before the European oceanic expeditions of the 16th and 17th centuries, all the major islands in the middle of the Pacific Ocean had been inhabited for several centuries and possibly for millennia. The settlement of Polynesia may have begun as early as 1500 BC, and by AD 1000 the Polynesians were the most widespread ethnic group on Earth, settling an area of over 20 million square kilometres. The colonisation of the Pacific islands was gradual: it is speculated that as populations grew to the point where they could not be supported by the resources available, small groups of pioneers set off in search of new island homes. How did they manage to navigate accurately and cover such enormous distances without even the most basic equipment used by the Europeans? Magellan and his crew had almost come to grief on this route, despite the fact that they and their ship were accompanied by the best of European seafaring technology.

In May 1976, the *Hokule'a* (named after the star Arcturus, which shines over Hawaii), a faithful replica of a traditional Polynesian twin-hulled canoe, set out from the Hawaiian island of Maui on an experimental voyage across the Pacific Ocean. *Hokule'a* had two 19-metre hulls; eight *iako*, or crossbeams, joining the two hulls; *pola*, or decking, lashed to the crossbeams between the two hulls; rails along the decking; and two masts. All the materials that were used to build this boat came from the Pacific islands: it was constructed from wood, leaves and plant fibres, all held together by adhesive plant resins. The sails, woven from leaves, enabled the boats, which could be up to 30 metres long, to reach considerable speeds with a favourable following wind. They could cover distances of between 60 and 100 miles in a single day, even with a full passenger complement of as many as 50 people. The performance of the craft easily matched that of the elegant Viking 'dragon boats' which terrorised the coasts of Europe from the early Middle Ages onwards.

Simple single-hulled dugout canoes, carved from wooden logs, were stabilised by outriggers, which prevented them from capsizing in the open ocean. Traditional canoes are still made in the Pacific islands.

The *Hokule'a* was helmed by Mau Piailug, a Micronesian who steered her without recourse to any modern navigational aids. He navigated mainly using the stars but also by observing other natural signs: the wave patterns would tell him which side of an island he was sailing off. Clouds were another important pointer. Tall clouds massed on the horizon almost unfailingly indicated a large, mountainous island beneath. Clouds with a milky green base usually had a low-lying atoll underneath them. After 31 days, the *Hokule'a* arrived safely in Tahiti 2500 miles away, proving beyond doubt the seaworthiness of this ancient type of craft and the accuracy of traditional methods of navigation.

BACK TO THE ROOTS

One question remained unanswered: where did the Polynesians come from? There is evidence to suggest that they travelled in several waves from southeast Asia – and perhaps specifically from the island of Taiwan where DNA has shown links to indigenous peoples. Norwegian Thor Heyerdahl believed that the islands were colonised from South America. He reinforced his arguments with spectacular voyages. His view was widely supported, but recent findings based on linguistic, architectural, DNA and botanical studies have disproved his theory.

Over recent centuries, the ancient traditions of the Polynesians have largely been forgotten. The colonial authorities forbade trade with other islands and prohibited the construction of traditional vessels. As a result there are now only a handful of people on the islands of Oceania who are fully versed in the arts of navigation and boatbuilding. But now Polynesians are looking to their ancestral heritage with pride, and seeking to revive ancient skills and traditions.

The settling of Polynesia

Settling Fiji, Tonga and Samoa

By the 16th century BC, the ancestors of the Polynesians, who almost certainly came from Southeast Asia, had reached Fiji. By the 14th century BC, they had progressed to Tonga, and by the 11th century to Samoa, from where they opened up the rest of the region from 1000 BC onwards.

Easter Island and Hawaii

Easter Island was first settled in around 400 AD, the Hawaiian archipelago in c.800 AD, and New Zealand by the end of the first millennium AD.

European settlement

The first European to discover the Pacific Ocean was the Spaniard Vasco Núñez de Balboa in 1513 who claimed it for the king of Spain. European navigators then explored and opened up Oceania on behalf of the European colonial powers.

Catastrophe
in the Baltic

The sinking of the *Estonia* in the Baltic in 1994 may have been caused by stormy seas, which ripped off the insecurely-fastened bow doors, allowing a great volume of water to surge into the ferry's car bay, capsizing the ship. But there was a suspicion that the ship was carrying a top-secret cargo and that an explosion on board was the reason for the ship's rapid submersion.

ESTLIN

At 1.24 on the morning of September 28, 1994, several ships picked up a distress call from the *Estonia*: 'There's water rushing into the car deck... we are listing at an angle of 30 degrees.' Then the radio transmission abruptly broke off. Immediately, a number of ships altered course and steered towards the last reported position of the *Estonia*, which had been sailing from the port of Tallinn to Stockholm. The weather was rough, with a wind of 45–60 miles per hour and waves up to 10 metres high. Radar operators frantically checked their equipment, looking for any sign of the ferry, which had disappeared so abruptly from the screens that they feared their own systems were faulty.

There was no problem with the radar screens, it was simply that the *Estonia* had gone down in just a few minutes. It was thought that only a hit by several torpedoes or bombs dropped from planes, huge explosions on board, or catastrophic technical failures could have caused such serious damage to a 155-metre-long ferry like the *Estonia*. But in 1994, with the Cold War a distant memory and Europe at peace, bombs and torpedoes were scarcely a plausible explanation for a maritime disaster that cost the lives of 852 people.

DREADFUL PERIL

A commission was set up in Sweden to investigate the sinking and the official verdict was that the massive bow door had suffered a technical failure. It had given way under the pressure of pounding waves when the ferry was sailing at full speed. Huge volumes of water surged into the car deck through the open door, and the extra weight of the water prevented the *Estonia* from correcting the severe list of about 30 degrees that had developed.

In the seventh-deck cabin of Sirje, an employee in the ship's restaurant, a tumbler of water slipped off the table and smashed on the floor. She woke with a start, wondered why the *Estonia* wasn't righting herself, and knew at once that they were in terrible danger. With some difficulty, she opened the porthole of the cabin and scrambled out. By this time the *Estonia* was listing so heavily that she was able to walk almost upright on the ship's side. She clambered up to the railings where a man helped her over onto the top deck.

DESPERATE SURVIVORS

Reaching the deck was no guarantee of safety, as the *Estonia* was listing more heavily by the minute. When Sirje spotted a red rubber raft, she jumped into the icy waters of the Baltic and a sailor named Silver Linde quickly dragged her on board the emergency raft. For seven hours she lay there, buffeted by rough seas in the tiny craft, which was finally spotted by a helicopter at around 8.30 am. She was one of only 137 people: 94 passengers and 43 crew members – who survived the catastrophe.

Karin Bergquist, a civilian employee of the Swedish police, was sitting in front of a karaoke machine on the ship when she realised that they were in difficulties. Fearing the worst, she ran up to the top deck. She was only aware how severely the *Estonia* was listing when she reached the deck. The ship's funnel appeared to be almost parallel with the horizon. Bergquist grabbed a lifejacket and clambered over the railing. Just then, a huge wave swept her off the vessel. Bergquist, a trained lifeguard, quickly swam to one of the ship's large self-inflating emergency rafts. She pulled herself on to it, and then helped six other survivors haul themselves on to the raft. Four hours later, she was rescued by the ferry *Mariella*, which had responded to the *Estonia*'s desperate Mayday signal.

Educational psychologist Rolf Södermann only survived the disaster because he was sitting next to an emergency exit. As the *Estonia* plunged, he was forced to jump from the upper deck into the water. He swam to an emergency raft that was bobbing on the waves just 70 metres away from him. The suction created as the ship went down dragged Södermann backwards in the icy water. Distress flares shot into the sky and he found himself surrounded by floating bodies. Somehow he made it to a capsized lifeboat, which he clung on to for the next four hours. He was finally taken on board a Finnish helicopter suffering from hypothermia.

At the time, the Estonia *was the largest and most up-to-date ship sailing under the Estonian flag.*

Urban Lambertson hadn't been unduly concerned about the stormy weather on board the *Estonia*. As a former naval officer and now head of navigation with the Swedish–Estonian shipping line that owned the ship, he had had plenty of experience of

The passenger ferry *M/S Mariella* arrived at the scene of the accident at 2.12 am, and was the first vessel to do so. Some survivors had clambered aboard an emergency life raft equipped with a chute, other people were in the icy water. A total of 15 people were transferred directly from the rafts to the *Mariella*.

worse conditions. When, some time after midnight, the ship failed to right herself from a list of some 20 degrees, he knew that something was terribly wrong. While other passengers in the karaoke bar skidded down the smooth wooden dance floor away from the door, Lambertson grabbed hold of the carpet and worked his way up to the exit. As the ship listed ever further to starboard, Lambertson pulled on a lifejacket. The lights were suddenly extinguished, the emergency lights were illuminated on the bridge and a warning signal was sounded – all signs that the ship was doomed. He leapt into the water, made it to an emergency raft just 20 metres away, and hauled himself onto it. Five hours later he was rescued, together with an Estonian man whom he had pulled aboard the raft.

After the disaster it was established that weak, poorly constructed attachments on the 50-tonne bow door, or visor, snapped under the weight of unusually powerful waves. At 1.15 am the huge bow door ripped away from the ship completely and crashed into the sea, bouncing off the bulbous bow which extended outwards from the ship.

THE RUMOURS FLY

These survivors were lucky; the ferry went down too quickly for most to be rescued. It is precisely the speed of the sinking that continues to fuel speculation about the cause of the disaster. There were three further decks below the level of the car deck. With the bow door detached, a huge volume of water would have rushed into the ship, and she would have 'turned turtle'.

The three lowest decks would have been exposed and the air trapped inside them would have kept the ship afloat for a while. But this did not happen; the *Estonia* sank like a stone. So, it was reasoned, her hull must have been holed, allowing air to escape.

THE PLOT THICKENS

A Swedish customs officer, Lennart Henriksson, had noticed some strange activity in the weeks leading up to the sinking of the *Estonia*. On September 14 and 20, just hours before the ship entered the port of Stockholm, his superior had ordered him not to search certain vehicles. Although Henriksson obeyed the order, he was still curious. Stealing a quick glance at the cargo area of one of the trucks, he spotted crates that clearly contained munitions. But it was ten years before Henriksson, who had retired in the interim, approached Swedish television reporters with the revelation. Only in January 2005 did the Swedish government admit that his observation had been correct.

It seemed that military equipment was being smuggled from Russia across the inadequately policed border with Estonia, and from there was being ferried by the *Estonia* to Sweden. Immediately after the ferry went down, relatives of the victims voiced their suspicions, but the Swedish government denied any such connection. German television journalist Jutta Rabe suspected that neutral Sweden was just a staging post for the traffic and that the ultra-sensitive cargo, which may even have included nuclear-powered satellites, was being forwarded straight on from there to the USA.

Rabe's investigations revealed that, on September 27, 1994, at 18.41 pm, a Boeing 727 aircraft had landed at Sweden's Arlanda airport, where it waited for a cargo from the *Estonia*. Following the sinking of the ship, the plane took off again for the United States at 19.54 pm on September 28, its mission incomplete. The bill for the landing charges was sent to the US Embassy in Stockholm.

AN UNDERWATER SARCOPHAGUS

Everything else is pure conjecture. Sweden was – and remains – a non-aligned country and would never have admitted to helping the United States with a clandestine operation. Suspicion was fuelled by the controversy surrounding the treatment of the wreck and the hundreds of bodies still on board. At first the Swedish government gave a solemn undertaking to salvage the wreck and recover the bodies. This did not present any great technical difficulties, since the ship was lying at a depth of just 80 metres, less than 25 miles off the Finnish island of Utö. Neither the depth nor the currents would have hindered a salvage operation.

The families of the victims were therefore astonished when the Swedish government unexpectedly designated the spot where the *Estonia* had sunk as an official grave site. It was proposed to seal the entire wreck in concrete to ensure that it was never disturbed. The concrete sarcophagus was of the same type that had been used to enclose the exploded nuclear reactor at Chernobyl in the Ukraine – the suggestion bore the hallmarks of a cover-up operation. Did the ship still contain clues that would explain the true cause of the disaster? Rumours circulated that a hole might be found in the steel plating of the *Estonia*'s hull, made either by torpedoes or by explosions on board.

Such speculations have continued to proliferate. The Swedish government still keeps the wreck under close guard. Although it has not actually been encased in concrete, any vessel approaching the site is ordered by a Swedish patrol boat to leave the area, on the grounds that it is a cemetery. When divers commissioned by Jutta Rabe defied the ban and went to investigate the wreck, the Swedes issued a warrant for her arrest for 'desecrating a grave'.

Other investigators, such as Peter Holtappels, head of a German special commission, have also been warned off by the authorities. Holtappels, a former naval judge, argues that air trapped in the lowest three decks of the *Estonia* should have kept her afloat for far longer than the ten minutes she reportedly took to sink, unless a powerful explosive charge on board the ship or a torpedo had also ripped a hole in her hull. The Russian Mafia is frequently mentioned in connection with the disaster. Or perhaps one nation's security service was so desperate to get rid of a highly sensitive cargo that it was prepared to allow as collateral damage the deaths of 852 people.

The
hunt
for the
signs

For half a century clay tablets inscribed with the mysterious script of Minoan Crete remained undeciphered. The breakthrough was the work of a gifted amateur linguist, with a passion for Ancient Greece. His discovery sent shock waves through the academic community.

Classical legend tells of King Minos, who dominated the Aegean with his powerful navy and ruled his domain from a palace on Crete. The intriguing story of Linear B, an enigmatic script from Minoan Crete, began in 1900 when the archaeologist Sir Arthur Evans set out to bring the world of King Minos to light with his ambitious excavation of the magnificent Cretan palace of Knossos.

During the excavations, Evans came across a series of clay tablets marked with curious lines, the like of which had not been seen before. His digs at other ancient sites on Crete also unearthed tablets with

The symbols on clay tablets found in Crete and Mycenaean Greece were finally deciphered by Michael Ventris. The tablets, written in an archaic form of Greek, recorded economic transactions, distributions of rations and palace resources.

the same linear script. He soon realised that the tablets contained two superficially similar, but actually quite different, writing systems. The older, somewhat more ungainly script was classified with the letter A, while the newer script used the letter B.

A MESSAGE FROM THE PAST

For decades Evans sought to realise his dream: not merely to excavate the palace of King Minos at Knossos, but also to reconstruct it. In 1935 Evans released 120 tablets for public inspection and study, causing a ripple of excitement through the academic community. Scholars soon adopted the designation Linear B for the script. The name denoted the fact that the script, in contrast to the pictograms used in hieroglyphic script, was made up of lines that served as characters.

The palace of Knossos was built c.1700 BC. Arranged around a courtyard, it was four storeys high, with a sophisticated drainage and water supply system. A basement room had pillars decorated with the design of the double-axe, or labyrs, a sacred emblem in Crete. In Greek mythology, the palace of King Minos is described as the 'labyrinth', or house of the double-axe.

Specialists and amateurs alike threw themselves eagerly into the exciting business of deciphering the script. Some of the theories put forward concerning the roots of Linear A and Linear B bordered on the eccentric. The discovery of further tablets inscribed with Linear B on the Greek mainland was a further impetus to scholarship. The new tablets were found at the palaces of Pylos and Mycenae in the Peloponnese. These

> *'All manner of muddle-headed eccentrics from the fringes of archaeology.'*
>
> MICHAEL VENTRIS ON SOME OF HIS FELLOW RESEARCHERS.

sites had been leading centres for the warlike Mycenaean civilisation, which was at its height between 1400 and 1200 BC. The epic poems of Homer, written much later in 800 BC, incorporate oral history and traditions about the heroic Mycenaean age, including the Trojan war, when mainland Greece was ruled by King Agamemnon.

But how did all this fit together? Both Linear A and Linear B were discovered on Crete, which had a leading political and commercial role in the eastern Mediterranean between 2000 and 1450 BC. In mainland Greece, evidence of the use of Linear B came from a later period. It was possible that the tablets unearthed at Mycenae may have been imported from Crete. Was the language on the tablets in fact that of Crete's ancient Minoan civilisation?

THE HUNT FOR CLUES

Arthur Evans attempted to decipher Linear B, but with no success. Frustrated experts on the trail of the Linear B script hoped in vain for a sensational find of the kind that the early researchers into hieroglyphics had enjoyed.

A spectacular case was associated with Napoleon Bonaparte's 1798 Egyptian campaign. The French emperor set out to conquer Egypt with a force of more than 30,000 troops. During the expedition, a soldier made a sensational discovery near the town of Rosetta. He found a tablet inscribed with three different types of script. The tablet, which became known as the Rosetta Stone, was carved in 196 BC. It presented the same text in three

different versions: hieroglyphs, demotic (the script of the
common Egyptian people) and finally in Greek.

The Greek script could be easily read and understood and so
researchers used the Greek text to unravel the secrets of Ancient
Egyptian script. In 1822, after years of study, the French scholar
Jean-François Champollion succeeded in deciphering it. To this
day, the Rosetta Stone remains one of the most important
documents in the history of ancient languages.

A MOMENTOUS LECTURE

All attempts to reveal the secret of Linear A were unsuccessful.
Even now, no-one knows how the language works. The fact that
we have a far better understanding of Linear B is largely thanks
to the ingenuity of Michael Ventris, an amateur linguist who had
trained as an architect. Even so, he did have an extraordinary
aptitude for languages. By the time he started school, he spoke
French and German and at the age of six he taught himself
Polish. By seven, he was studying a book about hieroglyphics.

In 1936, at the age of 14, Ventris went to see an exhibit of
Minoan artefacts in London. There, he heard Arthur Evans give
an impromptu lecture. The talk inspired him to become a
linguistic detective and he devoted all his spare time to studying
texts from Crete and ancient Greece. When he was just 18, he
felt confident enough to publish a paper that was an introduction
to Minoan script, although he later came to realise that he was
still on the wrong track.

INSPIRED GUESSWORK

During the Second World War, Ventris served as a navigator
in the RAF, still carrying copies of Linear B texts around in his
knapsack. When the war ended, he immersed himself eagerly
in his obsession once again. Yet there were still no clues or help
available to enable him to decipher the script. Ventris's tenacity,
astonishing patience, and ultimately his courage in freeing himself
from established ways of thinking finally enabled him to come to
his ground-breaking conclusions.

The American linguist Alice Kober had been able to ascertain
that certain combinations of symbols were repeated time and

again on the tablets. In addition, these groups of symbols often had different endings, indicating that the tablets were written using an inflected language. Using this insight, Ventris was soon in a position to develop his so-called 'grid' of syllables, which organised the sounds into a systematic structure and allowed him to assign the status of vowels or consonants to individual characters. He was finally able to identify a total of 91 symbols for syllables, 160 symbols that formed words in their own right, and several symbols denoting numbers.

But what could the words mean? Perhaps, Ventris speculated, they were place names. So, as an experiment, he inserted a few geographical concepts such as 'Knossos', or the names of other ancient Cretan settlements. This strategy appeared to work well. As he studied the script more closely, he made a surprising discovery. He came to the conclusion that the language behind Linear B was neither Etruscan nor Minoan, as he had first supposed, but rather a very early form of Greek.

Many experts rejected the findings of Ventris, the 'amateur' researcher. But they were confounded by the discovery of an unusually clear tablet. Within the Linear B text were clear pictures of pots and jars, which the newly deciphered accompanying text described in detail. Ventris's findings were vindicated, and from that point his work began to be accepted by the academic establishment.

Other mysterious writing systems

The Vinca script
The oldest known writing system in the world is the Vinca script. The Vinca civilisation (c.5300–3500 BC) was based mainly in the Balkans, but also occurred in Hungary and Romania. The script has around 200 characters, which have yet to be fully deciphered.

The Indus Valley script
The script of the Indus civilisations was used for short inscriptions, such as those used on seals. It has been found all along the Indus Valley in Pakistan, but mainly in Harappa, one of the centres of the Indus civilisation. The script dates to c.2500–2000 BC.

The Discus of Phaestos
Found on Crete, this artefact, dating from c.1700 BC, is inscribed with hieroglyph-like symbols. Scholars think that it is a religious text. It has still not been deciphered.

This finding had major historical implications. Up to that point, other experts had been convinced that the oldest written examples of Ancient Greek had been produced 500 years later than the script on the tablets.

THE MYSTERY OF KNOSSOS
In 1952, Ventris finally cracked the secret behind Linear B. He did not dare to go public with the announcement on his own. Instead, he told the renowned language scholar John Chadwick of his discovery. The following year, they jointly published their findings – 'Evidence for Greek Dialect in the Mycenaean Archives' in the well-known specialist publication *The Journal of Hellenic Studies*. The 19-page paper created a furore in the academic world. Many researchers took exception to the apparently cavalier way in which Ventris had established the Greek provenance of the texts. Some commentators were also disappointed by the mundane content of his discoveries: the tablets contained unspectacular inventories of household goods or were balance-sheets kept by ancient bookkeepers.

The young architect was deluged with comments and questions by other researchers – ranging from furious rejection to enthusiastic agreement and breathless astonishment. But tragically, Ventris had little time to respond to his critics; aged just 34, he was killed in a car crash on September 6, 1956. Many other studies have been conducted on the subject since Ventris's breakthrough discovery, but today there are few scholars who would quibble with Michael Ventris's reputation as the 'Decipherer of Linear B'.

The bodies in the peat bogs

The bogs of northern Europe are the last resting place of many Iron Age people. Their uncannily well-preserved bodies bring us face-to-face with our ancestors, revealing information about health, diet and appearance. But some of the corpses are chilling reminders of the ritual practices of the distant past.

A cold, dry wind was blowing in from the Baltic, the sky was cloudless and blue, and the sun was shining on a May morning in 1950. It was ideal weather for cutting peat, since the moorland quickly became a morass when it rained. Brothers Emil and Viggo Højgård needed peat to burn in their stoves, and set out from the hamlet of Tollund in eastern Jutland, Denmark, to the moor at Bjældskovdal. They were making good progress when they came across something that froze the blood in their veins.

Many of the bog bodies are Iron Age farmers who once lived in small settlements made up of wattle-and-daub cottages on the coastal lowlands. Iron technology was introduced into the region in the middle of the first millennium, BC.

As they eased a large block of cut peat away from the side of the pit, they found themselves staring at the face of a corpse. Further investigation revealed that the head belonged to a man of around 40 who was lying between the layers of peat. His eyes were closed and he appeared to be sleeping peacefully, yet around his neck was a tightly wound leather rope. The body was so well preserved that the Højgård brothers were convinced that they had stumbled upon the victim of a crime and immediately informed the police in the neighbouring town of Silkeborg.

Almost exactly two years after the discovery of that body, who became known as the Tollund Man, a worker cutting peat on Domsland Moor near Eckernförde in Schleswig-Holstein, North Germany, made a similar find. Near the Windeby estate, he uncovered the so-called Windeby Girl. Externally, the girl showed no signs of violence, although she had a shaven head and had been blindfolded.

Just a few metres from the site where she was found, a second bog burial came to light in June of the same year, this time almost certainly the body of a man. Perhaps a drama of tragic passion

Tollund Man was found laid in a relaxed position, his legs bent against his abdomen. His face, with its wrinkles, reddish stubble and hair, was alarmingly well-preserved. His body was naked but he wore a leather cap and a belt round his waist. A braided leather rope around his neck revealed that he had been garrotted.

had been played out on the moor, with the young couple taking their own lives in a lovers' pact?

Small children have also been among the corpses found in peat bogs. In 1922 a peat cutter working on Kayhauser Moor in the Ammerland region of Germany felt his spade strike a hard object deep below the surface. He carefully dug down further with his bare hands, only to come upon a

The best-preserved mummies are found in upland or freshwater moors.

shocking discovery. The body of the Kayhausen Boy lay exposed in the brown soil of the bog. On a cursory examination, a doctor discovered three stab wounds in the child's neck. The murdered child had been seven years old at the most; although his teeth had mostly disintegrated, a milk tooth was found in his jaw.

MUMMIES FROM THE MOOR

Most of the discovery sites for the so-called 'bog-bodies' are found in an area covered by northern and central European upland moor, within a cool and moist climatic zone that begins in Ireland and passes through Britain, the Netherlands, Northern Germany and Denmark, extending as far as the Baltic States.

The first bog body was discovered in the 17th century. Since then, several hundred have been unearthed, some complete skeletons and bodies with well-preserved skin and hair and others dismembered skulls, arms and legs.

Modern techniques have enabled the remains to be accurately dated. The bodies of two women mark the beginning and the end of the era of bog burials. The oldest is the Kølbjerg Woman, who is thought to have drowned around 10,000 years ago at the age of 25 and whose body later drifted into the bog. The most recent is Rosalinde, who was roughly the same age, and found her last resting place on Black Spawn Moor near Peiting in Upper Bavaria. Her body dates from the Middle Ages.

The great majority of bog burials come from the Iron Age in Central Europe, from between 700 BC and the first years AD. Modern dating techniques do sometimes explode some seductive myths. The Windeby Girl, who according to the reconstruction work done on her skull was probably a finely-featured brunette, definitely cannot have known her supposed lover. He died in AD 185 at the latest, some 150 years before the young woman.

Bodies are not the only remains preserved in the bogs of northern Europe. Several deposits of war equipment, including warships, shields and iron spearheads, have been found that date as far back as the Ice Age in Germany. Other ritual deposits, perhaps made as votive offerings in sacred sites, have been uncovered: the most famous of these is the Gundestrup cauldron of the 2nd century BC, a massive silver vessel decorated with scenes of stags, snakes, warriors and deities.

VICTIMS AND PERPETRATORS

How did the people whose bodies have been found in the bogs meet their deaths? It has been suggested that many were simply accident victims, who became mired in the bogs and drowned. The Husbäke Man from Husbäke Moor near Oldenburg probably died in this way. Some may have died of other natural causes. The Windeby Girl probably perished on the moor at the age of 14 from hunger and exhaustion.

But a number of bodies show unmistakable signs that they met a violent end. They were evidently stabbed, beaten to death, throttled or hanged. Examples of such corpses are the Osterby Man, who was also found near Eckernförde, with a smashed, decapitated skull, or the Yde Girl, found in the Netherlands, who was clearly strangled.

Contemporary Roman accounts of the Nordic peoples suggest that these victims of violence were prisoners of war or criminals who, following execution, were disposed of in the moorland bogs. It is also suggested that the Iron Age people of northern Europe offered human sacrifices

Mummification in upland moors

Lack of oxygen
Layers of peat in bogs have virtually no oxygen. In the absence of oxygen, putrefaction occurs very slowly.

Acidic water
The extremely high pH value of the water in upland moors, which is caused by natural acids, has a similar preservative effect.

Preservatives in water
Tanning agents in peaty water transform skin into a kind of leather; hair often takes on a fiery tinge, such as in the case of 'Red Franz' found in 1900 in a bog near Neu Versen in Germany, but is well preserved.

Low temperatures
Even in summer, upland moors retain a cool ground temperature, since they lose a great deal of ambient heat through evaporation. Decay is slowed down at low temperatures.

to celebrate military victories, or to propitiate the gods – for example in the case of illness.

It is also possible that only the most prominent and respected members of Iron Age society were ritually killed and offered up as sacrifices to the gods of the moor. The Tollund Man had done no hard manual work during his lifetime, otherwise his hands would have been calloused. The careful way in which his eyelids had been tenderly closed and his body laid on a soft bed of moss also militates against the idea that

It is not known how many more bodies still lie undisturbed in their damp graves.

he was a criminal. Twenty-four hours before his death, Tollund Man had consumed a porridge made from more than 60 different grass varieties and herbs. The plants in question mature at different times of the year, showing that the seeds must have been collected over a period of several weeks, possibly deliberately gathered for the man's last meal before his execution.

Perhaps the people of the Iron Age were even aware that bodies become naturally mummified in upland bogs, and so deliberately chose such regions for high-status burials. The fact that people of the time set great store in preserving the mortal remains of their relatives for as long as possible is reflected in the man-made ice graves used by people of the same period from the Altai Mountains in Siberia.

SILENT WITNESSES

Whatever the cause of or reason for their deaths, these well-preserved bodies are often extremely revealing about the lives of Iron Age and other prehistoric peoples. Using modern investigative techniques, the bodies can tell us much about diet, clothing, hairstyles and even illnesses. Our ancient ancestors put a premium on their external appearance. Some bodies are clothed in woollen garments that are decorated with intricate embroidery work. The Osterby Man had his hair done up in elaborate braids.

Sometimes these findings can, in a roundabout way, cast light on the time and cause of the individual death. The stomach of the Kayhausen Boy, for example, contained two apple cores, indicating that he must have been killed in autumn or winter.

The bodies are also eloquent reminders of the sufferings of our ancestors. It is clear that the Yde Girl suffered from scoliosis, a lateral curvature of the spine that is associated with severe pain. A man found on the Danish island of Seeland had been subjected to an excruciatingly painful operation: his skull was trepanned, or opened up. Although we know that he survived this surgery, why was it carried out in the first place? Was it to clear a blood-clot that had formed in his brain after a blow from an axe? Or did the person who operated on him want to release an evil spirit through the hole he had made in the man's head? The answer to this question is one of the many mysteries that bog burials still hold for researchers of the 21st century.

Pushing
back the frontiers

8

Julius Caesar
and the Gauls

According to Plutarch's account, Vercingetorix donned his finest armour and rode out through the the town to the enemy lines where Caesar waited for him. He leapt from his horse, stripped off his armour, and sat silently at Caesar's feet, until he was taken away as a prisoner. The actual surrender was far from the account enshrined in legend.

Vercingetorix, the young chief of the Averni tribe, organised Gaulish resistance to Roman occupation and became a national legend. He took up his last stand at the siege of Alesia, where the Gauls were defeated by Julius Caesar's Roman forces. Six years later the proud warrior was paraded through the streets of Rome and publicly executed.

In 52 BC, Vercingetorix assumed supreme command over all the tribes of Gaul and was proclaimed king by his supporters. The sheer ambition of the head of the Averni had alarmed many established tribal leaders, who feared that their own influence would decline if he came to power. From time to time his opponents tried to edge him out into the political wilderness. But the riposte from Vercingetorix was convincing. Who, he asked his compatriots, could possibly benefit from these internecine struggles? Wasn't there a far more pressing task at hand – to liberate Gaul from the Roman invaders? They should unite together to fight Julius Caesar.

> *'I embarked on this war in the name of freedom for all the Gauls.'*
>
> VERCINGETORIX TO CAESAR

THE REVOLT AGAINST ROME

The Gauls believed that the Roman invasion of their homeland in 58 BC had been unlawful and ordered on the flimsiest of pretexts. Caesar claimed that the migration of a few Germanic and Celtic tribes, on the lookout for new places to settle, constituted a threat to the Roman provinces in northern Italy and southern France.

In his account of the invasion, *On The Gallic War*, Caesar painted a convincing – if inaccurate – picture of the occupation as a pre-emptive defensive measure to protect the security of the Empire. But this was merely a pretext. In fact, he badly needed to secure some military victories and build up a force of loyal legionaries around him so that he could pursue his real aim – to gain ascendancy over his rivals in Rome.

The war had been raging for six years when Vercingetorix assumed command. The Gauls' only hope against the Roman legions lay in concerted action. By this time Caesar, a brilliant field commander and military planner, had already inflicted several defeats. Caesar even claimed, although this may well have been Roman propaganda, to have discovered that the Averni tortured insubordinate Gauls and used violent deterrents, such as cutting off the ears of disloyal foot-soldiers.

OFFENSIVE AND CATASTROPHE

By 52 BC Vercingetorix had completed his preparations for a major counteroffensive. The Romans now faced an effective and highly motivated army. To stop the invaders from replenishing supplies, the Gauls adopted a scorched earth policy, razing their own villages and farmsteads to the ground. Even setbacks such as the capture of the key city of Avaricum by the Romans earlier that year did little to dampen their fervour. The Romans subsequent siege of the city of Gergovia ended in a fiasco, when they were forced to withdraw after suffering heavy looses. The city henceforth became a powerful symbol of Gaulish resistance.

But the key battle of the war still lay ahead. Vercingetorix assembled 80,000 men in Alesia, in present-day Burgundy. Here he determined to fight a decisive engagement with the Romans in the summer of 52 BC. The signs looked favourable: the city was well fortified and was located in a protected position on a hill.

Caesar wasted no time in engaging the enemy. The legionaries constructed a siege encirclement of the town. As Vercingetorix exhorted the defenders of the city with rousing speeches, the Romans encountered some unexpected difficulties beyond its walls. The besieging army now found itself under siege. Caesar received intelligence that Gaulish warriors were flooding in from all directions towards Alesia to help compatriots trapped there. At this point, Caesar implemented an innovative solution. He divided his troops into defensive and offensive units. To keep the Gaulish relief forces at arm's length, a defensive perimeter of deep pits, entanglements, wooden stakes sharpened to spikes, and water-filled moats was swiftly constructed. In just six weeks, the Romans had thrown two encirclements around the town – a

Caesar's Gallic wars

58 BC
Caesar attacks the Helvetii as a danger to the Roman Empire and subdues tribes of the Franche Comté and Alsace.

57-53 BC
He invades Belgium and Normandy. A revolt amongst the Belgae is put down after fierce fighting.

52-51 BC
A revolt breaks out in Central Gaul. In the spring the Romans beseige Avaricum, killing most of the 40,000 inhabitants. Caesar then besieges Gergovia but is forced to abandon the attempt. In late summer; Vercingetorix attacks the Romans near Divio (modern Dijon). Caesar counters with his Germanic cavalry and sends the Gauls racing back to their own infantry lines. The Gauls regroup at Alesia. Vercingetorix surrenders to Caesar after the Gaulish relief force flees. By 51 BC the last remnants of Gaulish resistance were extinguished.

10-mile-long siege ring and, beyond this, a defensive ring 12 miles in circumference.

A Gaulish force of as many as 100,000 warriors gathered to relieve the town. But they found it difficult to co-ordinate their actions and the Romans were able to repel the attack. Vercingetorix was forced to look on helplessly as Roman forces edged ever closer. With enough provisions for only 30 days, the Gauls were in a desperate situation. Roman soldiers carried armfuls of Gaulish shields and bloodstained pieces of armour into their camp as war trophies, and the demoralised defenders could only look on in despair – ancient accounts of the siege speak of 'men weeping and women wailing'. When their food ran out, even the relief troops began to flee. To break the deadlock, the troops caught in Alesia decided to take the chiefs, including Vercingetorix to the Romans. They were surrounded and forced to surrender with all their weapons.

Gaius Julius Caesar (100–44 BC) was a brilliant military tactician, a courageous warrior and a skilled orator and politician. His military success in Gaul gave him the means to achieve absolute power in Rome in 46 BC.

VERCINGETORIX LIVES ON

For the next six years Vercingetorix was held in a Roman dungeon, well aware that he would be subjected to a final public humiliation before his execution. When Caesar vanquished his enemy Pompey after a bloody civil war and returned to Rome in 46 BC, the Gaulish hero was doomed to play his part in Caesar's triumph. The vanquished warrior was taken from his cell and paraded through the streets of Rome as part of the dictator's triumphal procession.

Vercingetorix's bravery and charismatic leadership assured his position as a national hero. In times of danger the French have repeatedly invoked his memory. He became a figurehead for the nation's struggle for independence in the same way as Joan of Arc, who led France into battle against the English invaders over 1000 years later.

Hard times
for **criminals**

Pinkerton's Detective Agency played a key role in the fight against the crime wave that was sweeping across the Wild West. Many agents were also effective spies for the Union side during the American Civil War.

Paul Newman and Robert Redford as Butch Cassidy and the Sundance Kid, who led the Hole-in-the-Wall-Gang. Pinkerton's men ran the gang to ground in Fort Worth. Many surrendered or died fighting. The leaders escaped to Bolivia, where they may have been shot by the Bolivian army.

Abraham Lincoln, President-Elect of the United States, had been
warned: on February 23, 1861, he was to be the intended target
of an assassin, who would murder him as soon as his train pulled
into Baltimore station. He had the agents of Pinkerton's National
Detective Agency to thank for this tip-off, which saved his life.
While conducting investigations on behalf of a railroad company,
they had learned of the assassination plot which was being
planned by Confederate supporters.

On the evening of February 22, he attended a ball in
Harrisburg as planned. He slipped away through a side door into
a coach with blacked-out windows which promptly sped off into
the night. Waiting for the President on the outskirts of the city
was an unlit railway train manned by armed Pinkerton agents.
One of the detectives cut telegraph wires so that anyone watching
them could not inform Confederates in Baltimore of the arrival of
the President there earlier than scheduled – it was only 3.30 in
the morning when Lincoln's train pulled safely into Baltimore
station. Four years later he was not to prove so lucky: he was
assassinated by John Wilkes Booth on April 14, 1865.

Allan Pinkerton was an
adept publicist. He used
the motto 'We Never
Sleep!', which was
accompanied by a graphic
of an open, watchful eye.
The logo was used in
advertisements in the
pages of magazines,
newspapers and circulars,
and featured on billboards
and wanted posters. It
soon gave rise to the
term 'private eye'.

A NOSE FOR CRIME

The 22-year old Scot Allan Pinkerton emigrated from
Glasgow to America in 1842. A trained cooper, he set
up a lucrative business near Chicago making barrels, but
he soon grew tired of his trade. Then quite suddenly and
purely by chance, a new career opened up for him. On
an excursion to an island near the town of Dundee, near
Chicago, Pinkerton came across a path. He found this
curious, since the island was supposed to be uninhabited.
Could it be that this spot was the hideaway of a notorious
gang who had been flooding the surrounding area with
counterfeit currency? Keen to solve the mystery, he rowed to
the island with the local sheriff day after day. They concealed
themselves in a safe hiding-place and staked out the path.
Pinkerton's hunch was correct: the counterfeiters showed up
and the delighted sheriff was able to arrest them.

The former cooper was rewarded with a job as an investigator
in Chicago and proved to be a success in his new role. The city

was widely regarded as a gangsters' paradise, yet could not call upon even a dozen officers to ensure the safety of its 30,000 citizens. By the end of 1848, Pinkerton had caught more criminals than any of his more experienced colleagues. Observant, tenacious and able to keep a cool head in a crisis, he was also incorruptible, a rare quality in mid-19th-century Chicago. But stopping crime did not pay. So, in 1850, he opened his own investigative bureau, Pinkerton's National Detective Agency, carefully handpicking his colleagues. He even engaged the first female detective in America. Before long Pinkerton's had extended its operations across the whole country, and some high-profile cases generated good publicity for the fledgling agency.

The Adams Express investigation was a case in point. The firm dispatched mail and registered items throughout the USA by railroad. In the autumn of 1858, substantial sums of money went missing, despite the fact that the cars in which the mail was being transported were locked and sealed. It seemed that $50,000 had vanished into thin air. Pinkerton's detectives kept watch on the employees of Adams and soon focused their attention on a security guard by the name of John Maroney, who appeared to be flush with money. Pinkerton discovered the whereabouts of the stolen hoard and arrested Maroney.

In an era when many law-enforcers openly accepted bribes to turn a blind eye, Pinkerton's had a reputation for honesty and integrity. New operatives were told never to accept bribes or compromise with criminals. They were always to co-operate where possible with local law enforcement agencies. They were to refuse divorce cases, or any cases that might involve clients in scandal. They were always to turn down reward money – they were well paid enough.

A SECRET MISSION

Following the outbreak of the American Civil War in April 1861 between the southern Confederate states and the northern Union, Pinkerton's worked for the Union side. They infiltrated the highest levels of command in the Confederate states, transmitting information about southern spies, army bases and plans for military operations. It was a dangerous enterprise and Pinkerton was close to being unmasked on several occasions. Back in Washington, he was charged by Abraham Lincoln with a new task. Spies from the South were at least as active as their northern counterparts, and Pinkerton was commissioned to find out who was responsible for security breaches. So he set up a network of agents that is now regarded as the forerunner of the FBI.

> *'I hated them with the same passion that corrupt policemen did.'*
>
> GEORGE WHITE, A BURGLAR, ON PINKERTON AGENTS

His colleague Elizabeth Baker acted in the guise of a naïve Southern belle to discover one of the South's key weapons. Unsuspecting gentlemen friends showed her around the Tredegar Ironworks in Richmond, Virginia, where she was able to see that the foundry was busy building submarines. The vessels were a threat to northern gunboats, as they could pass unnoticed under any port blockade. Baker also spotted that the newfangled craft had an Achilles' heel: their ventilation systems protruded above the surface of the water, so that a keen-eyed lookout could easily spot an approaching submarine.

Pinkerton's agents were not universally successful. On one occasion, the authorities in the North released an important woman spy from the South – but did so much sooner than planned. She duly unmasked three of Pinkerton's employees in Richmond, who were immediately arrested and hanged. Shaken by this incident, Pinkerton retired from espionage.

NO RESPITE

When the war ended, Pinkerton once more turned his attention to apprehending criminals. Over the following years his detectives, the famous Pinks, were instrumental in taking a whole string of notorious underworld figures out of circulation – among them Jesse James, Butch Cassidy and the Sundance Kid.

After Allan Pinkerton's death in 1884, his two sons continued to run the business. Today, the firm's employees are mainly concerned with investigating white-collar crime and insurance fraud, and offering security consultancy, preferring to leave the business of hunting down criminals to the police or the FBI.

A trapper's life becomes the stuff of myth

A skilled hunter, trapper and explorer, Daniel Boone instinctively understood the possibilities of the unknown expanses of America. In pioneering the Wilderness Road to Kentucky he opened up the gateway to the Wild West.

Daniel Boone was born on November 2, 1734, in a log cabin in Pennsylvania. The wild countryside provided the boy with a perfect education for his later career. Despite his aunt's efforts to school him, he preferred to amuse himself in the woods nearby, carving spears that he used to kill small game animals. On his forays into the wilderness he met local Indians, who taught him about hunting and reading tracking signs.

LIFE ON THE MOVE

When Daniel was 15, his family moved to the Yadkin River in North Carolina. Their arduous travels through rolling grasslands, sandy prairies and dark forests only served to heighten the young man's sense of adventure. Within a few years Boone had begun to earn his living accompanying wagon trains of settlers. His first assignment was of a military nature. In 1755, European colonial rivalries between France and Britain were being enacted on American soil. The British commander General Edward Braddock led an expedition to capture the French Fort Duquesne. In the baggage train accompanying his force, Boone drove a supply wagon and was engaged to repair harnesses and get damaged carts back on the road again. The expedition ended in disaster. Braddock and most of his troops were wiped out in an ambush, with only a few men, including Boone, escaping the massacre.

'One man was destined to lead the first settlers to the West, and that man was Daniel Boone.'

THEODORE ROOSEVELT

Shortly after this incident, Boone married and settled down. For ten years, he devoted himself to his family, life on the farmstead and hunting. Yet at the back of his mind he still harboured a dream of a land full of bison and deer, a land of freedom and adventure, a land that lay waiting for him beyond the Appalachian range.

THE PATH THROUGH THE WILDERNESS

In 1767 Boone travelled with his old friend, a hunter and trader named John Finley, to the edge of Kentucky and camped for the winter at Salt Spring near Prestonsburg. In May 1769 Boone,

Finley and four other men set off to go further west, beyond the Cumberland Gap. It was nearly two years before Boone returned home. During this time he thoroughly explored Kentucky, going as far west as the Falls of Ohio (present-day Louiseville). He made further trips to Kentucky in 1773 and 1774.

In 1775 Colonel Richard Henderson of the Transylvania trading company hired Boone as his agent and commissioned him to open up a passable route to Kentucky. Using axes, Boone and a party of 30 men hacked their way through the wilderness for 300 miles, right into the heart of Kentucky, the so-called 'Great Meadow'. It was a hunter's paradise, filled with buffalo, deer, wild turkey and meadows ideal for farming. The route they pioneered, originally no more than an impassable Indian trail, was the legendary 'Wilderness Road'. Soon, wagon trains of settlers were using the new route to get to the West. One of the first groups of newcomers to arrive was Boone's own family, who established a small settlement known as Boonesborough at the end of the Wilderness Road.

THE BLOOD BROTHERHOOD

But the local Indians declared war on the new arrivals, believing them to be intruders and attacked the settlement. Shawnee warriors kidnapped Boone's daughter and two other girls. He set off in pursuit, and freed all three girls in a surprise attack. Shortly afterwards, Boone himself was taken prisoner and spent four months in a Shawnee village. His skills as a hunter and backwoodsman so impressed Chief Black Fish that he adopted Boone into his own family. They even swore an oath to become blood brothers. But Boone had learnt that the tribe was planning further attacks against the settlers and so he made his escape from the village, and returned to Boonesborough.

The 'land of dreams'

A name for a state
Kentucky is taken from the Indian word 'Ken-tah-ten', meaning 'Land of the Future'.

Early explorations
The first expeditions to reconnoitre the region were in 1750–51.

Early settlement
The region, which was claimed by Virginia, was permanently settled from 1775 onwards. Boonesborough and Harrodsburg were among the first settlements.

The War of Independence
In the War of Independence (1775–83), Kentucky settlers fought against an alliance of the local Indian tribes and the British.

Kentucky joins the Union
On June 1, 1792, Kentucky entered the Union of the United States of America as the 15th state, after ceding the western parts of its territory to Virginia.

Aware that an Indian attack was imminent, he organised the region's defences, strengthened the palisades and stored provisions. When the Shawnee eventually appeared at the gates of the settlement talks were held over several days and, on September 9, 1778, a peaceful settlement seemed likely. But a nervous settler, alarmed by a Shawnee warrior, let off a shot. Salvoes of gunfire immediately followed, and war erupted. The Shawnee laid siege to Boonesborough for eight days, making repeated attempts to burn it down. But the settlers' sustained fire was eventually to prove too much for the Indian warriors. On September 18, the besieging force withdrew.

LEGAL ROBBERY

Daniel Boone was to have no future in Boonesborough. When Kentucky became part of the Union in 1792, he, like many settlers, lost his land as a result of legal loopholes in the title deeds. In 1799, he joined his son in Missouri. He acquired new land there, but subsequently lost this as well, when Louisiana and Missouri, part of the original territory of Louisiana, were sold by the French to the United States in 1803 for $15 million. Once again, Boone's title deeds turned out to be worthless and bureaucracy proved his undoing. Hunting remained his sole consolation and livelihood, as it had been throughout his life. Just two years before his death on September 26, 1820, he could still be seen roaming the forest in his own inimitable style, his flintlock slung over his shoulder.

Boone became a legend after his death with the appearance of *The Leatherstocking Tales* by James Fenimore Cooper, published between 1823 and 1841. His hero, Natty Bumppo, a rugged hunter, scourge of Indians, and scout for the British army, is based on Daniel Boone. Lord Byron also paid tribute to Boone in a series of stanzas in his poem, *Don Juan*.

A man-made flood disaster

William Mulholland was the engineering genius who brought water to the city of Los Angeles, transforming it into a boom town, and ultimately a major metropolis. Yet when the waters of the St Francis Dam burst in 1928, killing nearly 400 people, his reputation was destroyed.

Shortly before midnight on March 12, 1928, the St Francis Dam in the Santa Clara Valley north of Los Angeles broke. Over 55 billion litres of water flooded into the valley, cutting a swathe 2 miles wide and 62 miles long. It swept away people, animals, houses, bridges and sections of railway, before flowing out into the Pacific Ocean. The catastrophe claimed the lives of almost 400 people and left an area of devastation that was submerged in several metres of mud. The person responsible for the disaster was soon identified: William Mulholland, chief engineer on the construction of the St Francis Dam in 1926 and now head of the Los Angeles Water Authority.

AN AMERICAN CAREER

The collapse of the St Francis Dam inflicted lasting damage on Mulholland's reputation. Before the disaster, he had a string of remarkable achievements to his name. Born in Belfast in 1855, he left school at 15 to go to sea. Arriving in New York City at the beginning of the 1870s, he worked in various parts of the United States as a lumberjack, in textile mills and as a miner. In 1877 he moved to California and settled in Los Angeles. There, in the city's waterworks, he found an occupation that was to engage him for the rest of his working life. Los Angeles was criss-crossed by a system of open drainage culverts and Mulholland was given responsibility for maintaining one of these culverts. He taught himself mathematics and engineering, and just eight years later became chief engineer of the city's waterworks. His colleagues dubbed Mulholland 'the Chief', a man who managed to combine devotion to duty with humour and an affable nature.

He was also an innovator and creative thinker. In 1906 when building the barrier that formed the Silver Lake Reservoir, Mulholland was the first American engineer to use hydraulic sluices in the construction of a dam. The new method of

In the aftermath of the tragedy, William Mulholland argued that the collapse of the dam must have been caused by sabotage. When a State Commission found that the dam was built on unstable bedrock, he accepted the blame and resigned, a broken man. Yet none of the explanations for the tragedy satisfied him: 'There was a hoodoo about the place', he said.

construction gained acceptance right across the USA and was adopted when the Gatun Dam was built on the Panama Canal.

MULHOLLAND'S MASTERPIECE

By the end of the 19th century, Los Angeles had almost 100,000 inhabitants and a stream of immigrants arriving daily. Along with his former boss Fred Eaton, the one-time mayor of Los Angeles, Mulholland warned that the water supply would soon be inadequate for the growing population. The two men looked around for suitable sources of water in the area and investigated the Owens Valley, 230 miles north of the city. Mulholland realised that water from this valley could be used to supply Los Angeles. Since the valley was 1200 metres above sea level, water would not need to be pumped, but could be transported using the force of gravity. They decided to build an aqueduct.

Eaton negotiated the purchase of land and Mulholland directed the construction of the aqueduct. Around 5000 men worked for eight years, installing roads, railway links, power lines and sluices, and digging 164 tunnels with a total length of over 62 miles through the mountains. At 231 miles, the aqueduct was the longest in the world and the most challenging engineering project ever undertaken in America, yet remarkably it was completed within the allotted schedule and under budget.

On November 5, 1913, the aqueduct was officially opened. Water flowed from the Owens Valley into the San Fernando Valley, where it was stored in an underground reservoir. In 1921, several small reservoirs were built to supply the city in the event of a drought or damage to the aqueduct, but it was clear that a major reservoir was needed. Mulholland chose the San Francisquito Canyon, about 30 miles north of Los Angeles, as the site of the new dam. The aqueduct ran conveniently along the canyon and two electrical generating stations located there used aqueduct water to provide power for Los Angeles. In 1924, the construction of the St Francis Dam was started.

WATER WARS

In the years immediately after the completion of the aqueduct, Los Angeles did not need all the water now at its disposal. The surplus was used to irrigate the arid San Fernando Valley. Land prices in the valley rose steeply, enriching two syndicates of Los Angeles speculators, some of whom were friends of Mulholland. In the meantime the Owens Valley languished, becoming more arid and infertile. Its inhabitants felt betrayed: Mulholland had pledged that only essential water would be diverted to cater for the city. In May 1924, an explosion damaged a section of the aqueduct. Thereafter, acts of sabotage increased in frequency and the press began to speak in terms of a war in the Owens Valley.

The crisis came to a head in November 1924, when 70 armed men from the valley closed off a key lock on the aqueduct, shutting off the water flow. The next day there were 700 protesters at the site, demanding compensation for their now worthless land. Lengthy negotiations ensued, but no agreement was reached. In 1927, another part of the aqueduct was blown up. The 'providential' St Francis Dam and Reservoir saved Los Angeles from a severe water shortage and water from the reservoir also continued to generate electricity.

DISASTER STRIKES

During 1927 and 1928, several cracks appeared in the dam but Mulholland was not unduly concerned. On March 7, 1928, the dam was completely filled for the first time and further cracks appeared. At 11.57 pm on March 12, 1928, scarcely 12 hours after Mulholland last inspected it, the dam crumbled. The dam-keeper, Tony Harnischfeger, and his wife were swept away by a

Without Mulholland's technical genius, the growth of Los Angeles into a metropolis of ten million would have been impossible. In this arid region, development has followed water supply: the San Fernando Valley, irrigated by excess water from Mulholland's aqueduct, was annexed by Los Angeles in 1915, almost doubling the size of the city.

flood wave at least 38 metres high, the first of hundreds of people to die in the catastrophe.

A commission was set up to investigate the collapse. Experts found evidence that water had leaked from the dam the very day before it burst. Mulholland admitted that he had visited the dam the day before the accident, but swore that he had not noticed anything untoward. The experts concluded that the bedrock on which the dam was built was unsuitable as a foundation for such a structure and that the engineers were guilty of errors in their assessment of the geology of the site and the construction of the dam itself. Although not convicted of any crime, Mulholland resigned shortly afterwards. Deeply wounded by the accusations, he spent the rest of his life as a recluse. He died in 1935.

> 'If human error was at fault, then I am the human in question.'
>
> MULHOLLAND ANNOUNCING HIS RESIGNATION IN 1928

THE REHABILITATION OF MULHOLLAND

In 1992, the causes of the 1928 disaster were re-examined. Scientists came to the conclusion that Mulholland could not be held responsible for any negligence. In the light of the geological knowledge of the time, it would have been impossible to ascertain that foundations could not be safely sunk into the bedrock formation at the eastern end of the dam.

Mulholland remains, in equal measure, a legendary and controversial figure in the history of California. He created the conditions that enabled Los Angeles to develop into a major city, yet today people are also aware of the environmental problems that were caused by diverting water from the surrounding valleys into the city. Concerns such as these were simply not considered during the building boom of the 1920s.

Anyone visiting Los Angeles cannot help but stumble across Mulholland's name, since the most picturesque of the city's boulevards, Mulholland Drive, was named after him in 1924. From here it is possible to view the sprawling metropolis which, without his vision and determination, could not have achieved the prosperity and prominence it has today.

Rogues
and
adventurers

9

Caravaggio's self-portrait as sick Bacchus, god of wine and pleasure in Greek and Roman mythology, combines artistic virtuosity and palpable suffering. He painted it in 1593-94, soon after his arrival in Rome.

A
genius
who turned to
murder

The Italian Renaissance painter Caravaggio was an artist-rebel whose tempestuous life matched the drama of his paintings. Even as he attempted to capture divine light on canvas, the sublimely gifted artist descended into a vortex of criminality and violence.

Enraged, Caravaggio stood on the beach at Porto Ercole, on the Tuscan coast, and hurled abuse at the ship disappearing over the horizon with all his belongings on board. Sailing from Naples to Porto Ercole to await a papal pardon that would allow him to return to Rome, he had clearly walked into a trap. No sooner had he come ashore than he was arrested and held in custody. Now he found himself with no money and no papal reprieve to bring his four-year exile to an end. By midday, his rage had become a fever. For the next few days the artist fought for his life, but died on July 18, 1610, his colourful and violent career at an end.

A BRAWLER, PHILANDERER AND GANGSTER

Accounts of the final months of the life of the painter known as 'Il Caravaggio' after his birthplace are very contradictory. What is certain is that just as the artist displayed a masterly use of light and shade in his paintings, so his life was characterised by dramatic ups and downs. Tellingly, the principal source of information about Caravaggio's life and character are police reports of the period, full of charges including insults to honour, illicit love affairs, brawling and even manslaughter.

Michelangelo Merisi da Caravaggio was born near Bergamo in Lombardy, northern Italy, on September 28, 1571. Just before his 13th birthday, he was apprenticed to the painter Simone Peterzano. His career as an independent artist only began after his move to Rome, in around 1590. Caravaggio's paintings showed talent from the very beginning. But he was one among many struggling young artists in the city, and was often too poor to buy food. He also made enemies by pouring scorn on his colleagues' artistic efforts and showing no respect for recognised masters. In spite of his arrogance, before long Caravaggio secured powerful patrons in Rome's aristocratic and ecclesiastical circles, who supplied him with major commissions.

FAME AND RECOGNITION

By the end of the 1590s it was impossible for the artistic establishment in Rome to ignore Caravaggio. His early subjects were scenes from everyday life which, in their naturalistic depiction of human figures, shunned the idealisation that was conventional at the time. Within a few years, Caravaggio had found his characteristic style. His use of *chiaroscuro* (dramatic contrasts of light and shade) typified all his major works. His painting became dominated by themes from Christian history. Between 1599 and 1602 he produced three large canvases for the Chapel of Cardinal Contarelli in the Church of San Luigi dei

Artists' trials and tribulations

Rembrandt
The Dutch artist purchased so many objets d'art, costumes and rare collectors' items for his own art collection that he was forced to declare himself bankrupt in 1656.

Renoir
Although his hands had been crippled by rheumatoid arthritis, in the final years of his life the French painter Auguste Renoir (1841–1919) continued to turn out a large number of paintings and bronze sculptures.

Van Gogh
In 1889, after suffering a series of fits, and cutting off part of his ear, the Dutch painter Vincent van Gogh voluntarily committed himself to an asylum.

Francesci. The *Inspiration of St Matthew*, *The Martyrdom of St Matthew* and *The Calling of St Matthew* were consummate expressions of his skill. He also created his celebrated works, *The Crucifixion of St Peter* and *Conversion on the Road to Damascus*, in the Chapel of Tiberio Cerasi in the Church of Santa Maria del Popolo in Rome.

OUTLAW ON THE RUN
But despite his divine subject matter, Caravaggio was a drinker, womaniser and a hot-blooded brawler. In May 1606, in a duel following either a disputed tennis match score – or over a prostitute whose services both men sought – he fatally wounded the painter Ranuccio Tommasoni. Caravaggio fled Rome with a price on his head. He went to Naples and then Malta, where he was given a hearing by Alof de Wignacourt, Grand Master of the Order of St John Hospitaller. He was even received into the order as a Knight Second Class. But before long, after insulting and wounding one of his superiors, he was held in Valletta's fortress. He managed to escape, fleeing to Sicily, fearing pursuit by vengeful knights.

In exile Caravaggio continued to paint, his art becoming darker and more deeply shadowed. He longed to return to Rome, but only the Pope's pardon could end his desperate exile. Encouraged by news that influential people were interceding on his behalf, Caravaggio moved north to Naples in the autumn of 1609. There he was attacked and so seriously disfigured that it took him months to recover, all the while hoping for eventual forgiveness by the Pope. So it was that in July 1610 he sailed to Porto Ercole. By a cruel irony of fate, a letter containing the papal pardon arrived from Rome just three days after his death.

Fateful journeys
across the ice

A pioneer of Arctic aviation, Umberto Nobile
designed and piloted the first airship to fly over the
North Pole. On his return he was acclaimed a hero –
only to be later reviled as a coward. What went wrong?

It was a sight that polar bears would certainly never have seen
before: by the light of the midnight sun on May 11, 1926, an
airship more than 100 metres long appeared above the Arctic
pack ice. The *Norge* had a single goal – to reach the geographical
North Pole. At 2.20 am on the following day, the airship flew
over its objective. For Lincoln Ellsworth, it was the perfect way

The airship that Umberto
Nobile captained on his
second polar expedition,
in 1928, never returned to
its point of departure, the
island of Spitsbergen (now
Svalbard).

to celebrate his 46th birthday. On board with him were 15 other crew members, including the Norwegian polar explorer Roald Amundsen and the Italian engineer Umberto Nobile.

Ellsworth, a wealthy American had funded the expedition. It embarked from Kongsfjord on the island of Spitsbergen, north of Norway, and ended some 3200 miles later, in Alaska. Nobile, designer of the *Norge*, was also its captain. Amundsen, who 15 years earlier had won the race to the South Pole against Captain Robert Falcon Scott, was the most experienced crewmember. Having spent decades on research expeditions across the Arctic and Antarctic, he was in charge of navigation – especially vital on an Arctic flight since the magnetic North Pole pulls the compass needle in the 'wrong' direction, causing navigational errors. Explorers also had to provide evidence that they had actually reached the Pole, or risk being branded as frauds.

TENSION AMONG THE CREW

On board the *Norge*, Amundsen made no secret of his dislike for Nobile and criticised every aspect of the expedition, including the fact that Nobile had brought his terrier Titina along, grumbling that the dog was 'unnecessary ballast'.

Nobile suffered numerous humiliations and found himself increasingly sidelined. On May 12, 1926, Amundsen's antipathy was aggravated by the news that he had been thwarted in his goal to be the first aviator to reach the North Pole: the American Richard Byrd had flown over the Pole in an aeroplane three days ahead of him. Amundsen vented his disappointment on Nobile. Even after they returned safely, he continued to slander him in public. The two former travelling companions became bitter enemies. Nationalistic undertones were never far from the surface of this acrimonious dispute. Once the *Norge* reached the

The race to the poles

Roald Amundsen
The Norwegian was the first person to reach the South Pole, on December 14, 1911.

Robert Falcon Scott
The next month, on January 18, 1912, the Englishman reached the South Pole.

Richard Byrd
According to his own account, the American was the first person to fly over the North Pole, on May 9, 1926.

The airship *Norge*
Three days later, on May 12, 1926, the airship *Norge*, with Umberto Nobile, Roald Amundsen and the American millionaire Lincoln Ellsworth on board, passed over the North Pole.

North Pole known as Tigishu (the Great Nail) by the indigenous Inuit – three countries' flags were dropped from the airship: the Italian and Norwegian flags and the American Stars and Stripes. On his return to Italy, Nobile was fêted as a national hero, promoted to the rank of General, and shamelessly exploited by the Fascists for propaganda purposes – although all his life his political sympathies had tended to the left.

AN ITALIAN 'CONQUEST'

Umberto Nobile was born in Lauro, near Naples, on January 21, 1885. His study of maths, physics and engineering science led to an interest in aeronautical engineering. During the First World War, he worked as a designer in factories that built dirigibles for the Italian armed forces. He avoided active war service because he was declared physically unfit on three occasions by the conscription board. Yet a strong will lurked within Nobile's slight frame, fuelling a dream that progressively took shape from the mid-1920s onwards: Nobile was determined to reach the North Pole by airship.

Umberto Nobile in full military uniform, with airship blueprints rolled up under his arm. His first polar flight won him acclaim and promotion from Colonel to General. After the failure of the 1928 expedition, he was forced to resign his commission and faced ignominy.

After his painful experiences on the *Norge*, Nobile's second trip to the Pole two years later was conceived from the outset as an almost exclusively Italian venture. The airship was called the *N2 Italia*. Following a flight from Milan to Spitsbergen, the craft lifted off from Kongsfjord on its polar journey on May 23, 1928. Nobile first headed west then, on reaching a longitude of 27°W, turned due north. Aided by a stiff southerly breeze, the *N2 Italia* made rapid progress to its goal. But the joy of the crew members was soon tempered: if that strength of tailwind was maintained, then their return journey would be into a strong headwind which would slow their progress and drain fuel reserves. They could only hope for a change of wind speed and direction. The airship reached the North Pole on May 24 at around 12.30 pm and circled it for about two hours.

Although the original plan to land on the Earth's most northerly point was abandoned because the deeply fissured surface of the pack ice made it impossible, the crew of the *N2 Italia* savoured their triumph. They dropped the Italian tricolour, the city banner of Milan (the airship's home base), a small medallion depicting the Virgin Mary, and a large wooden cross given to the expedition by Pope Pius XI. With the mission completed, they awarded themselves a ration of egg-nog.

NIGHTMARE FLIGHT INTO THE UNKNOWN

Nobile was keen to set off south again, but the next morning the return flight ended in disaster. The wind direction had not changed and it was now blowing even more fiercely, burning up more fuel and causing the airship's internal framework to shake violently. The greatest danger they faced was icing. As the *N2 Italia* flew through freezing clouds, ice formed on the exterior surfaces. At intervals, chunks of ice broke loose, threatening to tear holes in the airship's envelope.

The greater risk was that the control surfaces would freeze up. Eventually, the elevator jammed, the nose of the airship dipped and, out of control, she headed straight for the pack ice. The captain ordered the engines to be set at full revs, which gave the airship greater lift and raised her nose just enough to avoid a crash. Yet the second time this happened, repeating the

The *Italia* crash prompted an international search and rescue operation. Six countries contributed planes and ships. Yet the survivors spent seven weeks stranded on the rapidly disintegrating polar ice flow with minimal protection against the cold. Among them was Franz Behounek (right), a Czech explorer.

manoeuvre failed to correct the ship's altitude and the *N2 Italia* dropped like a stone straight onto the pack ice, with her nose pointing skywards.

DOUBLE DISASTER

On impact, most of the crew of 16 were flung out of the airship's gondola onto the ice. Nobile suffered several broken bones, but the most seriously hurt was Chief Engineer Vincenzo Pommella, who died of internal injuries. Only the dog Titina escaped the crash unscathed. As the crew who had been thrown clear of the ship lay dazed at the crash site, the second act of the tragedy unfolded. Six men were still trapped in the gondola, which was hanging from the holed and crumpled fuselage. Before they could react, the wind picked up the damaged *N2 Italia* and carried it off over the ice floes. The men on the ice could only look on as the wreckage with their comrades inside disappeared into the distance. They were never seen again.

MAYDAY CALLS FOR HELP

The crew trapped in the gondola must have realised immediately that they had no chance of survival, and so threw out cans of fuel, food and various pieces of equipment onto the ice. Their selfless act gave their comrades a slim chance of survival. When they went down, Chief Petty Officer Giuseppe Biagi had instinctively seized the emergency radio transmitter. Once he had regained consciousness, he signalled 'SOS Italia, SOS Italia', hoping that the mayday call might be picked up by their supply ship, *Citta di Milano*, lying at anchor in the Kongsfjord.

The crash had occurred at roughly 81°N and 25°E, some 60 miles off Nordaustlandet Island in the Spitsbergen archipelago. The ice floe, on which the survivors put up a red tent, drifted due south before floating off on a tortuous course through the sea of ice. Hunger, the intense cold and the injuries they had sustained, coupled with the constant fear that the ice floe might break up, made this enforced voyage a torment for the shipwrecked men. On June 6, 1928, a Russian radio ham picked up their distress calls. He alerted the world to their plight, prompting an international search and rescue mission.

SEARCH AND RESCUE

One of those who took part in this mission was Roald Amundsen. On June 18, he and ten companions took off on a reconnaissance flight from northern Norway on board a French seaplane. The continuing feud between him and Nobile would explain why Amundsen was not put in charge of the better-equipped official Norwegian search team. As a further tragedy, Amundson lost his life on this mission: a few hours after take-off from Norway, his plane radioed its last signal before disappearing without a trace into the sea of ice.

Eventually, on June 20, an Italian pilot who had spotted the red tent dropped food supplies and blankets to the survivors. Three days later, the Swedish pilot Einar Lundborg landed his aeroplane, equipped with skids, on the treacherous surface of the ice floe. He could take only one passenger with him and selected the badly injured Nobile. On his return for more survivors Lundborg damaged his plane and he had to be rescued.

Three of the men then set off to try to reach Spitsbergen. Only two were later picked up, one, Finn Malmgren having dug his own grave in the ice before he lay down to die. The other two men survived a further 12 days without food, leading some to conjecture that they may have been forced to eat their dead companion. It was three weeks before the remaining five members of the airship's stranded crew were rescued. On July 12, 1928, they finally embarked on their homeward journey on board the Soviet icebreaker *Krassin*.

SHUNNED AND BETRAYED

On his return to Italy, Nobile, who had aged significantly during the weeks he spent drifting on the ice floe, faced further ordeals. He was shunned even by his former Italian Air Force comrades, accused of conducting a series of foolish manoeuvres that led to the airship crashing. Many Italians regarded the accident as a national disgrace and wanted a scapegoat. It was seen as particularly shameful that Nobile had allowed himself to be rescued from his icy prison before the others. It stood to reason that only a coward would have allowed such a thing to happen. The extent of his injuries was not considered by his critics.

Relieved but suffering from severe exhaustion, Umberto Nobile and his dog, Titina, celebrate their rescue from the ice flow on June 20 by the Swedish pilot Einar Lundborg.

In 1931 following the death of his wife and having resigned his air force commission, Umberto Nobile left Italy for Russia. He initially acted as an adviser to the Russian airline Dobroljet, working on the Soviet semi rigid airship programme. In 1936, he came back to Italy, then in 1939 moved to the United States where he taught aeronautical engineering. He returned to Rome in 1943. In 1945 the Italian air force cleared him of all charges and promoted him to the rank of major general. He then taught at the University of Naples until his retirement.

Nobile died on July 30, 1978, at the age of 93, surrounded by memorabilia from his polar expeditions and the embalmed remains of his four-legged companion Titina who, in contrast to his compatriots, had remained loyal to him to the last.

Highwaymen and plunderers

The knightly virtues – loyalty, courage, justice and humility – are an integral part of what we understand by chivalry. Yet in the Middle Ages, supposedly noble knights seldom fought unless there was something in it for them. In reality, they ruthlessly pursued their own interests.

In the early months of 1462, the forces of Count Ulrich of Württemberg, the Margrave of Baden, the Bishop of Metz and the Bishop of Speyer cut a swathe of destruction through the territories belonging to Frederick I, the Elector Palatine, as they advanced towards the city of Heidelberg. No town, village or

farmstead was safe from the ravages of their troops and only their defeat and capture at the battle of Seckenheim on June 30 put an end to their rampages.

To their surprise, Elector Frederick treated the captives with respect. At his castle in Heidelberg, he entertained them in a manner befitting their noble rank, only refusing them bread. When they questioned this, he pointed towards the scorched fields and burned villages that could be seen from the city walls, saying: 'Now, tell me whose fault it is that the provisioning of my daily bread is in such a bad state. You will have to remain here until you have sowed my fields and seen their recovery.'

Although the battle itself and the events that preceded it are historical fact, what is commonly referred to as the 'Heidelberg Banquet' is actually legend. However, it vividly illustrates how the feudal system could break down and degenerate into more-or-less private wars between feuding groups of nobles and their supporters. Such abuses resulted in those who once had been seen as pure and chivalrous knights now being denigrated as nothing more than avaricious robber barons.

FROM KNIGHTS TO ROBBER BARONS

The term 'robber baron' probably originated in Germany in the 12th and 13th centuries. During the Interregnum – the period in the history of the Holy Roman Empire when there was no emperor on the throne – some powerful feudal lords along the River Rhine took advantage of the absence of authority to levy unauthorised and exorbitant tolls on the shipping that plied the busy river. They were prepared to back up their demands by force. Iron chains would be stretched across the river just below the surface to prevent ships getting past the castles they had illegally constructed on the riverside. Nor were these greedy pirate lords above stealing the actual ships, stripping them of their rich cargoes and kidnapping their passengers. It was lawlessness on a grand scale.

Eventually the Rhine League put the robber barons of the Rhine out of business after laying siege to their castles and destroying them. But the German experience was by no means unique. Throughout medieval Europe, many noblemen made

A party of medieval travellers is set on by a band of outlaw knights. Weak rule often led to the breakdown of law and order and the emergence of over-powerful nobles, impelled by self-interest and personal ambition.

their livings by robbing unfortunate travellers who crossed their vast estates, or worse, imprisoning them in their castle dungeons until a ransom was paid.

WEAK KINGS AND AMBITIOUS NOBLES

In France, the first Capetian kings were weak rulers who failed to master their kingdom for a century. As a result, dukes and counts ran their own regions almost wholly independently. The resulting disorders grew to such an extent that the kings, fearing for their lives, rarely left the safety of Paris. Only with the accession of Louis VI, who reigned from 1108 to 1137, did the French robber barons begin to be brought under royal control.

The situation was similar in England, with barons quick to take advantage of weak kings, notably Stephen, to usurp royal authority and fight each other – and the king – using their castles as their bases. It was little wonder that the *Anglo-Saxon Chronicle* described Stephen's reign as the time 'when Christ and his saints slept'. A similar sequence of events was repeated later under Henry III, Edward II, Richard II and Henry VI.

CHIVALRY AND REALITY

Baronial power was particularly strong in the area between England and Wales known as the Marches. The Marcher Barons enjoyed more power than lords anywhere else in the country. They were allowed to build castles without royal permission and to wage war against the Welsh without the king's assent. As a result, they could keep any land they conquered for themselves. They were ruthless men, who were ruthlessly ambitious.

What happened to chivalry in all of this? The short answer is that, at least as depicted in romanticised form, it never really existed. The notion was essentially the invention of medieval poets, while the 19th-century Romantic movement, with its love of Gothic castles and other chivalric symbols, ensured its continued survival. Even the robber barons turned into folk heroes. Not for the last time, what people wanted to believe was at odds with the unvarnished historical truth.

The tragic obsessions
of a tycoon

The entrepreneur and movie producer Howard Hughes could afford anything he wanted. He was a legendary aviator, movie mogul and womaniser. Yet he spent the last quarter of his life as a recluse, addicted to drugs and teetering on the brink of insanity.

Born on December 24, 1905, in Houston, Texas, Howard Hughes learned from an early age that money talks. His millionaire father owned the Hughes Tool company, which manufactured equipment for the oil industry and he had a comfortable childhood. Yet Hughes never graduated from high school and was only able to attend classes at the California Institute of Technology because his father gave a generous endowment to the Institute.

Pictured in 1936, Hughes was associated with Hollywood's most glamorous actresses and the American public was fascinated by him.

James Hall and Jean Harlow in a still from Hughes's epic war film *Hell's Angels* (1930). Directed by Hughes, it was the most expensive movie of its time, at a cost of $3.8 million. Although it lost $1.5 million at the box office, the film made Howard Hughes a major Hollywood player.

Hughes returned to Texas and enrolled at the Rice Institute in Houston, but when he was 18 his father died – and he left without his degree. His father's will decreed that Hughes was to take over the Hughes Tool Company at the age of 21. But after having himself declared to be of legal majority, Hughes appointed former racing driver Noah Dietrich as the company's head of finance. It was a stroke of genius; over the next few years, Dietrich was instrumental in driving the company's prosperity.

MOVIES AND WOMEN

Besotted by the burgeoning movie industry, in 1925 Hughes went to Hollywood. He produced three films, then turned to writing and directing. In his first film, *Hell's Angels*, the largest private airforce in the world was used to re-create aerial dogfights from the First World War. Two of his later films tested the limits of public morality. *Scarface* (1932) was censored because of its violence and Hughes had to sue to allow its release. *The Outlaw* (1941) was controversial for its sexually explicit advertising and content, featuring a sensational décolletage worn by its star Jane Russell. Hughes had used his engineering expertise to create the half-cup bra modelled by Russell.

In 1948 Hughes took over the RKO studio. During the McCarthy era, as Hollywood was investigated for its supposedly pro-communist leanings, he was staunchly anti-communist. The studio was closed for six months while the politics of his employees were investigated – and completed pictures were re-shot if Hughes felt that their anti-communist politics weren't sufficiently clear.

Hughes's affairs with women were legendary. Although married to Ella Rice, a Houston socialite, in 1925, from 1928 he was linked to a string of movie stars: Jean Harlow, Katherine Hepburn, Ava Gardner, Terry Moore, Lana Turner, Rita Hayworth and Janet Leigh.

'I can buy anyone I like in the world.'

HOWARD HUGHES

There were also rumours of gay liaisons with a number of actors. He divorced Rice in 1929. In 1957, he married actress Jean Peters, but they divorced in 1970.

ROUND THE WORLD IN RECORD TIME

Towards the end of the 1920s, Hughes acquired a fleet of aircraft. In 1932 he formed the Hughes Aircraft division of the Hughes Tool Company. The firm went on to pioneer many innovations in aerospace technology. Hughes had acquired his pilot's licence during the filming of *Hell's Angels*. From then on, the most exhilarating hours of his life were spent in the air. A childhood illness had left him with tinnitus and a continual ringing in his ears. Too proud to wear a hearing aid, only in the cockpit of a plane did the ringing cease.

Flying became an obsession. Hughes set a number of world records, often in aeroplanes designed by himself. In 1935 he reached a speed of 350 miles per hour in the *H-1 Hughes Racer*. In 1938, he flew round the world in 3 days, 19 hours, and 17 minutes. But in 1946, Hughes was piloting an experimental US Airforce spy plane, the *XF-11*, when it developed an oil leak. Crash-landing to save the plane, he suffered numerous injuries included a crushed collar bone, six shattered ribs and third-degree burns. Only morphine made the pain bearable and Hughes became dependent on the drug for the rest of his life.

FLYING INTO TROUBLE

As a designer, Hughes constantly strove for superlatives. In 1942, with government support, he decided to build a series of huge flying boats to ferry troops and military equipment to Europe. But his obsessive perfectionism hindered the project; only one such aircraft was ever completed – after the end of the war. In

1947, in Long Beach Harbor, California, he made a test flight to prove that his flying boat – the largest aircraft in the world – really was airworthy and stop a Senate investigation. That short hop remained the only flight it ever made. The monster aircraft, the *H-4 Hercules*, became known as the *Spruce Goose*.

In 1939, at the urging of Jack Frye, president of Trans World Airlines (TWA), Hughes purchased a majority share for nearly $7 million and took control of the company. In 1956, seeking to take TWA into the jet age, he placed orders for a fleet of Boeing 707s at a cost of $400 million. To cover the cost, his outside creditors required Hughes to cede total control of TWA. He was unwilling to relinquish power and his empire began to crumble. In 1960, he was forced out of TWA, although he still owned 78 per cent of the company and battled to regain control. In 1966, he was ordered by a US federal court to sell his shares, netting him a profit of $547 million.

MONEY TALKS

During the Second World War Hughes turned his aircraft company into a major defence contractor and developed close links with the government and the CIA. In 1957, he appointed Robert Maheu, a former FBI agent, head of company finance without having met him. Through Maheu, Hughes placed bribes to influential politicians, and became a CIA contractor and

Hughes and his team designed a single hull flying boat capable of carrying 750 troops, with eight 3000 horsepower engines, a mammoth fuel storage and supply system, and wings 6 metres longer than a football field. Few people believed that the *Spruce Goose* could actually fly. On November 2, 1947, Hughes piloted the giant flying boat across a 3-mile stretch of water at Long Beach, California.

facilitator. He granted Vice-President Richard Nixon's brother a loan of $205,000 that was not repaid, and Nixon lost the 1960 presidential election largely because of the scandal over the debt.

In 1966, Hughes decided to move to Las Vegas to become a casino baron. He took over the top two floors of the Desert Inn. After only ten days, the owners asked him to leave, because he was taking up suites intended for high-rolling gamblers. So he bought the hotel for $13,250,000, twice its market value. Over the next two years he acquired several other hotels and casinos from the Mafia, effectively ending mob control of the gambling city. A campaign donation of $100,000 to Nixon in 1971 ensured Hughes an easy ride from a Congressional hearing on cartels.

LONELINESS AND OBSESSION

As early as the mid-1950s, Hughes' paranoid fear of germs began to rule his life. Before touching anything, he had to wipe it with paper towels. He spent days on end sitting naked in a white leather armchair that he called his 'germ-free zone'. From 1958 he was not seen in public and restricted communication to telephone calls and letters. He eventually became a complete recluse, locked away in darkened rooms in a drug-induced daze.

Hughes died on April 5, 1976. The official cause of death was kidney failure, but he was malnourished and dehydrated, with broken hypodermic needles in his arms. His appearance had changed so dramatically over the years that the FBI had to take fingerprints to confirm his identity. Hughes did not leave a will, and there were 400 claimants to his estate. His fortune of $2 billion was shared out among his 22 cousins. But all his wealth and talent could not save Hughes from obsessions that must have made his life a living hell.

The entrepreneur

1932
Founded the Hughes Aircraft Company.

1938
Takes control of the airline TWA. He sells it in 1966.

1948
Buys film studio RKO. He sells it in 1955.

1953
The Hughes Medical Institute is established. All shares in Hughes Aircraft transferred to the foundation, so making the aviation company tax-exempt.

1961
Foundation of Hughes Space and Communications Corporation.

1972
Sale of Hughes Tool shares and renaming of the firm as the Summa Corporation signals Hughes' withdrawal from business life.

A carpenter on the throne of Russia

Why did Peter the Great become an apprentice shipwright in the Netherlands? On the surface, it was a strange decision – none of his predecessors had ever left Russia in time of peace, let alone taken up a trade – but it fitted in with his dream of learning from the West so that he could modernise his backward country.

The news spread like wildfire. People came in droves from all over the country to the small town of Saardam – now Zaandam – to see if the amazing story they had heard was really true. A famous person from abroad, so it was rumoured, had arrived in town and was living and working there as an apprentice in the shipyards under an assumed name. Nobody wanted to miss the chance of catching even a glimpse of this extraordinary figure, always assuming that the gossip was true.

Presently, the narrow streets were packed with curious onlookers. Then, suddenly, a hush fell as they stared in respectful silence at an imposing young man – he was 2 metres tall – who was edging his way forward through the crush. It was Peter the Great, tsar of all the Russias, dressed as a humble workman on

Amsterdam, where tsar Peter undertook his apprenticeship as a shipbuilder, was one of the wealthiest cities in the world in the 17th century. Ships sailed from her harbour to North America, Africa, present-day Indonesia and Brazil and formed the basis of a worldwide trading network. By 1700, the city's population had grown to almost 200,000.

The creator of the 'killer whale'

Herman Melville made his adventures at sea into the stuff of literature. But most of his efforts won him little recognition in his own lifetime. It was long after his death that *Moby Dick*, his greatest novel, finally won immortality as one of the glories of 19th-century American literature.

In a raging sea, after months of fruitless searching, the lookouts on board the whaler *Pequod* finally sighted the hump of the notorious white whale Moby Dick. A life-and-death struggle ensued. The fanatical Captain Ahab, who had lost one of his legs in an earlier clash with the beast, ordered his men to take to their whaling boats to exact his vengeance. Yet nature rather than man prevailed. Moby Dick turned on his attackers, dragged the captain down into the ocean depths and sank the *Pequod*. Ismael, the only survivor, told the story to the world as the narrator of Herman Melville's most celebrated novel, *Moby Dick*.

When Melville started to write the story of Captain Ahab's quest for revenge against the great white whale in 1850, he was well acquainted with his subject, having served on several whaling ships. His colourful life provided the source material for exciting tales of adventure: sea voyages, mutiny, desertion, and several sojourns among the exotic islanders of the South Seas.

FROM BANK TELLER TO CABIN BOY
While still a young man, Melville had embarked on more careers than most people manage in a lifetime. From an early age, he had to earn his own living. From the time of his birth, in August 1819 in New York, his once prosperous family found themselves in straitened financial circumstances. The trading company on which their fortunes depended fell deeper into financial difficulty, finally going bankrupt in 1830. Melville's father died insane two years later. The young Herman first tried his luck as a bank teller and later helped out on his uncle's farm. He spent a couple of weeks as a schoolteacher before starting to train as a land surveyor. When he failed to secure the job he hoped for, he decided to go to sea. In 1839, he signed on as a cabin boy on the *St Lawrence*, which sailed the transatlantic passage between New York and Liverpool.

ADVENTURES IN THE SOUTH SEAS
Thus began Melville's lifelong fascination with the sea, which survived even through some dreadful early experiences of life on board ship. In 1841, he joined the crew of the whaler *Acushnet*, which was sailing to the South Seas, only to discover that its

captain was a tyrannical despot. After 18 months, Melville and another sailor jumped ship while the *Acushnet* was anchored off the Marquesas Islands in French Polynesia.

Once onshore, Melville and his companion stumbled into an amazing adventure. In a remote valley on the island, they came across the mysterious Typee tribe, who were reputed to be cannibals. The two sailors did not appear to be suitable sacrificial victims so, though they were in constant fear for their lives, they spent several months among the natives without coming to harm. An opportunity for escape came in the form of the Australian ship *Lucy Ann*. Melville then sailed to Tahiti, where he served time in jail for deserting the *Acushnet*. For a short while, he worked on a farm on the island before signing on as a crew member on another whaler, the *Charles and Henry*. Later, he enlisted in the US Navy and served on the frigate *United States*, finally stepping ashore again in Boston in October 1844.

> *'There he blows! A hump like an iceberg!'*
>
> CAPTAIN AHAB IN *MOBY DICK*

DESKBOUND JOURNEYS

In the meantime, the Melville family's financial situation had improved. His brother had secured a lucrative government posting to London, which gave Melville the breathing space he needed to embark on a new career. In 1846, his first book *Typee, A Peep at Polynesia* appeared, recounting the tale of his adventures in the South Seas. Though critics assumed that much of the story must have been made up rather than drawn from the author's experiences, the new writer's combination of exciting plot and exotic setting captured the imagination of his readers.

Spurred on by his success, Melville wrote a sequel called *Omoo*, published in 1847. Its reception was equally enthusiastic. The same year, he married Elizabeth Shaw, the daughter of the Chief Justice of Massachusetts, and started his next book, *Mardi and a Voyage Thither*. Rather than the straight adventure yarn his readers had come to expect, Melville this time produced a more philosophical book. It was a flop. Hoping to win back his lost audience, he then wrote *Redburn* (1849), a novel about his time as a cabin boy, and *White-Jacket* (1850), about his experiences in the navy. Both were only moderately successful.

WHALING TALES

Melville dreamt of a secure future as a writer and landowner, living on his own country estate. With cash from his father-in-law, he purchased the small farmstead of Arrowhead near Pittsfield, Massachusetts. There, he spent many happy days writing, working on the farm, and occasionally preparing lectures for delivery about his travels. At Arrowhead, Melville got to know Nathaniel Hawthorne, an established writer who lived in seclusion nearby. Hawthorne was to become a close friend and confidant – and he persuaded Melville to embark on his great novel about the whale. 'I hope to have a new work ready for you by the end of this coming fall,' Melville wrote to his London publisher Richard Bentley in 1851, '... an adventure novel based on certain wild legends that abound among those who hunt sperm whales in the southern seas, interspersed with real-life experiences that the author has amassed over more than two years spent as a harpoonist... I am not aware that any novelist or other writer has ever done this subject proper justice.'

For day after day, Melville drafted and redrafted. Carried away by the drama of his story, he wrote feverishly about whales, the hunt and the sea and brought to vivid life the fictitious ship's crew, while weaving his own philosophical musings into the

From the end of the 17th century onwards, whalers ventured into the freezing Arctic Ocean in search of their prey. This enterprise could be a deadly business, both for the hunted and for the hunter.

narrative. The book was not a hit on either side of the Atlantic when it was published in November 1851 and was poorly reviewed into the bargain. In the 40 years that passed between its publication and Melville's death, only 3000 copies were sold.

FRUSTRATED AND FORGOTTEN

Failure and overwork gradually wore Melville down. He was also plagued by rheumatism and problems within his family. In the 1850s he took several recuperative breaks in Europe and the Holy Land. His main sources of income were the farm and short stories that he began to write for magazines. But these increasingly failed to provide him and his family with enough to live on. In frustration, Melville sold the farm in 1863 and moved to New York, where in 1866 he was employed as a customs inspector. For the next 20 years this provided his income. Disillusioned by his fiction's apparent lack of success, he began writing poetry, his principal subject being the American Civil War. Yet at the time, he also failed to make any real impact in that field.

When Melville died of a heart attack in September 1891, almost no one noticed his passing, save for a few surviving admirers. The *New York Times* wrote 'There has died and been buried in this city...a man who is so little known, even by name, to the generation now in the vigor of life that only one newspaper contained an obituary account of him, and this but of three or four lines.' None of Melville's books were still in print – indeed, his last great work, *Billy Budd*, did not find a publisher until 1924, long after his death.

It was around the same time that *Moby Dick* began to find a growing readership and garner critical acclaim. Over the years, it has become one of the most widely read books in American literature.

A history of whaling

Medieval whale hunts
The hunting of whales for their blubber began in the Middle Ages.

The Greenland voyages
Whalehunting in the Arctic had its heyday at the end of the 17th century when the renowned 'Greenland voyages' took place.

Whaling moves south
In the 19th century, whaling activity shifted to the South Atlantic and South Pacific. The first factory ships, which could process the catch directly, came in 1925.

Into the Antarctic
From 1934 Japanese whaling ships ventured into Antarctic waters in the hunt for whales.

Protection for whales
In 1946, the International Whaling Commission gave whales a protected status. In spite of this, all species of whale are today threatened with extinction.

Buffalo Bill and the myth of the Wild West

Acclaimed as the 'King of Prairiemen', William F. Cody was a legend in his lifetime. For millions, he embodied the spirit of the Old West, transmuting his personal experiences into a heady picture of frontier life that still captivates the imagination.

The bison thundered towards a flimsy wooden partition. Its awestruck audience was about to see first-hand how a bison was hunted down and shot. It was part of a great extravaganza that set out to show what it was really like to live in the Wild West. The spectacular shows staged by

Buffalo Bill is accepted as one of the greatest heroes of the Wild West. His exploits were immortalised in countless dime novels.

William Frederick Cody – better known as Buffalo Bill – gave ordinary people the chance to venture into his extraordinary world, and all for the price of an entrance ticket.

Cody was only 23 when his already eventful life started to become the stuff of legend. As time went by, fictional exploits attributed to him combined with adventures he had actually experienced to create a picture that was part truth and part fantasy. After 1882, when Cody started to tour the USA and Europe with his Wild West Show, he became one of the best-known personalities of the day. By the end of the century, Buffalo Bill was probably the most famous man in the world.

BIRTH OF A LEGEND

Following his father's death in 1857, Cody and his mother moved to Kansas. There he worked as a cattle herder, a wrangler and as a mounted courier for a railroad freight company. In 1859, he tried prospecting for gold during the Pikes Peak gold rush in Colorado before signing on the next year as one of the 200 riders employed by the Pony Express Company, the new mail delivery service, which prided itself on being the fastest in America.

For decades, Cody's Wild West Company enjoyed worldwide success, re-enacting vivid scenes and incidents from the Wild West's absorbing story, Cody himself played the role of his alter ego, Buffalo Bill, while other company members included Native American chiefs and cowboys.

The Pony Express advertised for 'skinny, expert riders willing
to risk death daily' and at the age of 14, Cody fitted the bill. He
then became a scout for the US Cavalry, scouting for the army in
campaigns against the Kiowa and Apache before serving with the
Seventh Cavalry during the
American Civil War
(1861–65), when he saw
action in Missouri and
Tennessee. After the war, he
married Louisa Frederici in
St Louis, and continued to
scout and serve as a despatch rider for the cavalry detachments
stationed at Fort Ellsworth in Kansas.

> *'I believe that man is closer to
> God in the great, wide-open
> spaces of the West.'*
>
> WILLIAM F. 'BUFFALO BILL' CODY

THE INTREPID 'BUFFALO BILL'

In 1867, Cody entered the service of the Kansas Pacific Railroad
Company – then called the Union Pacific Eastern Division –
which, in order to feed its hungry construction crews, was
advertising for marksmen to hunt American bison (buffalo).
Cody claimed to have shot 4280 bison in just 17 months. The
nickname 'Buffalo Bill' came as the result of winning an eight-
hour shooting contest with a rival buffalo hunter called William
Comstock. Presumably, the contest was to decide which of the
two deserved the name.

Two years later, Buffalo Bill made his debut on paper, when
the first novel featuring him as its hero appeared. Ned Buntline
penned the first in a seemingly endless series of romantic tales,
inspired by talk and newspaper reports of Cody's heroic exploits.
When Cody died, more than a thousand 'dime novels', had been
produced, most by Prentiss Ingraham and some by Cody himself.

Cody's reputation for bravery was well founded. He was
awarded the Congressional Medal of Honor for his scouting
work, having served as Chief of Scouts with the Fifth Cavalry
from 1868 onwards and taking part in no fewer than 16 battles
against Native American tribes. The Fifth Cavalry came to regard
him as a good luck talisman, as in all the battles that he fought,
he was hurt only once – with a 'a slight scalp wound'. Clearly
a Native American brave had been out to scalp him.

The founding of Buffalo Bill's city

A new town for a new frontier
Bill Cody was a keen proponent of progress in the American West. He had little time for nostalgic memories of what the West had been like in the frontier days before it became civilised.

The establishment of Cody
In 1896, along with a number of other investors, he founded the city that bears his name in Wyoming.

A water source
To supply the new city with water, the Buffalo Bill Dam was constructed in 1904. This was a key element in its future growth.

The gateway to Yellowstone
Nowadays, the city of Cody is a popular tourist destination, not least thanks to its proximity to the Yellowstone National Park.

TAKING TO THE STAGE

In addition to novels, Ned Buntline wrote a play about Buffalo Bill called *Buffalo Bill, King of Border Men*, which Cody saw in New York in the autumn of 1871. Though Buntline and other theatrical managers tried to persuade Cody to take to the stage, their advances were rejected. Cody wrote, 'I told them I would rather face a thousand Indians' – but Buntline's persistence and the lure of easy cash wore him down. In December 1872 in Chicago, Cody played himself in Buntline's new play *The Scouts of the Prairie*. It was a runaway success. Buffalo Bill had proved himself a natural showman.

The next year, Cody founded his own theatrical company, the 'Buffalo Bill Combination'. Two other famous scouts, Texas Jack and Wild Bill Hickok, appeared alongside him. Although the two did not remain with the company for long – Hickok had a penchant for 'shooting the supers in the legs with powder to see them jump' – Cody went on playing in melodramas about life in the West for many years. The performances usually took place during the winter, as in summer he was drawn back to the real West, to work as a scout again.

In the summer of 1876, there was heavy fighting between the US Army and the Native Americans, so the Fifth Cavalry sought Cody's help again. But in July, General George Armstrong Custer, the Fifth Cavalry's commander and a popular hero, was killed at the battle of the Little Bighorn and his command decimated. In the massacre's aftermath, Cody is said to have pledged that he would take the scalp of a chieftain in Custer's memory. Shortly afterwards he did indeed scalp the Cheyenne chief Yellow Hair (Cody mistakenly called him Yellow Hand).

To this day, it is unclear exactly what happened. Cody claimed that he shot the chief with a rifle, stabbed him in the heart and finally scalped him 'in about five seconds'. Or it may be that Yellow Hair had already fallen in battle when Cody lifted his scalp. Regardless of the truth, the deed further enhanced Cody's reputation. The papers reported the incident widely and Cody immediately wrote a melodrama based on it: *Buffalo Bill's First Scalp for Custer*, which was premiered that autumn.

Even though show business was now Cody's main occupation, he did not totally abandon his career as a scout. In 1890, Cody and a number of Native Americans from his troupe succeeded in brokering peace following hostilities between the army and a number of tribes. He was also called upon to help to restore order after the Seventh Cavalry massacred more than 300 Sioux at the battle of Wounded Knee.

Chief Sitting Bull of the Sioux, and the tribes that fought with him, won an overwhelming victory over General Custer and the US Fifth Cavalry at Little Bighorn River in July 1876. Sitting Bull was granted amnesty by the US goverment in 1881. In later life he toured with the Wild West Show where he would curse the audience in his native Lakota language.

THE WILD WEST SHOW

The Wild West Show or the 'Old Glory Blow Out' appeared for the first time in North Platte, Nebraska, in 1882. It was a combination of rodeo, circus, pageant and play performed in the open air.

Dramatic scenes of life in the untamed West were played out – a bison hunt, an Indian attack on the Deadwood Stage involving real Indians, and a Pony Express ride – with each performance ending with a dramatic re-enactment of Custer's Last Stand. Some of the Lakota Sioux who had taken part in the real battle were involved in the restaging, while all the cowboys and cowgirls in the show were equally authentic. What was more, the cowgirls were paid the same as their male counterparts, almost unheard of at that time. A champion of equal opportunities, Cody called for women to be given the vote. Buffalo Bill's Wild West Show was as much a history lesson as it was entertainment. It satisfied the audience's cravings for sensation while at the same time stirring nostalgic feelings for the old days. By the end of the 19th century the West had been largely settled. Anyone who had never seen the country when it was still 'wild' and 'uncivilised' turned to Buffalo Bill's Wild West Show to find out what it had been like.

The show ran for 30 years – ten of them touring Europe – and it was a success everywhere. In 1887, it was the main attraction of Queen Victoria's Golden Jubilee. Attractions included sharpshooter Annie Oakley and for a season, the Sioux Chief Sitting Bull – billed as 'the slayer of General Custer'. In 1893, Cody renamed the show the 'Congress of Rough Riders of the World' and invited Cossacks and other horsemen to take part.

THE SHOW MUST GO ON

In 1908, Cody amalgamated his show with 'Pawnee Bill's Great Far East', a counterpart extravaganza with a vaguely Far Eastern rather than a Wild Western flavour. Two years later he embarked on a grand 'Farewell Tour', only to find that he could not afford to retire. Although he had earned a great deal of money from the show, he spent most of it in ranching, mining, irrigation, publishing and town building schemes that failed to pay off, at least during his lifetime. He was forced to take out a massive loan to keep the show on the road and, when he was unable to pay it back on time, the show had to be put up for auction.

For the rest of his life, Cody had to appear as a hired hand in other people's Wild West shows. But he was by no means a beaten man. In 1913, he founded a movie company to produce films about the Indian Wars. Despite having fought against the Native Americans for much of his life, Cody was an advocate of their cause, as early as 1879 warning the US government 'never to make a single promise to the Indians that is not fulfilled'. He never tired of pointing out that they, as the original inhabitants of America, had had every right to defend their territories.

Cody died in January 1917. In accordance with his wishes, he was buried at the summit of Lookout Mountain in a tomb blasted from the solid rock.

The legacy of our ancestors

10

Massacre in the Mediterranean

It was one of the greatest naval battles of
all time. At Lepanto in the Gulf of Corinth on
October 7, 1571, a Christian fleet halted the
seemingly inexorable Ottoman drive through
the Mediterranean. The victory was greeted
with acclaim throughout the Western world,
but history's verdict is that it was not as
decisive as it seemed at the time.

A ferocious sea battle raged in the Gulf of Corinth. Soldiers and sailors were dismembered on board their ships, the bodies of dead mariners floated in the sea, and the water was stained red with blood. Thousands of ill-fated galley slaves, still chained fast to their banks of oars went down with their ships.

It was the bloodiest clash between Christians and Muslims for centuries and the fiercest naval battle fought in the Mediterranean since Octavius Caesar and his admiral Agrippa defeated the combined forces of Mark Antony and Cleopatra at Actium in 30 BC. The Ottoman fleet, which consisted of some 220 to 230 war galleys, 50 to 60 galliots and other supporting vessels, was decimated. Only 40 of the galleys managed to escape and more than 25,000 Turks perished. For their part, the Christians lost 8000 dead, with some 16,000 of them being wounded. Some 10,000 Christian galley slaves were freed.

The last battle ever to be fought solely between galleys took place at Lepanto in October 1571. The Christian fleet finally prevailed over its Ottoman opponents.

THE DANGER FROM THE EAST

In 1565, 600 Knights of St John, and a supporting force of some 8000 seasoned warriors, prepared to defend their island fortress of Malta from Ottoman attack. The Turks had mustered a fleet of 181 ships, carrying 30,000 soldiers, for the purpose. Their aim, once they had secured the island, was to sweep the Mediterranean of Christian shipping and establish Ottoman dominance over the region once and for all.

All through the summer, the Turks laid siege to the island. Though they were eventually forced to withdraw, their ambitions were certainly not at an end. It was then that a new and powerful player – the newly elected Pope Pius V – came on the scene.

Christian and Muslim naval forces had never before faced each other in a major battle at sea.

Pius knew that there was no possibility of the Turks leaving Europe in peace. In the east, Vienna, the capital of the Habsburg Empire, was still under threat – the Turks had already besieged the city back in 1529. In the Mediterranean, it was a matter of when, not if, the Turks would strike again. Pius did not have long to wait.

FOUNDING THE HOLY LEAGUE

In 1570, a vast Ottoman force under Sultan Selim II attacked the Venetian-held island of Cyprus and laid siege to Nicosia and Famagusta, its two principal towns. Cynical observers suggested that the Sultan, who had won himself the unflattering nickname of 'the Drunkard', had chosen his targets because he wanted to bring the area where the renowned Cypriot wines were grown under his control. In fact, the Turkish plan was far more strategically motivated. Mehmed Pasha Sokollu, the Sultan's Grand Vizier and the real power behind the throne, was aiming to wipe out all of Venice's surviving outposts in the Eastern Mediterranean. As far as Cyprus was concerned, he succeeded in his goal: Nicosia was captured on September 15, 1570, while Famagusta fell into Muslim hands almost a year later, on August 1, 1571.

When they took Constantinople on May 29, 1453, so putting an end to the once mighty Byzantine Empire, the Ottomans sent a shock wave throughout Christian Europe. Their next step was to secure the Balkans and march into Hungary as a first step to attacking Habsburg Austria and then invading the rest of the West.

At the same time, the Ottomans attacked the city and port of Tunis on the North African coast, threatening Christian control of the narrow passage into the western Mediterranean. The twin threats proved more than enough to enable Pius to bring Spain, Venice and some other Italian states together into a military alliance. The result was the formation of a second Holy League against the Turks: the previous attempt, one between Pope Paul III, the Habsburg Emperor Charles V and Venice, had collapsed in 1540 as a result of poor relations between the Venetians and the Emperor. In a formal agreement signed on May 25, 1571, all the powers involved committed themselves to taking the fight to the Turks, rather than waiting for further attacks.

The League immediately began preparing for all-out war. Under the command of Don John of Austria, the half-brother of Philip II of Spain, a combined Spanish, Venetian and Papal fleet began to gather in the Straits of Messina, off the island of Sicily. Although only in his twenties, Don John had already shown himself to be a capable naval commander. All told, he had over 200 ships under him, more than 100 of them supplied by Philip II. The Venetian contingent numbered around 100 vessels, while Pius himself had personally outfitted 12 galleys and supplied the funding for many of the others.

On September 16, 1571, the great fleet was ready to weigh anchor. Despite its size and strength, commanders and crews both must have been nervous about the outcome. They were taking on opponents who, ever since their resounding victory over the Christians at the battle of Prevesa in 1538, had enjoyed the reputation of being as invincible at sea as they were on land. Ottoman spies had long since discovered the secret of the planned alliance and the Turkish fleet, commanded by Ali Pasha, had set sail westwards ready to meet the expected attack.

VENICE'S SECRET WEAPON

Fortunately for the Christian cause, Don John and his fellow admirals had a secret weapon. This was the galleass, a new kind of galley that possessed a significant sailing capacity rather than relying solely on banks of oars for its propulsion. It was also heavily armed with cannon. Six were hastily made ready in Venice's great arsenal and despatched to join the main body of the Christian fleet, were now sailing east across the Ionian Sea.

Despite the fact that battles had been fought at sea since ancient times, the tactics employed were still relatively

The Venetian shipwright Francesco Duodi developed the galleass. This new type of warship helped the Christians to secure their conclusive victory at Lepanto.

unsophisticated. As on dry land, two opposing squadrons confronted one another in rigid formation. The battle began with the firing of a salvo of shots from giant catapults, followed by cannon fire when the fleets were at close quarters. The aim was to try to inflict as much surface damage as possible. It was rare for a ship to be sunk by catapult or cannon fire. Eventually, the ships would get close enough together to be boarded. Hand-to-hand fighting followed until one side or the other had prevailed.

Traditional oar-powered galleys were considered the most suitable vessels for this stage of the battle. Equipped with stout rams on their prows, they ploughed into the side of enemy ships in a controlled collision. Then soldiers would swarm across the gangplanks lowered onto the decks of the vessel to be boarded and a fight to the death would ensue.

Galleys were far less useful early on. The one or two heavy guns they carried could only fire directly fore and aft. The galleass was designed to overcome the problem. Not only did such vessels carry more cannon, but their guns could fire in a variety of directions as well. They were also built with high sides, rather like the walls of a castle, which made it harder for an enemy to board them.

Key naval battles

The destruction of the Armada
In 1588, the Spanish Armada fought a losing running battle against an English fleet commanded by Lord Howard of Effingham as it sailed up the English Channel. While anchored off Calais, it was driven out to sea by English fire ships. During the enforced flight home via Scotland and Ireland it lost many of its ships to violent storms.

The battle of Aboukir Bay
On August 1, 1798, off the Egyptian port of Aboukir, the French fleet suffered a devastating defeat at the hands of Nelson's English fleet. With 14 ships under his command, he captured six and destroyed seven French vessels out of a total of 17

The battle of Trafalgar
Nelson confirmed British dominance at sea in 1805 when he destroyed the bulk of the combined French and Spanish fleets at Trafalgar. Shot down by a sniper in the rigging of a French ship, he died of his wound in the moment of victory.

A BATTLE OF GIANTS
On the morning of October 7, 1571, the Christian fleet entered the Gulf of Patras, where, having failed to intercept the Turks at Corfu, it was finally to confront its adversaries. It comprised 210 galleys and galleasses, along with a dozen supply ships, manned by a total of 80,000 sailors, oarsmen and troops. The Venetians made up the lion's share of the Christian force. The Ottoman fleet had around 330 ships, Ali Pasha's squadrons having been

Ali Pasha, the Turkish supreme commander, urges on his men. Bitter hand-to-hand fighting was conducted on board the warships at Lepanto.

reinforced by ships commanded by Uludj Ali, the Bey of Algiers and leader of the notorious Muslin corsairs (pirates) who had long terrorised Christian shipping. Ali Pasha stationed it off the fortress of Lepanto. The fort had been in Turkish hands since the third war between the Ottomans and Venice, and the Turks could retreat there if the battle went against them.

The Turks felt secure in their haven, but, with hindsight, their position was disadvantageous. They would probably have done better to engage Don John and his fleet in open water. Instead, they were forced to fight in the treacherous narrows off Navpaktos, which gave little room for manoeuvre. The gusty winds in the narrows also had a major influence on the course of the action. At its outset, they blew strongly from the east. Had the Turks taken advantage of this, they could still have advanced to meet the Christian fleet, but they hesitated and missed their opportunity. At around midday, the wind dropped, and then turned into a westerly. As a result, Don John's fleet now had the wind at its back while the west wind blew gunpowder smoke directly into the Turks' faces, obscuring their gunners' sightlines.

Once in position, battle was joined. Don John split his forces into three: the Venetians, under Agostini Barbarigo, on the left and to the north, Andrea Doria and the Genoese and Papal galleys on the right and to the south, with himself in the centre. Santa Cruz's 35 vessels were held in reserve. Having ordered his captains not to open fire until they were 'close enough to be splattered with Muslin blood', he readied himself for action. Ali Pasha had arranged his ships in a giant crescent formation but, seeing what the Christians had done, he ordered them to reform in three divisions with himself, like Don John, in the centre. The Venetian galleasses were the first ships to open fire and, almost immediately, eight Muslim vessels were hit and started to sink. As the galleys in the centre closed on one another, the Christian troops crowding the decks raked their opponents with arquebus and crossbow fire. Ali Pasha's men tried to board the Christian ships, but each attempt was beaten back with heavy losses. Then, Don John seized the chance to board Ali Pasha's flagship. His Spanish troops swarmed over its decks, captured Ali Pasha and beheaded him on the spot – against the wishes of their commander. The head was impaled on a pike and raised high for all the ships around to see. The demoralised Turks started to flee.

On the right, things had been going less well for the Christians. Uludj Ali and his pirates broke through their battle line and captured the flagship of the Knights of St John. But with the arrival of Christian reinforcements, he too decided to turn and flee. The story was much the same on the left, where Admiral Mahomet Sirocco at first managed to outflank the Venetian galleys, take their flagship and kill their admiral. The Venetians were saved when help arrived; Sirocco's galley was sunk, the Turkish admiral unceremoniously hauled out of the water and, like Ali Pasha, executed immediately. The battle went on for a few more hours until a thunderstorm ended the slaughter. The Christian victory was absolute.

A SHORT-LIVED TRIUMPH

When news of the great victory spread through Europe, church bells rang out in celebration in cities across the continent. In St Peter's Basilica in Rome, Pope Pius hailed Don John as the saviour of the Christian world. Yet its fruits were soon dissipated. Pius, who had inspired the creation of the Holy League, died the following year. Spain proved reluctant to commit more forces to the eastern Mediterranean and, in 1577, a financially exhausted Venice made its own terms with the Turks. As for the Ottoman fleet, it was swiftly rebuilt and soon regained its former strength.

At best, Lepanto was a psychological triumph, since it showed that the Turks could be beaten. It was to be many years before a final and lasting check would constrain Ottoman ambitions.

The best shoes in the world

In an age when *nike* meant 'victory', you could tell a lot about someone just by looking at their shoes – or you could in ancient Rome. The type of footwear worn by upper class Romans distinguished them from soldiers and plebeians.

Cobblers were highly respected in ancient Rome, their clients coming mainly from the upper echelons of society. Common people provided their own shoes – it was cheap and fairly straightforward to make simple footwear like the sandals worn by the standard bearer here.

The type of footwear a Roman wore clearly revealed his or her status in society. Slaves were not allowed to wear any shoes while convicts wore heavy wooden clogs – which may have helped to stop them from running away. There were other complex rules about who could wear what. Older men took care not to wear the kinds of shoes designated for younger men, while only senators were allowed to wear red boots.

By and large, Roman citizens wore sturdy, solid shoes called *calcei*. These had a leather sole – grain side down – and a soft leather insole – grain side up – sandwiching several more layers of leather. Winter shoes were often cork-soled to provide insulation. A major difference between the Roman *calceus* and a modern walking shoe was the lack of a raised heel; anyone wanting to look taller simply had the whole sole thickened. The uppers and soles of these shoes were not stitched together like a modern shoe, but nailed. If the uppers of a *calceus* reached over the ankles or even higher up the leg, the resulting boot, which kept the feet dry in wet weather, was known as a *pero*.

THE EMPEROR 'BOOTKINS'

The famous army boot, the *caliga*, was so strongly identified as a soldier's footwear that the terms *caligatus* or *caligatus miles* in Latin texts can be translated as 'common soldier'. The uppers of *caligae* consisted of a single piece of leather with slits cut into it to keep the foot cool in a hot climate. These military shoes used iron hobnails as treads. Each boot could have up to 90 nails with rounded heads hammered into the sole, so a pair of *caligae* weighed over a kilo (2lbs). A Roman soldier could cover record-breaking distances with just a single pair of sturdy shoes – one pair could survive up to 600 miles' worth of heavy marching. *Caligae* were tied on with leather laces that continued half way up the shin, and which, in cold weather, could be stuffed with wool or fur.

Caligae was the term from which the Emperor Gaius – Caligula – got his nickname. Son of the popular legate Germanicus, the boy accompanied his father's legions on several northern campaigns. The soldiers regarded the child as a lucky mascot and nicknamed him Caligula, or 'Little Boots'.

COOL AND COMFORTABLE

The favourite footwear of all Romans, rich or poor, was sandals (*sandalia* or *soleae*), often a simple affair with a thong between the toes. Sandals were meant to be worn indoors, not in public. Some contemporary moral guardians feared a complete moral collapse if the nation that aspired to rule and civilise the known world started wearing light sandals in public. The sandals-indoors-only rule had some exceptions – Romans could wear sandals on the street if they were on their way to a banquet or the public bathhouse – and with good reason: it was a slow business undoing and doing up the straps of some outdoor shoes. Once inside the bathhouse, bathers could put on wooden-soled *soleae* to protect their feet from the underfloor heating.

When out visiting, Romans generally wore outdoor shoes, which they removed at the door before slipping into the sandals that had been carried by their slaves. The rule didn't apply to Emperor Caligula, whose despotic rule over Rome lasted from AD 37 to 41. He is said to have liked nothing better than to don ordinary sandals and wander through the streets. And when he wanted to be even more provocative, he would dress in women's clothes and put on ornately decorated women's shoes. While there are no obvious gender differences in Roman footwear, women's sandals were often dyed and decorated and made from softer, finer leather than men's. Alternatively, women and children wore stitched *socci* indoors. These were slipper-socks made from thin leather or sometimes fabric.

The cheapest shoe – equivalent to modern flip-flops – were simply-constructed palm-leaf sandals called *baxae*. Contemporary historians report that these shoes were not only made and worn by the poor but, for some unfathomable reason, by philosophers and comic actors too.

The history of shoes

Prehistoric shoes
Early Stone Age rock paintings indicate the wearing of shoes made of animal hides.

The first sandals
The Egyptians invented sandals c.3000 BC.

Pointed shoes
In medieval times, the length of the pronounced pointed toe showed the social status of the wearer.

High heels
High heels first came into fashion in the 17th century.

Shoes for everyone
Shoes began to be mass-produced in the 19th century.

The pearl
of the Mediterranean

The metropolis of Alexandria, founded by Alexander the Great, was intended to be a fitting centre for the vast empire he was creating. Although he did not live to see it built, the city more than fulfilled his dream. Known as the 'shining pearl' of the Mediterranean, it was one of the intellectual and commercial hubs of the ancient world.

On his arrival in Egypt, Alexander, the all-conquering Macedonian general, was hailed by the Egyptians as a liberator. Mazaces, the Persian governor ruling in the name of the faraway Darius III, quickly capitulated.

His conquests had made Alexander the greatest hero of ancient times. Now, he sought to build a new metropolis that would immortalise his name.

Technologically advanced and much loved by sailors, the Pharos of Alexandria, one of the world's earliest lighthouses, became celebrated as one of the Seven Wonders of the ancient world.

He came in person to supervise his architect Democrates, the master mason Numenios and his technical adviser Hyponomos as they decided on the new city's ground plan. Alexander himself indicated the overall layout they were to follow, including the location of the market place, the number of temples and the gods they should serve, and the city's defences. He also stipulated where the royal palace should be built and worked out a drainage and sewerage system for the entire city.

Because they were pressed for time, they marked out the ground with barley flour instead of chalk, sprinkling it on the earth as the king led the way along the city's projected roads and avenues. Then a flock of birds descended and ate all the grains. Not a trace of Alexander's plans survived.

MESSAGES FROM THE GODS

Worried that the incident was a warning from the gods, Alexander was reassured by his soothsayer Aristander, who told him that it was a sign that Alexander's city would prosper and be able to provide for as many inhabitants as the vast number of birds that had just eaten their fill. Alexander immediately ordered building work to resume before setting off through the northern Sahara to the oasis at Siwah – the home of the world-renowned oracle of the god Amun.

'Alexander was convinced that if a city was built on the site it would certainly prosper.'

THE GREEK HISTORIAN ARRIAN IN *ANABASIS*

On the way, Alexander and his companions ran out of water, to be saved only by a sudden and unexpected rainstorm. Then they got lost in a sandstorm. They were saved again by the appearance of two black ravens that led them to their destination. Alexander believed that the gods had sent them as divine guides. His consultation with the oracle proved to be equally satisfactory.

Encouraged, Alexander and his army began the long march into Asia. His aim was to overthrow the Persian Emperor and take control of his dominions. He had invaded Egypt to give him a strong base so that he could secure his communications across the Mediterranean. It would also enable him to handle the

The Greek architect Democrates drafted the plans for the new city of Alexandria and supervised the construction.

lucrative sea-borne trade network he planned to take over from the Phoenicians who, up to then, had been the foremost Mediterranean merchants of the day. Having conquered Persia, Alexander pressed forward to India, only to die suddenly on the return journey in Babylon at the age of only 32.

THE CITY'S BEGINNINGS

Meanwhile, the city Alexander had left behind was growing steadily. The street pattern was modelled on a chessboard, so that all the streets intersected at right angles. The main boulevards were to be particularly imposing – it was specified that they should be no less than 35 metres wide. The orientation allowed cool northerly breezes to blow down the streets, while a low range of hills to the south protected them from the scorching desert winds. Ample space was allowed for wide public squares and important buildings such as palaces and temples, while the small offshore island of Pharos was linked to the city by a stone causeway 1300 metres long. Named the Heptastadion as it was seven stades long – a stade being one-eighth of a mile – its construction gave the city a second well-sheltered harbour. Nor did the planners neglect the problem of peopling the new city. By all accounts, this was no easy task – at least initially. Ancient records reveal that all the people within a 20-mile radius of Alexandria were ordered to abandon their villages and move *en masse* to the city. But it was not long before such coercion became unnecessary.

THE CAPITAL OF THE PTOLEMIES

Following Alexander's death, a bitter struggle broke out over who should succeed him as ruler of his vast empire, which stretched from Greece to the borders of India. He left no heir, so several of his generals vied for the right to the succession. The upshot of the protracted wrangling was the division of the empire. The warring generals – the *diadochi* (followers) – were reduced to grabbing individual fragments for themselves. No single figure succeeded in taking Alexander's place.

A great military hero and general, who became ruler of vast swathes of the known world, Alexander aimed to make his city the economic, cultural and population centre of his empire.

The person who came out of this process the best was Ptolemy, who had been one of Alexander's most loyal confederates during his campaigns in the East. He made a bid for control over Egypt and founded a dynasty that lasted until the death of Cleopatra 300 years later. He chose Alexandria as his royal capital. Unlike Alexander, Ptolemy could personally devote himself to furthering the city's development. It was his ambition to turn Alexandria into the most important city in the world – not least to gain the upper hand in the struggle for prestige between Alexander's successors. In turn, his heirs all took a personal interest in promoting the new city's growth and well-being.

The result of the constant concern for the city's welfare shown by its rulers was a metropolis that steadily expanded on all fronts. In particular, trade and commerce flourished. The bustling harbour played host to ships from far-off India and Arabia, bearing luxury goods from the Far East such as spices and fine textiles. At the same time the Egyptians supplied the whole of the Aegean and the western Mediterranean with corn, the country's main export, papyrus, linen, oils, jewellery and perfumes.

A WONDER OF THE WORLD

Ship's captains of the period were not only keen to put into Alexandria because of the good trading opportunities. It was also one of the safest ports in the region, thanks to its famous lighthouse, which became recognised as one of the seven wonders of the ancient world. The lighthouse, which was situated on the offshore island of Pharos, was the work of the engineer Sostratos.

Sostratos started work on the lighthouse in 290 BC during the reign of Ptolemy I, but it took him 12 years to complete, by which time Ptolemy II Philadelphus ruled Egypt. It was a technological marvel. The eight-sided tower was 110 metres high, while its constantly burning signal fire, so it was said, could be seen an amazing 30 miles away. According to various accounts, a huge mirror or even a vast lens was used to enhance the light's visibility. The seventh and last of the great wonders of the ancient world survived virtually intact for more than 1500 years, until it was finally destroyed by an earthquake in 1326.

A PARADISE FOR SCHOLARS

The Ptolemaic rulers supported scientific and artistic endeavours in Alexandria. Mathematicians, astronomers, geographers, writers and physicians were all provided with superb working conditions and paid handsomely by their royal patrons. The scholars conducted research in the Museion, or Temple of the Muses, which had been founded by Ptolemy I. As well as benefiting the wider world, their efforts contributed to the

The Seven Wonders of the ancient world

The following list of the grandest and most prestigious feats of architecture or works of art in the ancient world is thought to have been compiled in the third century BC.

- The Great Pyramid at Giza.
- The Hanging Gardens of Semiramis in Babylon.
- The Temple of Artemis in Ephesus.
- The statue of Zeus by the Greek sculptor Phidias.
- The Mausoleum of Halicarnassus.
- The Colossus of Rhodes.
- The Pharos of Alexandria.

Many of the treasures housed in the world-famous library at Alexandria were lost for ever in a devastating fire in 48 BC. The fire spread unchecked to other parts of the city, notably to buildings near the waterfront where some 40,000 books were being stored.

greater glory of the city. The mathematicians Euclid and Archimedes, the philosopher Plotinus, and geographers Eratosthenes and Ptolemy were all active there.

Perhaps Alexandria's most remarkable institution was its great library, which was the largest in the ancient world. Its shelves and archives held over 900,000 books – or, more precisely, papyrus scrolls – devoted to a host of different topics. An army of scribes was employed to make copies of the texts, which came from many diverse sources. Rumour also had it that the city's rulers were not above playing underhand tricks to augment the library's holdings. Visitors who came by sea to Alexandria had any reading matter they brought with them confiscated as soon as they stepped off the ship. These books were immediately sent to the library, where they were copied before being returned to their reluctant donors.

Disaster first struck the library during the course of Julius Caesar's campaign in Egypt in 48 BC, when the Roman forces set some 60 ships of the Egyptian fleet ablaze in Alexandria's harbour. The library itself survived until the 4th century AD, when it was probably destroyed by a Christian mob rampaging through the city bent on sacking all its pagan temples. The Museion came to an end around much the same time.

A MULTICULTURAL SOCIETY

According to some estimates, the population of the city reached a peak of 500,000, making it second only to Rome among the cities of the ancient world. As well as Egyptians, Greeks and

Macedonians, the colourful mix of different peoples also included Syrians, Persians, Arabs, Ethiopians, Indians, Jews and Romans. The city's streets and alleys resounded with a welter of different languages that rivalled the mix of tongues heard at the legendary fall of the Tower of Babel. Despite the best efforts to provide more housing – a list compiled as part of a census stated that there were exactly 47,790 houses in the city – space in the city was always at a premium. Nevertheless, all its inhabitants were proud to live there. With a disarming lack of modesty, they gave their teeming metropolis the honorary title of 'the world's city'.

ALEXANDER'S GRAVE

One of Alexandria's most popular sites for visitors was the grave of Alexander the Great. A decade after his death, Ptolemy I arranged for his body to be transported from Babylon to Egypt. This turned out to be a commercial masterstroke. As the canny Ptolemy had envisaged, well-to-do travellers now came from far and wide to Alexandria, eager to see the embalmed remains of the conqueror. Not all visitors were as careless as the Roman Emperor Augustus, who insisted on touching Alexander's body and in the process broke off the dead emperor's nose.

It was Augustus who brought the rule of the Ptolemaic dynasty to an end with his victory over Cleopatra in 30 BC. Alexandria became the capital of the Roman province of Egypt. Its prestige began to wane, accelerated by the Arab conquest of Egypt in AD 642. Though the Arabs admired the city, they were not seafarers. Moreover Amr Ibn-el-Aas, the first Muslim ruler of the country, was mindful of the instructions of his master, Caliph Omar, to 'establish the capital where you wish, but let there be no water between you and me'. Alexandria was on the wrong side of the Nile. The Arabs moved east of the river and chose Cairo as their new capital.

The seemingly inexorable decline continued. When Napoleon and his army entered Alexandria in 1798, it was no more than a small town. The population of the city that had once been the second largest in the world had shrunk to just 8000. It was not until the opening of the Suez Canal that it started to recapture some of its former glory.

Why did the Pope ban the crossbow?

Pope Innocent II and the Lateran Council of 1139 banned Christians from using crossbows against their fellows – but sanctioned their deployment against the Saracens and other 'infidels'.

The followers of Hermann Gessler, the all-powerful Austrian governor of Switzerland, were dumbfounded. Their master had been suddenly struck down by an arrow bolt, seemingly out of nowhere. Though the narrow lane known as the Hohle Gasse near the town of Küssnacht, was ideally suited for an ambush, but there was no sign of any assassin. Having felled his foe, the Swiss hunter and patriot William Tell made good his escape.

In 1307 William Tell had been arrested for refusing to bow to the governor's hat – stuck on a pole in the town of Altdorf as a symbol of Habsburg imperial authority. Gessler then ordered Tell, a noted archer, to shoot an apple off his own son's head with his crossbow. If he succeeded, he would be freed, but if he refused he would be executed immediately. Tell hit the apple. But he was not released. Asked by Gessler why he had stuffed a second bolt into his quiver, he replied that it had been intended for the governor himself if the first bolt had hit his son. Gessler had Tell clapped in irons and put on board a boat for his castle at Küssnacht. As the boat was crossing Lake Lucerne, a storm arose. The crew persuaded Gessler to let Tell take the helm. He promptly steered for a convenient rock, leapt ashore and fled. He then made his way to the sunken lane, where, hidden behind the bushes, he lay in wait for his intended victim. When the governor came into sight, Tell loaded his crossbow, pulled the trigger, and hit his target. The tyrant was dead.

CROSSBOW AND LONGBOW

The story of William Tell makes it clear what an insidious weapon the crossbow was – a person could use it to fire at their intended victim from an unseen position. The Italians of the time christened it the assassins' bow. A famous early victim was William Rufus, king of England, who was killed by a crossbow bolt while out hunting in 1100. What made the weapon special was the distance a bolt could travel and the speed it could reach in flight. A bolt could punch its way through even the sturdiest chain mail and armour, as Richard the Lionheart found to his cost when he was fatally wounded by a crossbow shot as he laid siege to Chalus Castle in France in 1199. Knights feared it, because it made them more vulnerable than before, challenging their battlefield supremacy. The use of such a weapon also flouted the accepted rules of chivalrous combat, in which opponents fought face to face at close quarters.

Above all, the crossbow was relatively simple to operate, so ordinary soldiers could be quickly trained to master it. Once the weapon – a bow and a short stock equipped with spanning and firing mechanisms – had been drawn using muscle power, a

The pride of the republic – Venice's *Arsenale*

Its mastery of shipbuilding enabled Venice to become the richest trading city in the Mediterranean and a leading power in medieval and Renaissance times.

Hidden behind the high walls of the *Arsenale* and under conditions of absolute secrecy, Venice's fleet was laid down from the late Middle Ages onwards. It was the cornerstone of the city's enormous wealth and continuing prosperity.

In its 16th-century heyday, Venice's celebrated *Arsenale* (arsenal) proudly claimed to be the largest shipyard in the world. It was enormous by the standards of the time. In 1104, following a series of fires that destroyed a number of the shipyards scattered throughout the city, Venice's rulers decided to concentrate

shipbuilding in one quarter. Work on the old arsenal was completed by 1300. The new arsenal was built between 1300 and 1400 and the most recent – the one that survives today – between 1473 and 1573.

In the 16th century, 2000 shipwrights, carpenters and other artisans worked at the arsenal. In times of war this could rise to 3000 or more. The workers were known as the *arsenaloti*. They built and maintained the merchant vessels and warships that made up Venice's all-powerful fleet – the basis of the city's power, prosperity and prestige.

THE 'QUEEN OF THE SEAS'

Founded on trade, Venice began its dealings with the East in the 10th century AD, when much of the Dalmatian coast came under its rule, giving the city control of the Adriatic. At the same time, Venice was laying the foundations for continued commercial expansion by winning trading and other concessions in ports throughout the eastern Mediterranean. The Venetians also consolidated their influence on the Italian mainland. After defeating Genoa, its main rival, in a great naval battle off the tiny island of Chiogga in 1380, Venice was recognised throughout Europe as the leading sea power. Convoys of merchant ships escorted by war galleys plied every major trade route through the Mediterranean, laden with precious cargoes from the furthest corners of the Earth. Not for nothing did Venice win itself the title 'Queen of the Seas'.

The Venetians worked hard for their success. Everything that they undertook was a communal, not an individual, concern. It was not only the merchants who benefited from a successful voyage. Sailors and oarsmen shared in the profits too. The setting-up of such trading partnerships was legally documented in a document known as a *colleganza* – so that participants knew where they stood and what they could expect. The system helped

The rise of Venice

A favoured location
Venice was sited in a sheltered lagoon and on the border between areas under Byzantine and Frankish control.

Trading privileges
The city deployed its fleet to aid Byzantium against its enemies. In recognition, the Byzantines granted many trading privileges, as a result of which Venice swiftly came to dominate trade with the East.

Rewards from the Crusaders
The Christian kingdoms established in the Holy Land after the First Crusade were also dependent on Venice's help, particularly the support of its navy. In return Venice gained control over further bases around the Mediterranean.

to turn a small town on a lagoon into the foremost trading city in Europe and Asia. Preserving its cherished status depended on the quality and size of the fleet that Venice could deploy to back up its merchants and to support its diplomats. To ensure their needs were met, the Venetians developed a method of manufacture – mass production – not used elsewhere until the beginning of the 20th century.

THE BIRTH OF MASS PRODUCTION

Many trades were involved in the building of the Venetian ships. Carpenters laid down the keel and hull. The hull was then manoeuvred onto rollers and progressed through the stages of fitting out as though on a conveyor belt. Each operation was controlled by a different trade guild. Caulkers made ships watertight by sealing their timbers with pitch. Sail makers and oar makers then took over. Finally, weapons were installed. Once a ship reached the end of the production line, it was ready for launching. The admiral, commanding the arsenal, carried out a last inspection and it was then permitted to make its maiden voyage. The system was so efficient that in the 16th century the shipyard could build or repair some 40 to 60 vessels a year.

THE DECLINE OF VENICE

Venice's maritime star eventually waned. The city had always lacked timber but a more serious problem was a shortage of men to build and sail the ships. The fall of Constantinople to the Ottoman Turks in 1453 struck a mortal blow at Venice's trade with the East, while the Portuguese discovery of a sea route around Africa to the Indies, and the Spanish conquest of the New World, dramatically changed the balance of commercial power. The fall of Cyprus, Crete and the Peloponnese to the Turks ended centuries of Venetian dominance in the eastern Mediterranean.

Venice became something of a backwater, seemingly content to live on memories of its past glory. When, in 1797, Napoleon occupied the city and then gave it and the surrounding area to Austria in the Treaty of Campo Formio, the once proud republic fell without putting up a fight. It was never to regain its independence. In 1866, it became part of a united Italy.

The age of the Moors in Spain

Following a successful invasion in 711, the Moors ruled much of medieval Spain for nearly 800 years. When not fighting their Christian adversaries in the *Reconquista*, they presided over a tolerant and sophisticated civilisation where Islamic, Jewish and Christian cultures could exist together.

The Straits of Gibraltar separate Europe from Africa by less than nine miles. In May 711, the Arab commander Tariq ibn Ziyad and his force of 7000 made the crossing. His troops chiefly comprised north African Berbers augmented by a handful of soldiers from Medina and Damascus. It was the first step in a speedy campaign of conquest that was to amaze and astound the Christian world.

Tariq was under orders from Musa ibn Nusair, the Arab ruler of the Maghreb in north Africa, to expand the bounds of his empire. But he also had a diplomatic pretext for his incursion. In around AD 415 the Visigoths had migrated to the Iberian Peninsula and gained control over the region. When their king, Witiza, died in 710, Roderic, Duke of Baetica, was chosen to succeed him instead of Witiza's son. The Witiza family, with Julian, governor of Ceuta, asked the Moors for help to overthrow the usurper. The family's motives were probably purely political, but Julian may have been motivated by personal considerations: according to the chroniclers, Roderic had raped his daughter.

The appeal turned out to be a major strategic blunder. Instead of helping Witiza's son to regain his father's throne, the Muslim invaders proceeded to overrun the Visigoth kingdom. Only a small strip of territory in the mountainous northwest managed to hold out against them.

In 1431, a pitched battle took place at Higueruela between John II of Castile and Moorish forces. Following the Christian victory, Granada was forced to agree to pay tribute money to Castile.

THE END OF THE VISIGOTHS

The decisive battle was fought at the Rio Barbate, south of Cadiz, on July 19, 711. Here, Tariq's invaders met Roderic's hastily mustered forces. The Visigoth king had been campaigning in the north against the Franks and the Basques when news of

the Muslim invasion forced him to march hurriedly south to meet it. 'Before us is the enemy, behind us the sea,' Tariq shouted to his men. 'We have only one choice – to win!' He was true to his word. The Christian army crumbled in the face of the Muslim onslaught. Roderic himself was slain. It was the beginning of the end for Visigoth Christianity in Spain.

One by one, cities fell to the Muslims, often betrayed by their own citizens who were weary of Visigoth rule. Early in 712 Toledo, the Visigoth capital, was captured after a brief siege and Muslim forces then overran almost the entire Iberian Peninsula. Their lightning advance encountered serious resistance only in the heavily forested mountains in the northwest, where the new kingdom of the Asturias provided a refuge for the beleaguered Christians. The Islamic triumph seemed to have been rapidly concluded.

Decisive battles

Rio Barbate, 711
Tariq ibn Ziyad defeated and killed the Visigoth king Roderic, paving the way for Muslim conquest of the Iberian Peninsula.

Tours, 732
In 732, the Frankish ruler Charles Martel halted the northward advance of the Moors into France at the Battle of Tours.

1236–48
Ferdinand III, King of Castile and León, captured Córdoba in 1236, Jaén in 1246, and Seville in 1248.

Granada, 1492
In 1492, the forces of Ferdinand II of Aragon and Isabella I of Castile retook Granada, the last stronghold of the Moors in Spain.

CHRISTIANS AND MOORS

It was from the Asturias that the *Reconquista* – the long series of wars fought by Christian forces to retake the Iberian peninsula – was launched. In 722, Pelayo, the Asturias' ruler, defeated a large Moorish force at the village of Coradonga. The ensuing struggle lasted for centuries and cost thousands of lives on both sides. Not until January 2, 1492, did Granada, the last Muslim stronghold, finally surrender to the resurgent Christians and Islamic rule on the peninsula came to an end.

Slowly but surely the Christians fought their way south. Eventually, they managed to establish five small kingdoms – Castile and León on the great central plateau, Navarre in the shadows of the Pyrenées, Aragon in the northeast and Catalonia on the eastern coast. In 1085, Alfonso VI of Castile and León wrested Toledo from the Moors and the *Reconquista* began in earnest. In 1212, at the battle of Las Navas de Tolosa, the armies

Rodrigo Díaz de Vivar, popularly known as El Cid, conquered the city of Valencia in 1094 and displayed great bravery in holding on to it. He came to epitomise the *Reconquista* and soon became the national hero of Spain.

of Castile and Aragon, with knights and infantry supplied by France and Germany following an appeal by Pope Innocent III, crushed the Moorish army. Some 20,000 Moors were killed. A generation later, Ferdinand III recaptured Cordoba, Seville, Jerez and Cadiz. The whole of Andalusia south of Castile became Christian – leaving the Moors with the kingdom of Granada in the far south.

Many brave men made their names in the long years of conflict, but the most celebrated was probably Rodrigo Diaz de Vivar – better known by his Arab nickname El Cid – who later became one of Spain's national heroes. At the time the fog of war often made it unclear who was fighting for which side. El Cid began his rise to fame when he slew the champion of the Christian king Sancho of Navarre in a war against fellow Christians in Castile. Eventually, El Cid became almost a soldier of fortune, sometimes campaigning for the Christians and sometimes for the Moors. In 1094, he laid siege to and captured Valencia from the Moors, although many of the soldiers he led against the city were Muslims.

Christians were frequently as much at loggerheads with one another as they were with the Moors – who were also deeply divided. As early as 40 years after the initial conquest, they split into supporters of the rival Umayyad and Abbassid dynasties, battling for control of the Caliphate in distant Damascus. The Umayyad faction invited Abd-al-Rahman I to set up his own emirate in Spain. It became the powerful Caliphate of Cordoba in the heartland of al-Andalus, as they had renamed Spain.

Eventually, the Almoravids, who ruled from 1061 to 1147, overthrew the Ummayads. They were supplanted by the Almohads, who, in 1170, had moved the capital to Seville. The final rulers, the Nasrids, managed to keep an uneasy peace with the Christians for 250 years until they were driven out.

PEACEFUL TIMES

During more peaceful times, the Muslim rulers of al-Andalus promoted the Islamic principles of tolerance towards people of other faiths, a liberal outlook, and an interest in the arts and sciences. Their libraries housed important manuscripts, while the foremost scholars of the day taught in Spanish universities.

Cordoba was one of the jewels in the Muslim crown. As early as the 10th century, it had almost half a million inhabitants – one of the most heavily populated cities in the world, with 500 mosques, 300 public baths, 70 libraries and miles of paved, lamp-lit streets. At a time when 99 per cent

Muslims, Christians and Jews all helped bring Spanish culture to a peak of sophistication.

of the Christian population was illiterate, there were 800 public schools and it was difficult to find even a Moorish peasant who could not read and write.

With Baghdad and Constantinople, Cordoba was one the great cultural centres of the civilised world. The Arab philosopher, theologian, legal expert and physician Ibn Rushd – or Averröes – lived in the city. He was renowned for his commentaries on the teachings of Aristotle. Another Cordoban, Abu-I-Hasan, known as Ziryab (blackbird) was one of the leading Islamic composers; other luminaries included the Jewish physician Hidai ibn Shaprut, the Jewish lexicographer Menachem ben Saruk, and Abu al-Qasim, the greatest Muslim surgeon of the Middle Ages.

THE MOORISH INHERITANCE

Not all of the magnificent treasures of Moorish Spain were preserved for posterity. Christian iconoclasts destroyed priceless and unique works of Islamic art during and after the reconquest of the country. But some did survive – at least for a time.

In Cordoba, the lavishly appointed Mesquita (mosque) remained more or less unscathed for three centuries after the city's recapture. The Christians simply reconsecrated it as a church. Then, despite protests from Cordoba's civic leaders, the clergy persuaded Emperor Charles V to authorise the building of a new cathedral in its precincts. The result was a travesty. 'By installing something that is commonplace', said Charles, 'you have destroyed something that was once unique.' But despite the graceless addition, much of the original Mesquita remained intact around it. In Seville, the imposing minaret of the main mosque became the bell-tower for a new church, the largest Gothic cathedral in Europe – a visible symbol of the final triumph of the 'faithful' over the 'unbelievers'.

Such zealotry was not confined to the Christians. The Almoravids set fire to the 10th-century grand summer residence of the Umayyad Caliph Abd-al-Rahman III. Lying northwest of Cordoba at the foot of the Sierra Morena, it was the Versailles of its day. Luckily, the Alhambra in Granada came through the entire *Reconquista* and its aftermath relatively unscathed. Built by the Nasrids between 1248 and 1354, this fortress-palace situated on its high hill still dominates the city.

The Moorish legacy was wide-ranging. They set up the first paper and pottery manufactories in Europe, built the first windmills and laid out terraced fields watered by irrigation systems. Their long presence left its mark on several European languages – common words like 'mattress,' 'alcohol,' or 'algebra' were originally derived from Arabic. By their introduction of rice

Muslim artists developed the decorative arts to a high degree of perfection. Basic geometrical shapes and also plant forms adorn the magnificent buildings they created such as the *Mesquita* in Cordoba with its 'forest' of columns made from marble, jasper, and porphyry.

they helped to transform the culinary scene, as did the cultivation of plants like lemons, apricots, bananas, aubergines and watermelons. Although the Prophet Mohammad had forbidden the consumption of alcohol, they encouraged winemaking.

A TERRIBLE SEQUEL

How did Ferdinand and Isabella, the 'Catholic Kings' who presided over the final stages of the *Reconquista*, repay the Moors for the rich gifts that they had brought to Spain? The answer was simply with repression and expulsions. Agreements that the last Caliph of Granada – Muhammad Abu-Abdullah, or Boabdil – had negotiated were quickly violated. Muslims and Jews were dispossessed and forcibly converted to Christianity. Muslim uprisings were brutally suppressed, and those who took part slaughtered, turned over to the newly established Spanish Inquisition, or deported to other parts of Spain.

Though many Muslims returned to North Africa, thousands hung grimly on until, in 1609, Philip III conducted a religious and ethnic 'cleansing' of his realm. Some 300,000 'Moriscos,' or baptised Moors, were expelled to the Maghreb. The cross had replaced the crescent and the Moors had faded into history. But their legacy left Spain – and the West – forever in their debt.

Keeping
it in the family

In ancient Egypt, many Pharaohs married their sisters or daughters, leading to highly complicated family relationships. Later, the Romans condemned and outlawed such practices.

Gaius Julius Caesar, Rome's greatest general, was totally smitten: the Egyptian queen, the clever and beautiful Cleopatra, had turned his head completely. They had come together as the result of two hard-fought civil wars – one between rival factions in Rome – the other between royal Egyptians. In the course of the former, Caesar pursued his rival Pompey to Egypt. Pompey was murdered by the Egyptians, keen to please the winning side. Caesar was still determined to secure Rome's interests in the area. Egypt was the granary that kept Rome fed and Caesar was anxious to end any disruption that might hinder grain exports.

Cleopatra VII had been toppled by her elder brother Ptolemy XIII from the throne that their father had decreed on his deathbed they should share. Civil war ensued. Cleopatra was determined that Caesar should support her claim. According to Plutarch, she was smuggled past Caesar's bodyguards rolled up in a carpet. Regardless of the accuracy of the account, Cleopatra did gain admission to Caesar's presence and swiftly succeeded in bending him to her will. He agreed without more ado to help her to secure sole occupancy of the Egyptian throne. He must have been flattered – Caesar was 31 years older than Cleopatra and bald into the bargain. Whatever his motives for intervening, the consequence was that Cleopatra regained supreme power. Her brother was drowned in the Nile while attempting to flee from his sister's victorious forces.

MARRYING HER BROTHER

Two factors still gave Caesar cause for concern. He was uncertain whether the Egyptian people would consent to being ruled by Cleopatra alone. Despite her brother's death, his followers still commanded substantial support and this might be transferred to a new male claimant to the throne. His affair with Cleopatra was now an open secret. The knowledge that their queen was in love with a foreigner – a Roman – might stir up even more trouble among the Egyptians.

Then Caesar had a brainwave. He knew that it was an Egyptian tradition for royal siblings to marry one another. He had even heard that, in former times, pharaohs had been known to marry their own daughters – with, in Roman eyes, the grotesque result that such rulers were at the same time husbands, fathers and fathers-in-law, and their daughters likewise were both wives and daughters-in-law. Assuming that children resulted from such a union, the king in question would have achieved the peculiar feat of being both father and grandfather to his own children.

Cleopatra, the mysterious and strikingly beautiful Egyptian queen – as shown in this 19th-century painting – had no trouble winning Caesar's heart and securing her hold on power.

In order to pacify the Egyptian populace, Caesar and Cleopatra arranged, in best Egyptian royal tradition, that the queen, who was then 22 years old, should enter into a sham marriage with her younger brother, the 12-year-old Ptolemy XIV. Although the marriage existed only on paper, the demands of convention were satisfied and the Egyptian people mollified.

Caesar and Cleopatra continued their affair. The union produced a son, Caesarion. When Caesar was assassinated by Marcus Brutus and other discontented Roman senators in 44 BC, Cleopatra had Ptolemy murdered and established Caesarion as her co-ruler. The little boy was only four. After his mother killed herself following defeat by Octavius Caesar and the suicide of Mark Antony, her new lover, Caesarion was strangled. Egypt became a province of the Roman Empire and the long line of the Pharaohs finally came to an end.

The trouble with a limited gene pool

The royal disease
Haemophilia is referred to as the 'royal disease' for good reason, since it affected several interrelated royal families in 19th-century Europe. Prince Leopold, Queen Victoria's eighth child, suffered from it, while two of her daughters – Princess Alice and Princess Beatrice – were carriers of the disease. Through them, the condition was passed on to other royal families, notably those of Spain and Russia. Alexis, Russia's last Tsarevich, was a haemophiliac.

The royal jawline
The Habsburgs paid the price for selecting from too limited a gene pool. Charles II (the Bewitched), the last Habsburg ruler of Spain, came to the throne in 1665. He had the most pronounced case of the Habsburg jaw on record – so large and deformed that he was unable to chew. He was also impotent and mentally retarded.

PRECEDENTS SET BY PAST PHARAOHS
Caesar and Cleopatra had historical precedent on their side in planning such a union. The Pharaoh Ahmose, who liberated his country from the invading sea-peoples, the Hyksos, and founded the New Kingdom married his sister Nefertiri in around 1552 BC. The Pharaoh Tuthmosis II, who reigned from 1494 to 1490 BC, also married his half-sister Hatshepsut. Although like many Ancient Egyptian rulers he had more than one wife, she was undoubtedly his favourite. When Tuthmosis died, she acted as regent for the son of another of his wives, whom he had named as his successor but who was not old enough to ascend the throne.

But she enjoyed her new role so much that she was loath to abdicate once her nephew had reached his majority. In 1473 BC she had herself proclaimed

The gods Osiris (centre) and his wife and sister Isis (right) were the model for royal incest in ancient Egypt. They are shown here on a pectoral ornament from the 9th century BC along with their son Horus.

Pharaoh, dressing in the traditional garb of a male Pharaoh and wearing a false beard in an attempt to legitimise her position. Her achievements once on the throne made her one of ancient Egypt's greatest rulers.

Amenophis III, who ruled Egypt from 1402 to 1364 BC, married his daughter – for an entirely different reason. His favourite wife, Teje, was the daughter of a Nubian general – Egypt had recently conquered Nubia – and was generally considered unworthy of her status by the priests and nobles of the Pharaoh's court. Amenophis decided to placate them by taking his daughter Satamun as another wife.

Ramses II lived to the age of almost 90, ruled for 66 years from 1290 to 1224 BC, and left an indelible mark on his country's architectural heritage. His wives and concubines bore him more than 100 children. His favourite wives were Nefertari and Istnofret. The former is thought to have been the daughter of a Theban nobleman, so Ramses may have married her to strengthen his power-base there. Another theory is that she was a daughter of Seti I, so she would have been Ramses' half-sister.

Ramses called Nefertari 'the one for whom the sun shines'. After her death, he married Meryetamun, her eldest daughter. Istnofret gave birth to Merenptah, who succeeded Ramses as pharaoh, Khaemwese, who became high priest of the temple of Ptah at Memphis and a daughter, Bent' anta, who became another of Ramses' consorts after her mother's death.

MYTHICAL MODELS

In most cases, such marriages were a matter of form. The key consideration was to safeguard the future of the dynasty by giving as few outsiders as possible the chance to gain influence by marrying into the royal family. As a precaution, a Pharaoh would probably marry only one of his half-sisters.

'It is a great thing to erect one monument after another.'

RAMSES II

The practice also had religious overtones. Belief in a 'sacred union' between the divine siblings Isis and Osiris set the pattern for subsequent marital relationships within the ruling dynasties. As a loving sister and wife, it was Isis who brought Osiris back to life after his murder by his evil brother Set.

ROYAL INTERMARRIAGE

By Cleopatra's time, the practice of marrying a sibling had become common in all echelons of society. But the ancient Egyptians were one of the few societies to condone the practice. The Greeks and Romans regarded incestuous marriages as decadent and perverse. In Tudor England, one of the false charges laid against Anne Boleyn, Henry VIII's second wife, at her trial for treason was that she had committed incest with her brother George.

On the other hand, among royal families, intermarriage was viewed as the best means of preserving – or expanding – a particular dynasty's power and influence. The Habsburgs were virtually unparalleled in the degree of their interbreeding – although they stopped short of marrying their siblings.

Greyhounds
of the sea

Tea clippers were characterised by a sharply-raked bow, an overhanging stern and acres of sail.

In the mid-19th century tea clippers battled the high seas as they raced to deliver their valuable cargo from China to the tea-drinkers of London. The first ship to come home with the tea brought riches and prestige for its owner.

In the era of the tea clippers, voyages that might once have taken a year could be completed in 100 days. Speed was everything. Competing importers were desperate to be first back with the new season's crop. The tea races captured the British imagination and huge bets were placed on the outcome. And smart Victorian hostesses across London were willing to pay a premium in order to be able to serve tea from the winning ship.

On June 18, 1872, as the cry of 'anchors aweigh' rang out on the deck of the *Cutty Sark*, Captain George Moodie may have been looking forward to the weeks at sea that lay ahead but he would also have been under considerable pressure. Although the *Cutty Sark* was technically the fastest tea clipper afloat, she had yet to take on her greatest competitor, the *Thermopylae*.

The *Thermopylae* was built in 1867 by the owner of the Aberdeen White Star Line, George Thompson, who wanted a winning clipper. His ship's iron framework supported a streamlined wooden hull and a huge acreage of sail. In 1868, on her maiden voyage, the *Thermopylae* made the journey from Gravesend to Melbourne in a record-breaking 63 days.

In a few hours, both clippers – their holds laden with the new season's China tea – would be sailing on the same high tide from the port of Woosung (now Wusong) on the Yangtze delta. Woosung was the starting point for a race that, over the next three to four months, would take the two tall ships through the

After harvesting, China tea was loaded onto small boats, which ferried the bails out to the tea clippers anchored offshore.

South China Sea and the Indian Ocean, round the Cape of Good
Hope into the Atlantic Ocean and from there up the English
Channel to London. Captain Moodie knew that his ship's owner,
John Willis, was banking on the huge bonuses that the winner of
this race would earn – and was determined not to let him down.

As the anchor was winched up, Moodie was not the only one
keeping an eye on the procedure. Robert Willis, the shipowner's
brother, had appeared on
deck. Over the next few
hours, the two men watched
from their vantage point on
the bridge as the *Cutty Sark*
was towed out of the harbour

*With her 43 sails, the Cutty
Sark was the fastest tea clipper
in the world.*

at Shanghai and 14 miles downstream to Woosung. From there,
within sight of the *Thermopylae,* she would set sail. The crew of
the *Cutty Sark* scrambled up the rigging and unfurled the sails.
One square sail after another billowed in the wind and the
clipper began to gather speed. A final signal was sent between
the ships and then they were off.

Over the following days, the two ships caught sight of one
another on several occasions. When they entered the Indian
Ocean, the *Thermopylae* – under the command of her
experienced captain, Robert Kemball – was one-and-a-half
nautical miles ahead, a negligible lead in view of the *Cutty Sark*'s
potential top speed of over 17 knots. In London, countless
wagers on the race made the *Cutty Sark* the favourite; she was
newer than the *Thermopylae* by a year and, being narrower in
the beam and having a larger sail area, faster, too. But would
these advantages be enough? And did Moodie, who had a
reputation as a responsible and calm master, have the competitive
spirit to push his ship to her limits?

A BROKEN RUDDER
Initially, it looked as though he did. With a steady southeasterly
trade wind behind her, the *Cutty Sark* had, by August 14, put
400 nautical miles between herself and her rival as they crossed
the Indian Ocean. But the weather was beginning to make
Moodie anxious. The wind was freshening to storm strength and

The Cutty Sark

The last of the clippers
The *Cutty Sark* is the world's only surviving tea clipper. She is now a standing museum exhibit on the quayside at Greenwich in southeast London

Specifications
Cutty Sark was launched from Dumbarton on November 22, 1869, displaced 983 gross registered tonnes, and was 85.3 metres long. She could carry a cargo of 6000 tonnes of tea and was sailed by a crew of 35.

The career of the Cutty Sark
The *Cutty Sark* was used on the tea run from China until 1877. From 1885, after being reassigned to carrying wool from Australia to England, she beat her old rival the *Thermopylae* five times.

waves broke ceaselessly over the ship's bows. The clipper was not deflected from her course and ploughed steadily ahead. As the wind grew increasingly strong, Moodie trimmed the sails – a dangerous operation for the crew, who had to climb more than 40 metres up the rigging to fasten the sails as the ship pitched heavily beneath them.

All of a sudden a violent shudder ran through the ship. The helmsman could no longer hold his course and turning the wheel had no effect. The rudder had broken; the *Cutty Sark* was virtually out of control. Now it was no longer a question of being first in London and winning the race; what mattered was getting the ship and her crew home in one piece.

As the *Cutty Sark* wallowed in heavy seas, the crew fought to get her under control. To make matters worse, a row erupted between the captain and the owner's brother. Willis wanted to put into Cape Town and have the rudder repaired there. Moodie disagreed. He wanted his experienced shipwright, Henry Henderson, to rig up an emergency rudder. The captain believed that putting in to Cape Town would scupper any chance of victory, and that the necessary repairs could be done at sea. Willis was intransigent. His overriding concern was the safety of the ship – and with good reason. He was probably the only person on board who knew that neither the ship nor its cargo were insured. The argument grew more violent, and it was not until Moodie charged Willis with mutiny and threatened to clap him in irons that he finally yielded to the captain's authority.

Henderson and the crew carried out the repairs efficiently, and the *Cutty Sark* was underway after just five days – but the captain now had to exercise more caution than he would have liked. With an emergency rudder in place, he couldn't chance pushing his ship too hard through the Atlantic. His rate of progress, about

200 miles a day, was well below the 300 miles that the *Cutty Sark* was capable of. Moodie knew that he now stood only a slim chance of overtaking the *Thermopylae*. On the other hand, perhaps the *Thermopylae*, too, had lost valuable time through running repairs.

With a steady hand, Moodie guided the *Cutty Sark* safely through the unpredictable Atlantic. On October 18, 1872, 122 days after setting sail from China, the *Cutty Sark* passed Gravesend at the mouth of the Thames. She was just seven days behind the triumphant *Thermopylae*, whose 115-day passage had won the race.

In the meantime, news of the dramatic events at sea had spread throughout London, and when she finally docked a wildly cheering crowd greeted the *Cutty Sark* and her crew, almost more enthusiastically than they had welcomed the *Thermopylae*.

THE END OF AN ERA

When the *Cutty Sark* was launched in 1869, it was already an Indian summer for tall ships. The Suez Canal had opened the same year, providing a short cut for all eastern trade. This was bad news for the sailing ships, as they could not navigate the narrow passage.

The new steamships that were being developed could manage the canal, but their technology was so inefficient to begin with that the clippers were safe – at least in the short term. But before long, the increasing speed and larger cargo capacity of steamships would make sailing ships obsolete. The journey from China to England no longer depended on favourable winds and could be completed by plodding steamships in just 60 days. The great tea race had had its day.

The *Cutty Sark* was built in Scotland at Dumbarton and Greenock on the River Leven and launched in 1869. Her timber and iron hull was strong and sleek. Her three masts could hold a spread of canvas that propelled the ship at more than 17 knots. She now lies in dry dock at Greenwich.

A **race** to remember

Towards the end of the 19th century kings, emperors and tycoons acquired luxury racing yachts as symbols of their prestige. Among the greatest enthusiasts was the German emperor Wilhelm II. Between 1887 and 1914, he sailed five fabulous yachts, which he raced in all-out competition against the finest British and American yachtsmen of the day.

On a fine June day in 1904, hordes of spectators packed the harbour wall in the north German port of Cuxhaven, craning their necks to glimpse the yacht *Meteor III*, the latest racing schooner owned by Emperor Wilhelm II. A cannon shot would signal the start of the Lower Elbe Regatta – the prelude to Kiel Week, the sailing event founded by Wilhelm in 1895 in emulation of Britain's Cowes Week. He had attended the latter religiously from 1889 until his growing unpopularity ended his personal participation in the regatta. His competitiveness so irked his uncle the Prince of Wales that the future George V sold his own yacht *Britannia* and gave up sailing for good.

Ever since then, the sailing-mad Wilhelm had taken part in Kiel Week. His enthusiasm helped to establish the popularity of sailing in Germany, even though his first two yachts were built in Britain and *Meteor III* in the United States. His crews were British too until 1906, when the rising tide of anti-British feeling led to their replacement by German sailors while *Meteor IV* and *Meteor V* were designed and built at German shipyards.

But in June 1904 all minds were concentrated on that day's racing, which promised to be thrilling. The freshening wind was now blowing straight down the Elbe estuary. The ebb tide, just beginning to flow, gave rise to a heavy swell that would tax the seamanship of those taking part in the race to the utmost.

THE AMERICAN CHALLENGE

Meteor III was tacking her way up to the starting line under full sail, followed by one of her keenest rivals, the American yacht *Ingomar*, owned by Morton F. Plant and helmed by the legendary Charlie Barr, who had shown his talent in a number of America's Cup races, and was certain to be going all-out for a win.

From the start, the prospect of the American yacht's participation worried the organising committee, since it was by no means certain that the emperor would manage to defeat his rival. The builders of the *Ingomar* had put a premium on speed at the expense of comfort – in stark contrast to Wilhelm's yacht, which was fitted out in the opulent style befitting an emperor and whose deck always stayed dry, however much she heeled in the

Emperor Wilhelm II at the helm of his yacht *Meteor*.

wind. Accommodation on board included an imperial bedroom suite, two saloons and a dining room that could accommodate 24 at a sitting.

As the starting cannon fired, the 11 yachts crossed the line and the spectators were treated to a dramatic duel on the Elbe. With all their canvas spread, *Meteor III* and *Ingomar* headed directly for one another as the American yacht began to overhaul *Meteor III* on the starboard tack. The vast bowsprit of the *Ingomar* was closing on the bow of the Emperor's yacht with alarming speed. In a few minutes, the two would collide if neither altered course. But which would give way? To the onlookers' consternation, it became clear that the imperial yacht was in breach of the sea's highway code by trying to muscle in and illegally steal its rival's water.

COLLISION STATIONS

On board *Ingomar*, the crew's nerves were at breaking point. At the helm, Charlie Barr held steady, determined not to give an inch of seaway to his rival. Yet even he must have had a moment's doubt as he saw his vessel's bowsprit bearing down and threatening to skewer *Meteor III*. How seriously would a collision damage the imperial yacht and what would be the consequences if she sank, taking the Emperor with her, or left him swimming for his life?

Barr called out across the deck to his fellow crewmember Brooke Anthony Heckstall-Smith: 'Mr Smith, who has right of way?' 'The *Ingomar*' came the immediate reply. Though Barr knew the laws of seamanship as well as Heckstall-Smith, the two had previously agreed that the decision on any issue like this would be the latter's. 'Mr Robinson, what am I to do?' said Barr, turning to the vessel's racing skipper. Quick as a flash, Charles Robinson, the Vice-Commodore of the

Wilhelm II's racing yachts

Naming the yachts
Between 1887 and 1914, Wilhelm raced five yachts with great success, all of them called *Meteor*. The name commemorated a naval action in the Franco-Prussian War.

The first three Meteors
Meteor I and *II* were constructed in Scotland – Meteor I's original name was *Thistle* – but the Emperor had *Meteor III* built in the United States.

Max Oertz's Meteors
Both *Meteor IV* (1908) and *Meteor V* (1913) were designed and built by the brilliant German shipwright Max Oertz. His work helped German yacht construction to gain an international reputation.

New York Yacht Club, a man with nerves of steel, replied: 'Hold on'. 'By God, Charlie', suddenly chimed in Morton F. Plant, 'you're the boy. I'll give way to no man!'

A LAST-DITCH MANOEUVRE

Had the crew of *Meteor III* not come to their senses, things could have taken a disastrous turn. As a keen sailor, Wilhelm was fully aware of the rules and that he was in danger of breaking them. Despite the determination he liked to display, he had absolutely no intention of damaging *Meteor III* and risking injury to himself and his crew, especially as the really serious business of Kiel Week was due to start a few days later. Moreover, he was scheduled to take the salute at the review of the Imperial High Seas Fleet that was to be the highlight of the festivities. One of the many prominent guests invited to witness the occasion was King Edward VIII himself.

Perhaps it was such considerations that lay behind the *Meteor III* putting her helm down at the very last minute, when the *Ingomar*'s bowsprit was barely a metre away from her rigging. The *Ingomar* also jammed her helm down as quickly as the wheel could be turned and the two vessels ranged alongside each other, their sides almost touching as they shot into the wind.

Meteor III was the ultimate victor, though for Wilhelm the triumph must have been tainted by the apology he had to make to the *Ingomar*'s skipper after the race. His enthusiasm for the sport remained undiminished. The following year, he was instrumental in founding the first trans-Atlantic yacht race for the Admiral's Cup, when 11 crack yachts set sail from Sandy Hook, New Jersey, USA, for the Lizard in Cornwall. This time, the American vessel *Atlantic* came first and the German contender *Hamburg* second. And, though he never took part personally again, Wilhelm continued to enter his yachts in British regattas until the outbreak of the First World War in 1914 put an end to his participation once and for all.

Before Wilhelm (below) came to the throne, Germany had a tiny navy. Inspired by Grand Admiral Von Tirpitz, the Emperor fought hard to build a fleet big enough to rival Britain's Royal Navy and to help Germany to win its coveted 'place in the Sun'.

Spreading
the word

Using thousands – sometimes even millions – of pieces of coloured stone, known as *tesserae*, to create elaborate pictures was a painstaking and expensive way to advertise a business – but one that was widely used in ancient Rome.

About 2000 years ago Ostia was the principal port serving Rome, then the most important city in the world. Located at the mouth of the Tiber, Ostia was densely populated with a broad cultural and racial mix. A combination of immigration and the import of slaves – mainly taken from Egypt, the Middle East and Turkey – added up to a population of some 50,000.

The city had a variety of buildings but, because it was a port, there was plenty of warehousing (*horrea*), for storing imported goods before they were transported to Rome and elsewhere in great barges towed up the Tiber by oxen. Ships docked at Ostia from all over the world, bringing cargoes of consumer goods such as corn, oil, wine, dates and papyrus – and luxury commodities such as gold, silk and ivory. Roman goods were also exported through the port.

A COMPETITIVE MARKET

The city's heart was in the theatre district. There, built around a large square – the Piazzale delle Corporazione – were the various guilds' headquarters. The offices housed trade associations of craftsmen and merchants, from shipbuilders to corn traders. The most imposing buildings were the elegant offices of the shipowners or *navicularii*, who drummed up business by hanging carved or painted signs outside and using wall paintings to advertise their services. Then someone had the novel idea of using the floor and commissioned a mosaic – an image made up of tiny tiles – to illustrate the services on offer.

This expensive publicity stunt proved so successful that, before long, other *navicularii* around the square followed suit. Ultimately, the entrance to almost every one of the 70 or so businesses in the city's port area was adorned with a mosaic floor. Passers-by could see what sort of goods or services were available within and, in some cases, could read a clear inscription naming the owner or his country of origin.

A cosmopolitan range of businesses advertised in this way. Mosaic inscriptions show that traders came from Gaul, North Africa and Egypt – and they often reflected aspects of their homelands in their floor designs. The *navicularii* from the North African region of Missua suggested the nature of their business

Merchants from Sabratha (in modern-day Libya) used a picture of an elephant. This is thought to imply that Sabratha exported elephants – and probably other wild beasts – as well as ivory.

with sea creatures, ships and a lighthouse at a harbour mouth. They also invited the potential customer to stop and browse by placing the simple word *hic* (here) in the mosaic. Carthaginian shippers – *navicularii Carthaginenses* – showed grain ships typical of those used to cross between Africa and Italy.

Mosaics unearthed

Gladiators in Germany
In 1852, a publican in Nennig in the Saar region of Germany unearthed a large finely coloured mosaic depicting gladiatorial scenes, dating from the 2nd century AD.

Satyrs at the cathedral
In 1941 a mosaic showing Dionysus, maenads and satyrs was discovered at the southern entrance to Cologne Cathedral during the building of an air raid shelter.

Mosaics in every room
In 1960, a Roman palace was discovered at the village of Fishbourne near Chichester in West Sussex during the digging of a main water trench. Dating from the 1st century AD, every one of the villa's 100 or so rooms has a mosaic floor.

MARKETING TOOLS
The use of mosaics for advertising and public relations was not restricted to shipping. The owner of a thermal bath enticed customers with the simple invitation *bene lava* (bathe well), while reminding people not to forget to take off their shoes when entering – and to take them with them when they left.

The restaurant trade touted for custom with simple signs in doorways – some of which blatantly drew attention to the poor service or high prices of competitors.

The classic motto in mosaic form was *cave canem* (beware of the dog) which adorned the entrance of many Roman houses, and was designed both to warn the unwary and deter unwanted guests.

313

The **fall** of the impregnable **castle**

A carrier pigeon bearing a false message spelled doom
for the Crusader castle of Krak des Chevaliers, which
had withstood no fewer than twelve Muslim sieges.

The soldiers manning the ramparts desperately scanned the
horizon for any sign of relief forces. Muslim besiegers had broken
through the outer ring of fortifications and were now preparing
to storm the castle's inner defences. Suddenly, a carrier pigeon
appeared in the sky. The note was from the Grand

Master of the Knights of the Order of St John of Jerusalem – the Knights Hospitaller – in Tripoli. He told the defenders that no relief could be despatched, and advised them to make the best terms they could with their assailants. So the garrison accepted the offer of safe conduct back to the coast and surrendered. The mightiest Christian stronghold in Syria had finally fallen.

AN OUTPOST OF CHRISTIANITY

Perched high on a windswept mountain spur, dominating the strategic pass between the Mediterranean coast and the inland cities of Homs and Hama, Krak des Chevaliers was a great prize. Such was its reputation for impregnability that many centuries later, T. E. Lawrence – Lawrence of Arabia – described it as 'the best preserved and most wholly admirable castle in the world'.

In 1031, the Emir of Aleppo built a Muslim stronghold on the site. Crusader forces under Raymond of Toulouse captured it during the First Crusade in 1099, but abandoned it when they marched on Jerusalem. The castle fell into Christian hands again in 1110, when Tancred of Hauteville, Prince of Antioch, retook it and in 1142 Raymond II, Count of Tripoli, gave it to the Knights Hospitaller, who remodelled it into the most powerful Crusader fortress in the entire Holy Land.

Krak des Chevaliers was fortified with two ingeniously engineered concentric lines of defence, the inner ramparts lying close enough to the outer ones to continuously overlook and dominate them. The 30-metre-thick outer wall, had seven massive guard towers. Deep under the castle, vast storage rooms were carved out of solid rock. They held sufficient food and other provisions to enable the Hospitallers to withstand a siege for as long as five years. Nor did the garrison risk perishing from thirst. A special aqueduct was built to feed fresh water to deep reservoirs in the underground cellars.

The Crusades

A call from the Pope
In 1095 Pope Urban II called for a Crusade to be launched as a 'holy war' against Islam.

A crusade for Christ
Crusaders aimed to liberate Jerusalem and reconquer the Holy Land for Christianity.

A short-lived success
Territories captured in the first years of the Crusades – such as Antioch in 1098, and Jerusalem, in 1099 – were all eventually retaken by the Muslims.

The eighth Crusade
The final Crusade ended with the defeat of Louis IX's army and the French king's capture in 1270. In 1291, Acre, the last Christian stronghold, fell to Muslim forces.

The Crusaders suffered numerous defeats at the hands of their Muslim adversaries in the 13th century. This 14th-century illustration from a French manuscript shows a battle scene, with the Muslims in control.

The castle withstood Muslim onslaught for well over a century. In 1163, Nur ad-Din, Sultan of Damascus, laid determined siege to the place, only to be driven off by relieving Crusader troops in a battle in the valley below the castle. In 1188 Saladin, Nur ad-Din's successor, began his own siege, but quickly decided to end it, reckoning that his forces would be better employed fighting the Crusader armies in the field. Nevertheless, in Muslim eyes it was still imperative that the fortress – the 'bone in the throat' as it had been nicknamed by those who had tried to take it – be captured if they were to succeed in eradicating the Christian presence in the Holy Land. Fate decreed that Bayburs I, a one-time soldier-slave who had risen inexorably from his humble origins to become the Sultan of Egypt, would be the man who succeeded where all others had failed.

A SLAVE ON THE THRONE

Born on the steppes of far-off Turkestan in around 1223, Bayburs was captured as a young man by the Mongols and sold into slavery in Egypt. He ended up in the service of the Ayyubid Sultan where he became known for his military skills. In 1250, he led an audacious attack by the Mamelukes – the warrior-slaves who fought for the Sultan – on the Crusaders and routed them at the battle of Monsrah. Louis IX of France, commander of the Crusader army, was captured on the battlefield and released only after payment of a heavy ransom. A decade later, Bayburs defeated the Mongol armies at the battle of Ain Jalut in 1260. After the battle, he murdered Sultan Qutuz on the return journey to Cairo and took his place on the throne.

Baybars' first move was to establish his rule over Egypt. That accomplished, he pushed into Palestine and Syria to destroy the remains of Crusader power. He chose his moment well. Support for the Crusaders had long since waned in Europe. Though Baybars failed to capture Acre, the capital of what remained of the kingdom of Jerusalem in 1263, he went on to decimate the Crusader armies in the field before successfully laying siege to Antioch in 1268. Once the city had fallen, he had it razed to the ground. Its people were enslaved.

Finally, in 1271, the Mamelukes stood before the gates of Krak des Chevaliers. The Hospitaller forces that confronted the onward march of Baybars' army were by now seriously depleted. In its heyday, 2000 handpicked knights had garrisoned the castle, but, by the latter half of the 13th century, it and Margat, the only other important fortress still in Crusader hands in the area, could muster only 300 knights between them. Nevertheless, Krak des Chevaliers initially withstood the Muslim attack. It took four weeks for Baybars' troops to break through the vulnerable southern section of the outer wall. Given the rate of progress, Baybars must have wondered how many lives it would take to force the garrison into submission.

This consideration prompted Baybars to devise a ruse to achieve his objective. It was he who dispatched the carrier pigeon with its message urging surrender. Even though the Hospitallers were in all probability aware that the message had not been sent by their Grand Master, they were all too keen to comply with its demand in the light of their hopeless situation. Preserving their dignity – and, more importantly their lives – they fled unmolested to Tripoli. The impregnable bulwark had fallen. On April 8, 1271, the banner of the Prophet Mohammed flew for the first time over Krak des Chevaliers.

Arbitary acts of fate

11

The decade of dust storms

In the 1930s, vast tracts of the Great Plains – the 'breadbasket' of the USA – turned into desert. Decades of intensive farming had removed the prairie grass and a series of extremely dry years turned the once fertile soil into dust. Then, during successive violent storms, the dust simply blew away.

On the 14th day of April of 1935,
There struck the worst of dust storms
That ever filled the sky.
You could see that dust storm comin',
The cloud looked deathlike black,
And through our mighty nation,
It left a dreadful track.

So sang the American folk singer Woody Guthrie in his ballad, *Dust Storm Disaster*, recorded in April 1940. Five years had passed since 'Black Sunday', the day a catastrophic storm hit the Midwest, but Guthrie's memories were vivid. He was not the only American who would never forget it.

A CHOKING CLOUD OF DUST

On April 14, 1935, a family from Boise City, Idaho had planned a trip to the country. As Ed and Ada Philips and their six-year-old daughter drove out of the city the weather seemed set fair – a cloudless blue sky stretched overhead – and they spent the day sunbathing and enjoyed a picnic. But during the afternoon they began to feel uneasy. The temperature suddenly dropped; birds began twittering in alarm. Then on the horizon a black cloud appeared, rolling swiftly across the flat landscape, engulfing everything in its path like a gigantic steamroller. The family quickly packed their things into the car and started for home.

During this dust storm in Colorado, the clouds appeared on the horizon with a thunderous roar before rolling in and dumping a layer of fine silt all over the land. People tied handkerchiefs over their noses and mouths. They shut themselves in their houses and wedged rags into the cracks around doors and windows – but still the dust found a way in.

They were already too late; the storm caught up with the car, reducing visibility to a few feet and turning day into night. The fine dust filled their ears and eyes and clogged their mouths and noses, making it difficult to breathe. Fortunately they stumbled on a ruined house and went in to take refuge – joining ten other people who had also been caught unawares. It was four hours before the storm died down and they could make their way home.

> '*We live with the dust, eat it, sleep with it, watch it strip us of possessions and the hope of possessions.*'
>
> AMERICAN JOURNALIST, AVIS CARLSON

The next day, a reporter coined the term 'dust bowl' to describe the driest region of the Plains – south-eastern Colorado, south-west Kansas and the panhandles of Oklahoma and Texas. Here, throughout the 1930s, the so-called 'black blizzards' raged each spring, blowing up roughly every other day during March, April and May. In Oklahoma, 102 such storms were recorded in a single year. In June 1935, *Reader's Digest* magazine published a letter from a woman in Oklahoma. 'In the dust-covered desolation of our No Man's Land here, we have been trying to rescue our home from the wind-blown dust which penetrates wherever air can go. It is almost a hopeless task, for there is rarely a day when at some time the dust clouds do not roll over. Visibility approaches zero and everything is covered again with a silt-like deposit which may vary in depth from a film to actual ripples on the kitchen floor.' That year, dust storms were responsible for the failure of 46.6 million acres of crops on the Great Plains.

THE WIDER IMPACT

In May 1934, a four-day storm laid waste to more than 50,000 square miles of fertile farmland in the Great Plains – but its effects were noticed much further afield. The winds whipped up a cloud that covered an area around 15 times the size of Britain, and gathered enough momentum to send 350 million tonnes of airborne soil at speeds up to 100 miles an hour towards the East Coast. The cloud towered almost three miles high; migrating birds that flew into it suffocated in mid air and dropped out of the sky. In Washington DC black dust rained on the White House. The wind currents dumped an estimated 12 million tonnes of dust on Chicago. The next day, New York City was engulfed for several hours. The dust even fell on ships lying more than 300 miles offshore.

In the early 1930s, farmers had ridden out the storms with a degree of stoicism and even a morbid humour. But as their wheat fields were destroyed on a regular basis, fodder for livestock dwindled and hundreds of thousands of starving animals had to be slaughtered, the farmers' sense of humour deserted them. Incomes slumped, but the banks still insisted on interest payments being made on farm loans. Many families faced ruin and were forced to abandon their farms.

A column of refugees from the dust bowl made their way to California, driven out by dust storms that could sandblast the paint from weather-boarded houses. People caught outside when the storms rolled over vomited clods of soil – and ministers preached that the storms signified the end of the world.

A huge migration began. Nearly 40 per cent of the people living in the rural area around Boise City in Idaho left for an uncertain future. By 1940, two-and-a-half million people from the Great Plains had upped sticks, 200,000 of them moving west to California. But the whole nation was in the grip of an economic depression following the 1929 Wall Street Crash, and the last thing the people in California

> *'The people came out of their houses and smelled the hot stinging air and covered their noses from it.'*
>
> JOHN STEINBECK IN *THE GRAPES OF WRATH* (1939).

wanted was an influx of desperate 'Okies' and 'Arkies' – disparaging terms used to describe the Oklahoma and Arkansas refugees. The only work to be had was in the cotton fields and fruit groves, where the migrants laboured for starvation wages, and had to find extortionate rents for dreadful lodgings.

The disaster not only inspired John Steinbeck and Woody Guthrie. It also resulted in an unusual film. Sponsored by the US government, *The Plow that Broke the Plains* was a short documentary made in 1936 by Pare Lorentz. This early propaganda film, whose soundtrack incorporated many folk tunes, aimed to drive home the message that the misuse of land had serious repercussions.

WILL IT HAPPEN AGAIN?

Periods of drought were nothing new in the Great Plains – they were as much a part of the climate as tornadoes and blizzards. From 1880 to 1885 and again from 1906 to 1912, the region had

Large scale agribusiness is still used to grow grain in the USA. Immense farms, high-level mechanisation and an intensive use of pesticides predominate.

suffered long dry periods. But once the rain and snow returned, the farmers would trundle out with their tractors and ploughs to turn the fertile prairie grasslands into fields of wheat.

Grain prices were high during the First World War and with new heavy agricultural machinery making farming easier, the farmers grew rich. In Kansas alone in 1919, more than 12 million acres of land were being used to grow wheat – almost double the area of a decade earlier. Ten years later, the climate pendulum swung once more and the farmland that had provided such high yields was gradually transformed by water shortages and storms into desolate badlands.

PREVENTING THE DUST BOWL

It took a long time for the US government to grasp the seriousness of the situation and put relief programmes in place. The Roosevelt administration provided as much aid as it could, and also targeted the causes of the dust bowl. Rows of trees were planted to act as windbreaks and protect the soil from drying out completely. Soil conservation became a big issue, and farmers were taught the benefits of terracing and contouring. The dust bowl years finally ended in 1941 with the arrival of drenching rains on the southern and central plains.

There have been a number of droughts and dust storms since 1941, in the early 1950s, the 1970s and the 1990s. In dry years towns in the core of the region are still badly affected by dust storms. Careful land management has meant that the effects of these storms are far less dramatic than they were during the 1930s, but environmentalists and critics of modern agricultural systems warn that unless modern farming is drastically reformed, the dust bowl may return.

America's 'breadbasket'

The Great Plains states

The Great Plains are an arid region in the US Midwest. They cover about half a million square miles in ten states – New Mexico, Texas, Oklahoma, Colorado, Kansas, Nebraska, Wyoming, Montana, South Dakota and North Dakota. Ever since the area was first farmed it has been regarded as the 'breadbasket' of the United States.

Thousands of miles of 'nothing'

Today, barely one million people inhabit the region, making the Great Plains one of the most sparsely populated agricultural areas on the planet. Its farming population is now one-eighth the size it was in 1930.

Reasons for depopulation

The population decline has occurred in response to droughts, to the mechanisation of agriculture, and to the fact that previously cultivated land has been allowed to revert to prairie grasslands.

Mortal danger
on the
high seas

When the *Andrea Doria*, an Italian luxury liner collided with a Swedish ship in dense fog off the eastern seaboard of the USA, prospects looked bleak for her 1706 passengers and crew, even though the disaster was played out in front of the world's media.

With a terrible rending of metal, the bow of the *Stockholm* buried itself in the side of the *Andrea Doria*, tearing a massive gash in her flank, her steel plating crushed like an eggshell. On board, internal walls collapsed, burying bunks as they fell. Tastefully furnished cabins were transformed into a deadly maze of twisted metal, splinters of glass and shattered furniture. On the lower decks, a thousand tonnes of water gushed in. Eleven hours later, the *Andrea Doria* finally slipped beneath the waves.

THE LUXURY LINER

The pride of the Italian Line left Genoa on July 17, 1956.
The *Andrea Doria* called at Cannes, Naples, and Gibraltar before
setting course for New York, a crossing she had made 50 times.
A total of 1706 passengers were on board, enjoying the ship's
three outdoor swimming pools or drinking cocktails at the bar.
In the evenings there was live music and dancing. Safety was at a
premium: no expense had been spared in fitting the floating hotel
with the latest equipment, including a brand new radar system.

FOG AND DANCING

The nine-day voyage passed without incident. The weather
was fine and the sea calm. Only on the afternoon of the last day,
July 25 did a bank of fog appear off the American coast. But the
ship's new radar system was capable of pinpointing every hazard,
even in the worst visibility. Captain Piero Calamai set up the
usual safety procedures; the foghorn sent out a warning blast at
regular intervals and a lookout was posted at the ship's bow to
keep a watch for approaching danger. But the captain only
reduced the ocean liner's speed marginally.

    On the final day of the crossing, passengers were getting
ready to bid farewell to life on board. Some retired early, while
others were determined to savour every last minute in the
ship's bars and ballrooms. Meanwhile, routine operations were
continuing on the bridge. At 10.20 pm the *Andrea Doria* passed
the Nantucket lightship, a marker point for all ships on their way
to dock in New York harbour.

Named after the 16th-century Genoese admiral, the *Andrea Doria* was the largest, fastest and supposedly safest of Italy's ocean-going liners. With a double hull, *Andrea Doria* was divided into 11 watertight compartments: any two of these could be filled with water without endangering the ship's safety. She also carried enough lifeboats to accommodate all 1706 passengers and crew.

Modern shipping disasters

The *Titanic*

After colliding with an iceberg on the night of April 14–15, 1912, the supposedly 'unsinkable' transatlantic liner *Titanic* sank on her maiden voyage, with the loss of more than 1500 lives.

The *Wilhelm Gustloff*

The German liner *Wilhelm Gustloff*, torpedoed in the Baltic on January 30, 1945, went down with the loss of at least 5348 – and perhaps as many as 9000 – people most of them refugees fleeing Nazi Germany.

The *Kursk*

On August 12, 2000, the Russian nuclear submarine *Kursk* was lost on manoeuvres in the Barents Sea with 118 crewmen on board. The explosion of one of the submarine's own torpedoes was almost certainly to blame.

The calm on the bridge was rudely interrupted by a telephone call. The lookout on the bow reported that he had heard the foghorn of another ship off the starboard side. Another 25 minutes elapsed before the small Swedish passenger ship *Stockholm* appeared for the first time on the *Andrea Doria*'s radar screen, confirming the lookout's sighting. 'Single vessel…distance 17 miles', the second officer called out.

A FATEFUL DECISION

The *Stockholm*, at 160 metres and 12,165 tonnes, was one of the smallest of the new postwar liners. She had left New York harbour that morning and set a course slightly to the north of the usual route taken by ships out of New York – probably to cut a few miles off her journey. The route would bring her into proximity with incoming ships in one of the busiest sea lanes in the world. On the bridge of the *Stockholm* the ship's third officer, 26-year-old Johan-Ernst Bogislaus Carstens-Johannsen, manned the 8.30 pm to 12.00 am watch, the only officer present. On the bridge of the *Andrea Doria*, Second Officer Curzio Franchini kept a close watch on the radar screen for the approaching ship. There seemed to be no cause for alarm.

There are clear rules of navigation governing evasive action. If two ships are approaching one another on the high seas, they are required to pass each other on the port side. But the radar showed the captain of the *Andrea Doria* that the other ship was sailing to the right of his vessel. To pass it on the port side, the *Andrea Doria* would have to cut across the path of the *Stockholm* – a risky manoeuvre. The liner would also have to sail close to the busy Nantucket coast. So at 11.05 pm Captain Calamai made the decision to make a slight alteration in his course that would ensure that the ships passed at a safe distance from one another on their starboard sides. Meanwhile the *Stockholm*'s radar operator had picked up the *Andrea Doria*. The ships had been approaching one another for many miles now but still had no visual contact.

THE DOOMED MANOEUVRE

On board the *Andrea Doria*, Third Officer Eugenio Giannini scanned the white wall of fog with a pair of binoculars. At first he could only make out a dim glow in the distance, then, gradually, the masts and navigational lights of the other ship emerged from the gloom. At this point, barely one nautical mile separated the two ships. As he gazed at the lights of the *Stockholm*, Giannini suddenly saw that the other vessel was changing course and heading directly for the *Andrea Doria*. On board the *Stockholm*, Carstens thought he was giving the oncoming ship a wide berth, but in fact he was turning his ship towards the *Andrea Doria*. Captain Calamai ordered his ship to

The *Andrea Doria*'s severe list complicated normal lifeboat procedures. Empty boats had to be placed in the water first, and evacuees lowered down the ship's hull to sea level to board. This was finally accomplished using ropes, Jacob's ladders and a large fishing net. Some passengers panicked and threw children to rescuers below or jumped overboard themselves.

turn hard to port, in the desperate hope that her superior speed and manoeuvrability would avert the impending disaster. His emergency manoeuvre made the situation worse. Instead of steering straight at the *Stockholm* with her bow, the *Andrea Doria* now presented a vulnerable flank to the rapidly approaching ship. On board the *Stockholm*, Carstens ordered the ship's engines to be set to full reverse. But it was too late. A collision was inevitable.

MASS PANIC

At 11.10 pm, the ships collided. The *Stockholm*'s sharply raked prow pierced *Andrea Doria*'s starboard side, penetrating three cabin decks to a depth of nearly 12 metres. The impact hurled people from their bunks: some were killed outright. The band playing to late night dancers in the ballroom toppled from their bandstand and the movie screen went dead. Panic ensued.

The interior of the *Andrea Doria* was divided into eleven compartments sealed off from one another by watertight bulkheads. If the ship was holed anywhere, the water would only flood one of these compartments. But the *Stockholm* had ripped open seven of the compartments. Barely five minutes after the collision the *Andrea Doria* had heeled more than 20 degrees to starboard. Water gushed into the damaged hull, flooding cabins and giving the ship a list that grew steadily heavier.

The chief engineer realised at once that with such a heavy list, the ship would eventually capsize and sink. They knew that they had already lost the battle against the huge volume of water that had entered the ship. At any moment the liner could turn turtle. It was essential that everyone abandon ship immediately: the captain ordered the crew to man the lifeboat stations.

A SPECTACULAR RESCUE MISSION

There was yet more bad news: the eight lifeboats on the port side could not be launched because the ship was listing too heavily. But the eight lifeboats to starboard could only accommodate 1004 people, and there were 1706 passengers and crew on board. People rushed up on to the deck in terror and confusion, some of them wearing their nightclothes, others still dressed in evening wear. Without outside help, the people on board would have been lost. The radio operator sent a distress signal giving the exact coordinates. It set in motion the greatest peacetime rescue mission at sea. Several ships in the immediate vicinity made straight for the accident. They included the *Cape Ann*, a freighter owned by the United Fruit Company, and the US Navy transport ship *Private William H. Thomas*. *Stockholm* also took part in the rescue despite the serious damage to her bows.

Dense banks of fog still rolled around the *Andrea Doria*. When the French liner *Ile de France* arrived, Captain Raoul de Beaudéan could only make out the vague outlines of the two damaged ships. When the fog suddenly lifted, de Beaudéan clearly saw the desperate plight of the *Andrea Doria*, by now listing to 40 degrees. He ordered ten lifeboats to be lowered, and most of the remaining passengers were rescued by the *Ile de France*.

Many families were separated during the evacuation because so many different ships were involved in the rescue. The entire operation, and the human dramas on the dockside of New York, was reported in vivid detail by the world's news media.

The media were quickly on the spot, photographing from planes and helicopters and beaming pictures of the rescue operation around the world. Once the surviving passengers were safe, the crew were evacuated. Captain Calamai ordered his officers to abandon ship, but he was determined to go down with the *Andrea Doria*. His officers refused to leave the ship without him and he was the last person to board a lifeboat, at 5.30 am.

The collision claimed 46 lives on the *Andrea Doria* and five crewmen from the *Stockholm*. Amazingly, all those who survived the force of the initial collision were rescued. The *Stockholm* was able to steam to New York under its own power, and was eventually repaired and brought back into service. The stricken *Andrea Doria* continued to slowly capsize, and eventually disappeared beneath the waves at 10.09 am on July 26.

A nuclear bomb goes missing

On January 17, 1966, an American KC-135 tanker plane and a B-52 bomber carrying four 1-megaton hydrogen bombs crashed while refuelling in the air over the Spanish Mediterranean coast. Pieces of wreckage and three of the bombs fell near the village of Palomares. But where was the fourth?

In 1966, the Cold War was at its height. Following the end of the Second World War, relations between the United States and the Soviet Union became increasingly hostile. During the 1950s and 60s both nations engaged in an arms race – a huge and expensive build-up of weaponry. The philosophy of the arms race – 'mutually assured destruction' or 'MAD' – was to give each nation the ability to annihilate its enemy in retaliation for an attack. The concept of 'the ultimate deterrent' was effective, as there was no one issue over which any country was willing to destroy itself. Maintaining the deterrent involved stationing as many nuclear weapons as possible close to enemy territory, in order to launch an immediate strike if the Cold War turned 'hot'.

Long-range ballistic missiles were still under development. Instead, nuclear bombs were carried on board aircraft patrolling the fringes of the boundary between eastern and western Europe – the so-called 'Iron Curtain'. Few Europeans were aware that, for decades, US bombers laden with nuclear weapons circled the earth ceaselessly. The bombers were on permanent red alert, and in order not to waste valuable time with take-offs and landings, it was routine to refuel in flight.

A CRASH IN MID AIR

During one of these routine flights, in this case over southern Spain, an American B-52 bomber and a KC-135 tanker aircraft manoeuvred themselves into position for a refuelling operation they had carried out countless times. Suddenly the sky resounded with an ear-splitting bang. The aircraft had collided. With its full load of fuel, the KC-135 exploded. All four crewmen were killed. The B-52 also exploded. Three of its crew members died, but four parachuted to safety. All four hydrogen bombs on board the plane plummeted to earth. Each had a greater explosive yield than the atomic bomb that had been dropped on Hiroshima at the end of the Second World War.

Some of the village's older residents still remember vividly the day the accident happened. Although it was more than 40 years ago, it remains a taboo subject for many. At first sight, it appeared that the village – Palomares, near the port of Almería on the southeastern corner of the Iberian Peninsula – had had a lucky escape. Both aircraft fell on to uninhabited farmland.

Since 1950, there have been 32 accidents involving nuclear weapons, known as Broken Arrows. After the incident in the remote Spanish farming community of Palomares, nearly 2000 US military personnel and Spanish civil guards were rushed in to clean up the debris.

On April 7, 1966, 80 days after the mid-air collision, the US navy salvaged the fourth H-bomb from the sea bed. The 3-metre-long warhead was brought aboard the *USS Petrel*, its parachute still attached. The bomb – known as 'Robert' or bomb #4 – had been damaged, but had not ruptured.

It appeared that there was relatively little damage and there was relief that no-one on the ground had been killed. But over the next few days, specialists wearing protective clothing and carrying unfamiliar equipment took numerous readings. Bemused farm labourers working nearby had no idea what was going on. But when 2000 people were told to leave their homes at once, and to stay away from them until further notice, it became clear that what they had witnessed was no ordinary plane crash.

The investigators knew what the locals did not – that the crashed bomber had been carrying H-bombs. Miraculously, when the warheads hit the ground, they did not trigger a nuclear explosion. But the high-explosive priming charges inside two of the bombs had gone off and plutonium dust had spread over several hundred acres of farmland. A third bomb was intact. But worryingly, the fourth was still missing. There were a number of conflicting ideas about what had happened to it, and only one clue to its location, given by a fisherman who apparently saw it hit the water.

Day after day, ships patrolled off the Spanish coast, while divers were sent down to search for the missing weapon. Weeks passed with no success. Then, two months after the crash, the US Navy's deep-diving research vessel located the bomb eight miles offshore and 800 metres down on the sea bed.

THE GREAT COVER-UP

Back on dry land, a major clean-up operation had quickly swung into action. Soil readings revealed that 558 acres, mainly used for tomato cultivation, had been contaminated with radioactive material. The US authorities were anxious to remove all trace of the accident from Spanish soil, whatever the cost. They undertook a huge decontamination effort over the next three months, involving around 1700 US servicemen and Spanish civil guards. Sixteen hundred tonnes of radioactive earth was taken to the United States and buried in South Carolina. The area underwater was left alone, even though its flora and fauna showed increased levels of radiation.

It was impossible to cover up the fact of the accident, but the military authorities kept a tight rein on the release of information to the media. Local villagers received no official notification as to what had happened, but not long after the accident they were allowed to return home. Rumours spread, though in the repressive atmosphere of Franco's Spain – with its reliance on harsh justice dealt by military tribunals – people were wary of asking awkward questions.

So everyone behaved as though nothing had happened and went back to work in their fields. But the name of Palomares had been tainted by the incident, and local farmers began to find it easier to sell their produce if they omitted to say where it came from.

Cold War hot spots

The Berlin Airlift
In 1948 the Soviet Union directly challenged the West by instituting a blockade of the western sectors of Berlin. The USA and its allies airlifted food and other supplies into the city until the blockade was withdrawn.

The Berlin Wall
To halt the embarrassing flow of East Germans to the West, the East German government built the Berlin Wall in 1961, sealing off Soviet-controlled East Berlin from the rest of the city.

The Cuban Missile Crisis
In 1962, US intelligence discovered the presence of Soviet missile installations in Cuba. This resulted in a tense stand-off, although direct conflict was avoided when the Russian premier, Nikolai Khrushchev, ordered Russian ships carrying rockets to Cuba to return home rather than confront US naval ships that had been sent to intercept them.

The Spanish government was also anxious in case rumour frightened away the tourists who had begun to visit Almería's coastal resorts. A few months after the crash, the public relations machine went into overdrive. Spain's minister for tourism and the US Ambassador even took a dip in the sea together for the cameras. Visitors were happy to believe the message that all was now safe and continued to flock to the area.

THE SHADOW OF THE PAST

On the surface, normality had returned, although even today some residents have regular blood and urine tests. Doctors have concluded that, more than 40 years after the crash, the local population does not suffer from a higher incidence of cancer than elsewhere. But the shadow of the contamination has not quite faded. Grandiose property development schemes are currently underway all over Almería, with hotel complexes, apartment blocks and golf courses planned for Palomares. But deep foundations are required for such major building projects, and measurements taken from beneath the surface at the crash site in 2004 revealed unexpectedly high levels of radiation. Building work has been halted for the time being while scientists ascertain whether the site can ever be properly decontaminated. Local people are outraged – once again, their town is making headlines for all the wrong reasons, just when the future seemed brighter.

'People here are fed up to the back teeth.'

JÉSUS CAICEDO, MAYOR OF PALOMARES

To prevent any contaminated areas from being built on, the Spanish government put a compulsory purchase order on the affected land; the plots won't be returned to their original owners until the experts have given the area the all-clear. For the people of Palomares the events of January 17, 1966, are still casting a lengthy shadow over their land.

Two Starfighters of the
Federal German Air Force
on a training flight.

From
star fighter to
widow maker

A new fleet of American fighter-bombers was supposed
to herald a bright new dawn for the revived German Air
Force, allowing it to play a key role in the NATO alliance
during the Cold War. But unusually high accident rates
turned a political triumph into a fiasco.

On July 19, 1962, the military airfield at Nörvenich was
a hive of activity. The first unit to convert to the Lockheed
F-104G fighter-bomber, 31 (Ground Attack) Squadron
'Boelcke', was due to be officially taken into commission
the next day. An air show would mark this key event in
the history of the German Air Force. Four pilots from the
display team took off for a last practice run before the big
day in their new Starfighters. But shortly after take-off, the

formation leader made an error and the entire display team crashed; all four pilots were killed. The festivities were cancelled. Before long, the Starfighter had acquired another name – the Widow Maker. It was also known as the Flying Coffin.

A DIFFICULT BIRTH

The nickname was coined in 1965–66, when Starfighters began to crash with depressing regularity. Difficult questions were asked. Why had the government ordered 916 aircraft that seemed catastrophically accident-prone?

In the immediate aftermath of the Second World War, it was inconceivable that Germany would play a significant military role again. But growing tensions between East and West caused the Federal Republic of Germany, immediately to the west of the Eastern Bloc, to become vital to the NATO alliance. Western Europe and the United States faced a new enemy: the Soviet Union and the armed forces of its satellite states. West Germany needed a new army, navy and airforce to support its NATO allies. It was particularly difficult to create an airforce from scratch as most of the German military-industrial complex had been destroyed during the war. The fledgling West German aeronautics industry was incapable of producing aircraft that could hold their own against an opposing force.

When negotiations began at the end of the 1950s over the choice of future combat aircraft, three planes made it onto the shortlist: the French Dassault Mirage IIIA, the American Grumman Super Tiger, and the American Lockhed F-104 Starfighter. Eventually the decision was made in favour of the Starfighter, not least because the aircraft could be built under licence in the Federal Republic.

A TECHNOLOGICAL MARVEL?

The new high-tech aircraft fitted perfectly into the West German rearmament policy. But from the outset, the Starfighter was blighted by misfortune. Shortly after licensing the Germans to build the aircraft, the Americans withdrew the plane from service in the US. The F-104G was also wholly unsuited to European weather conditions. Ninety separate modifications were made to the plane's construction, driving up the cost of each plane by nearly 30 per cent. But the project was seen as a milestone in the restoration of Germany's international standing. The plane could also deliver nuclear payloads – the real role envisaged for the aircraft officially designated as a 'multi-role combat aircraft'.

PAYING A HIGH PRICE

The Starfighter at first proved too technically complex for German pilots, with little experience of sophisticated aircraft. North European weather and operational restrictions hampered training. A *Luftwaffe* training operation was set up in the southwestern United States, where there was space, clear air and good weather; but it was an inadequate preparation for northern Europe; many of the problems were caused when flying low-altitude missions at high speed in conditions of poor visibility.

The question of where the expensive aircraft were to be housed had been largely neglected. With insufficient hangars, the aircraft, equipped with sophisticated electronics, were frequently left out in the wind and rain. The Starfighter needed many hours of maintenance for every hour in the air, and many of the ground crew personnel were hastily trained conscripts.

From its inception to 1987, when the Starfighter was withdrawn from service by the Germans, 116 pilots lost their lives flying the aircraft. The accident rate escalated as more operations were undertaken, with 28 crashes in 1965, an average of more than two a month. By mid-1966 61 Starfighters had crashed, with the loss of 35 pilots.

The crashes drew the media's attention to the plane's problems and prompted a debate in the German parliament. At the height of the Starfighter political crisis in mid-1966, the *Luftwaffe* chief had to resign after criticising the programme as being politically motivated. But when the number of crashes fell, thanks to technical alterations and better pilot training, public interest waned. In retrospect, the Starfighter's accident rate of one crash for every 6765 hours flown is a fairly average rate of attrition for operational fighter aircraft in peacetime. But the problems caused in the plane's first years of service were well publicised and it retained its notoriety as a 'widow maker'.

Disaster at Chernobyl

In April 1986, the unthinkable happened in Ukraine. A nuclear reactor blew up, turning an entire city into a deadly wasteland. It was the worst nuclear accident of all time, releasing 400 times more fallout than the Hiroshima atomic bomb, and sending a radioactive cloud across Europe.

Entire regions around the Chernobyl reactor, such as this residential area in Solnechnyy, have lain derelict and abandoned since the accident in April 1986.

At 11 am on April 27, 1986, the authorities finally ordered the residents of the Pripyat, in the Ukraine, to leave the area as quickly as they could. An explosion had devastated reactor block 4 of the Chernobyl nuclear power station a few miles away 33 hours before. The evacuation of Pripyat began at 2 pm and, two hours later, 1200 buses had cleared the city of its inhabitants. In three days, it was claimed, they would be able to return. Days turned into years. Today, Pripyat's former citizens have long been aware that their home is a radioactive no-go area, and will remain uninhabitable for generations.

THE CATASTROPHIC ACCIDENT

Everything seemed normal at the Chernobyl nuclear power station on the night of April 25–26. The employees responsible for reactor block 4 performed their tasks routinely. They were preparing to shut down the reactor to allow maintenance to be carried out. At the same time they were preparing to conduct a long-overdue test to ascertain whether the station's turbine, then close to the end of its life, still generated enough electricity to guarantee short-term operation of the plant's emergency cooling system in the event of a power cut. For various reasons, the reactor was running at well below capacity. This was risky, as the RBMK-1000 reactors installed at Chernobyl, were unstable at low power. The nuclear reaction was maintained and moderated by the use of graphite-tipped control rods and the fuel rods were cooled with light water. If the cooling system failed, then the reaction could quickly run out of control.

At 1.23 am it became clear that the reactor operation was becoming less stable and an emergency shut-down procedure was started. Paradoxically, this initially accelerated the reaction. Because of a design flaw in the construction of the reactors, the control rods activated by the procedure could only bring the reaction to a halt after first stimulating an initial increase in the reaction. The reactor had been running at just 10 per cent of its usual operational level. Just seven seconds after the emergency procedure, it shot up to ten times its normal output – and Chernobyl 4 erupted like a volcano. A massive steam explosion travelled along the channels in the reactor, rupturing coolant

Nuclear accidents

Windscale

On October 10, 1957, a fire broke out in the nuclear reactor at Windscale (now Sellafield) in Cumbria. A cloud of radioactive material was released, and spread over the British Isles and the European mainland.

Nuclear submarines

There have been repeated reports of serious accidents on nuclear-powered submarines. The Soviet submarine K-27 experienced a major reactor malfunction while at sea on May 24, 1968, which cost nine crewmen their lives.

Three Mile Island

Before Chernobyl, the most serious known reactor accident occurred on March 28, 1979, at the Three Mile Island nuclear power plant at Harrisburg in the USA. The core suffered a partial meltdown, and it took five days to bring the reactor under control. The accident released radioactive material into the environment.

tubes and blowing a hole in the roof. The reactor core, reaction chamber, and the main reactor hall were completely destroyed. For several days after the explosion, winds scattered radioactive particles in all directions, with some landing as far away as northern Italy, Finland, Scandinavia and western Britain.

FLAWED SYSTEMS

A series of investigations found that the operators had violated plant procedures, but this may have been due to their lack of knowledge of the plant's flawed design. Ignoring the guidelines, they switched off many of the reactor's safety systems. A government commission in 1986 found they removed at least 204 out of a total of 211 control rods from the reactor core, leaving just seven: guidelines prohibited the operation of the RBMK-1000 with fewer than 15 rods inside the core.

The Soviet engineers who designed the plant were fully aware of the potential risks. But they favoured hazardous graphite-moderated reactors of the type at Chernobyl for a very specific reason. While the plant was still running, the fuel rods could be taken out and processed to obtain plutonium for nuclear weapons. To conduct the same operation in a light-water-moderated reactor, it was necessary to run the core for a certain amount of time before shutting it off completely.

HEROES OF THE RADIOACTIVE HOLOCAUST

Within three and a half hours of the accident, the fire service had managed to extinguish the fire almost completely. During the operation, more than 230 men had received extremely high doses of radiation, and 29 of them died in the following weeks from the consequences of this exposure. But they had laid the foundations for the containment of the catastrophe. In the days following the accident, helicopters dropped 40 tonnes of boric acid onto the ruins of the reactor hall to stop the nuclear reaction, 800 tonnes of the mineral dolomite to absorb the heat it had generated, 1800 tonnes of sand and mud to extinguish the fires and 2400 tonnes of lead to screen the radiation. But this only succeeded in trapping the heat within the ruined building, which threatened to set off the nuclear reaction once again. So a tunnel was excavated under the reactor and a cooling system using liquid nitrogen was installed. Ten days after the explosion, the ruins of Chernobyl 4 were stabilised and all radioactivity contained.

Subsequently, 2000 construction workers and engineers, assisted by thousands of soldiers, built a protective concrete shield around the wreckage – the so-called sarcophagus. Three cement works were set up to produce enough concrete for the enormous task. The walls that now entomb the turbine building, the service building and the devastated main reactor hall are up to 15 metres thick in places. As a foundation, the workers put a layer of gravel and cement 6–12 metres thick under the melted reactor core, which also isolated it from the ground water. During the operations, workers were exposed to increased levels of radiation, but the long-term effects of this exposure are still not fully known.

Regular Geiger-counter readings to measure radiation levels are still taken today at the site of the destroyed reactor. About 95 per cent of the fuel (180 tonnes) in the reactor at the time of the accident is thought to remain inside the shelter. If the sarcophagus, which is deteriorating with age, collapses, another cloud of radioactive dust could be released.

THE RADIOACTIVE LEGACY

The former reactor core gave most cause for concern. Although it had been buried under a million tonnes of concrete, underneath the carapace the radioactive material continued to generate heat, causing stresses that fractured the concrete. Engineers feared that water might penetrate the cracks, setting off a new chain-reaction in the fuel still present in the core, so they set about constructing a roof for the sarcophagus.

The roof was installed using helicopters. The pilots lowered thick steel tubing, 30 metres long and 120 centimetres in diameter. The tubes were positioned to span the gap between the top of the western wall of the reactor hall, which had survived the explosion, and the ventilation shafts on the opposite side of the wrecked reactor. Then a light coating was laid on top of the pipes to repel the rain. It was impossible to work with complete accuracy from a helicopter, and as a result there were gaps between the steel tubes up to 25 centimetres wide, through which rainwater seeped. At first, it seemed impossible to seal the gaps, as anyone working on the roof would have been given a fatal dose of radiation within ten hours. Eventually most of the holes were plugged using a remote-control system.

'Chernobyl cost the Russian economy $500 million.'

FORMER RUSSIAN PREMIER MIKHAIL GORBACHEV

The ruins of the reactor were not the only radioactive legacy. A huge amount of radioactive waste such as vehicles, tools and other items accumulated at Chernobyl. The debris has been placed in trenches 100 metres long, 4 metres deep and up to 50 metres wide, with concrete bases to seal them off from the groundwater. Each dump can accommodate up to 15,000 cubic metres of waste, and to date around 1000 such dumps have been created in the surrounding area.

A RADIOECOLOGICAL NATIONAL PARK

A surprising beneficiary of the Chernobyl disaster has been the surrounding countryside. The authorities were obliged to evacuate around 350,000 people from parts of Ukraine, Belarus and Russia, leaving 3860 square miles of land almost

uninhabited. As humans left, wild animals came in to fill the vacuum. Ten years after the catastrophe, three times as many animals as before the event were living in the area around the reactor. Belarus has even declared the part of the 30-kilometre-wide exclusion zone around the reactor within its territory as a 'State Radioecological Reserve', which they have stocked with European bison and other wildlife.

Today, the animals show no external signs of suffering any ill effects from the catastrophe. But in the years immediately after the accident, tests on wild boar, birds and rodents within 6 miles of the reactor revealed an incidence of hereditary defects ten times greater than that in other regions. Scientists also found a large number of animals with six toes and other anomalies. The defects were clearly the result of irradiation of the foetuses in the womb. The incidence of such anomalies has now declined to a level not much higher than before the accident, and even the number of hereditary defects has fallen noticeably.

Firefighters who rushed to the scene were not told how radioactive the smoke and debris were. Even their vehicles were irradiated. Many of the vehicles deployed on rescue operations in the aftermath of the accident, tools and other equipment have been buried in huge trenches within the Chernobyl exclusion zone.

THE HEALTH FALLOUT

People living around the reactor also suffered high doses of radiation. The radioactive substance iodine-131, released by the explosion of reactor number 4, found its way mainly into victims' thyroid glands after the accident. There, the radiation altered the genetic make-up of the cells and eventually caused cancer. In the aftermath of the disaster in the worst affected areas in Belarus, doctors diagnosed incidences of thyroid cancer 40 times higher than in areas unaffected by the blast. In Belarus alone, it is reckoned that some 3000 people will contract such tumours over time, although these cases are relatively treatable. A further 1600 such cases are expected in Ukraine.

After ten years, the authorities had found around 1000 tumours of this kind among children. Two-thirds of them had been under five when the accident happened: at this age the thyroid glands are seven times more susceptible to the effects of radioactivity than in adults. In the years following the disaster, no higher incidence of other forms of cancer became apparent in the affected areas than elsewhere. Estimates of the final death toll from cancer vary from a conservative 9000 – in a report by the International Atomic Energy Agency and the World Health Organisation – to a potential 200,000 by Greenpeace.

The worst effects of the reactor accident for the former inhabitants of the region may be its psychosocial repercussions. A total of 350,000 people were displaced and resettled, some of

Many children in Belarus have been diagnosed with thyroid cancer following the Chernobyl disaster. Nine children who suffered from thyroid cancer have died, but the vast majority of those diagnosed with the condition have survived. One of the main causes of this cancer has been identified as drinking milk from cows that ate contaminated grass.

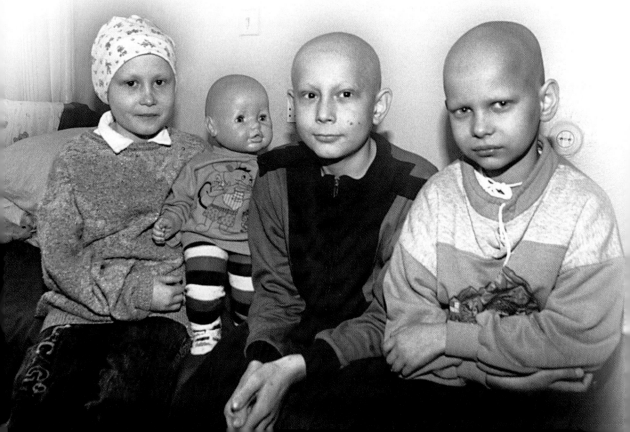

them within just a few hours, and their homeland was declared a radioactive exclusion zone. Up to 800,000 so-called 'liquidators' were involved in the clean-up operation following the accident, and many of them received high doses of radiation. Even today, few of these rescue workers know how they have been affected.

The effects of this uncertainty are dramatic. In the decade after the accident, the birth rate among the Chernobylis, as the survivors are known, fell to just a sixth of that in the rest of country. On the other hand, the suicide rate rocketed.

LIVING WITH RADIATION

Ten years after the catastrophe, the contamination of the area had decreased to an extent that made it possible to visit the city for brief periods. But readings taken in Pripyat in February 1996 still recorded radiation levels some 20 to 30 times higher than in any uncontaminated city – far too high for people to live there for any length of time. This situation has not changed in the interim. Two miles away, at the Chernobyl nuclear installation, radiation is an order of magnitude some 60 to 100 times greater than uncontaminated areas. In the summer, when a warm breeze whips up the radioactive dust, these readings can be five or six times higher, according to Alexander Krasnyuk, who for many years was the power station's press officer. As a result, the 10,000 or so employees of the nuclear plant, who continued to work in the immediate vicinity of the shattered reactor for a decade and a half after the accident, were housed 30 miles away in the uncontaminated town of Slavutitch, only coming into the Chernobyl area for the duration of their shifts. There they kept reactors 1, 2 and 3 running until the last of these was finally decommissioned at the end of 2000.

Faced with the continued uncertainty, some of the evacuees, especially older people, have taken it upon themselves to return to the exclusion zone. These returnees are now living in primitive conditions in the huge area that the explosion contaminated. The authorities turn a blind eye, at least to old people, even when they burn irradiated wood and so spread radioactivity again. It is thought that the high levels of radiation in the region will have little impact on people with only a few years left to live.

The train that fell into a swamp

In 1993 a barge towed by a tugboat collided with a steel pier and knocked a railway bridge out of alignment. A passing train full of sleeping passengers plunged into an alligator swamp in Alabama. Forty-seven people died.

About ten miles east of Mobile, Alabama, Willie Odom peered through the thick fog over the Mobile River. The skipper of a tug, the *Mauvilla*, which was towing six heavy barges upstream, he had completely lost his bearings. With no chart or compass, it was impossible to check his position, and his radar equipment wasn't helping as he didn't know how to use it properly. So he was unaware that he was gradually deviating from the main shipping channel and heading for the mouth of a small tributary not normally used by commercial river traffic. This creek, the Big Bayou Canot, was straddled by a bridge carrying the main railway line. Lost in the fog, Odom did not notice that a barge he was towing had hit a steel pier that supported the railway bridge.

Meanwhile, the Amtrak transcontinental service *Sunset Limited*, with more than 200 people on board, was trundling through the night at a comfortable 70 miles an hour. A few minutes earlier, the train had pulled out of Mobile on the final leg of its 3000 mile journey from Los Angeles to Miami via New Orleans – the so-called 'Scenic Southern Route'. Most passengers were asleep or dozing as dawn approached. A few people were still awake in the restaurant car, including two of the train's guards.

> *'I looked to my right – and saw water gushing into the carriage.'*
> ONE OF THE SURVIVORS OF THE BIG BAYOU CANOT RAILWAY DISASTER.

A SHOCKING AWAKENING

When the *Sunset Limited* reached the bridge at 2.54 am on September 22, 1993, the damaged pier buckled under the weight of the three locomotives pulling the train. The engines plunged into the water, dragging the baggage and dormitory cars and two of the six passenger carriages with them. The fuel tanks ruptured and the diesel ignited the baggage and dormitory cars. In an instant the quiet creek was transformed into a nightmarish scene of twisted metal, sinking railway carriages and burning diesel fuel. Inside the wrecked carriages that had fallen into the water, people were fighting for their lives. Many drowned; others were killed by fire and smoke. Some people were crushed by huge pieces of wreckage – including the train driver, who lay buried under one of the locomotives deep in the muddy riverbed.

The passengers in the rear part of the train had been violently shaken when the front carriages came uncoupled and the train ground to a halt – but at first they had no idea of their lucky escape. As the sun came up, it became clearer what had happened, but the scene took on a new, dangerous dimension – one of the carriages, which had come to a stop right at the far end of the wrecked bridge, was threatening to topple into the river. Disaster was averted by the two guards who had been in the restaurant car – maintaining calm and order, they managed to lead the passengers in the four rear carriages to safety.

One of the guards then radioed for help. At almost the same time, the US Coastguard received a distress call from the tugboat. A rescue operation swung into action, with helicopters, divers and river boats, including the *Mauvilla*, taking part. The creek water was so muddy that it was virtually impossible to see anything, so the rescuers – aware of the possible proximity of alligators and poisonous snakes – were often forced to rely solely on their sense of touch. It was a slow business salvaging the bodies from the wreckage, not helped by the lack of a proper passenger list. By evening it emerged that 42 of the passengers and five train crew had been killed; 103 passengers had been injured. The tug's crew of four were unhurt.

The public reaction was one of outrage. How could such an accident possibly have happened? The search for answers revealed the shocking truth – under existing law, tugboats were not required to carry accurate navigation equipment, or even to have a properly qualified skipper on board. A few weeks after the accident, safety legislation was passed addressing these loopholes – too late for the 47 unfortunate victims of the *Sunset Limited*.

2004: a bad year for railways

Iran
February 18, 2004: In the Iranian city of Nishapur, a freight train carrying chemicals and petrol exploded, killing 300 people.

North Korea
April 22, 2004: Two trains carrying fuel blew up in the city of Ryongchon, North Korea, killing 161 and injuring 1300

United Kingdom
November 6, 2004: A high speed train hit a stationary car at Ufton Nervet, Berkshire. Seven people were killed, 100 injured.

Sri Lanka
December 26, 2004: A packed passenger train, the *Queen of the Sea*, on the island of Sri Lanka was swamped by the tsunami created by the 2004 Indian Ocean earthquake, with the loss of 1800 lives. This was the world's worst rail disaster.

The
destruction
of Halifax

On December 6, 1917, a minor collision caused a munitions ship to blow up in the Canadian port of Halifax. It was the largest man-made explosion until the dropping of the atomic bomb on Hiroshima in 1945.

The small port of Halifax on the east coast of Canada may have been far removed from the battlefields of Europe during the First World War, but its large natural harbour was crowded with wartime shipping – loading cargo, awaiting convoys or under repair. Freighters assembled there every week before crossing to Europe in convoys escorted by warships. Halifax was easy to protect and defend: every evening at sunset its bottleneck entrance channel was simply blocked by anti-submarine nets to stop enemy U-boats from entering. It also prevented the passage of ships in or out of the harbour.

On December 5, 1917, the *Mont Blanc*, captained by Aimé le Médec, arrived just too late to be let into the harbour. At the same time an empty Norwegian freighter, the *Imo*,

The northern part of Halifax, including the cathedral, was worst hit. The explosion completely destroyed more than 1630 homes; 12,000 houses were badly damaged and 6000 people were left homeless.

under Haakon From, was due to embark for New York to pick up relief supplies for Belgium, but because of delayed coal supplies, this ship had also missed the sunset shutdown. On hearing that the *Mont Blanc* would have to spend the night at anchor outside the port, its captain was alarmed. His ship had more than 2400 tonnes of explosives in its holds and there were drums of benzene stacked on deck. Moored offshore, the ship was a sitting target.

A BATTLE OF WILLS

At daybreak on December 6, 1917, the *Mont Blanc* weighed anchor and headed in towards the narrow harbour mouth. At the same time, the *Imo* was heading out. The entrance and exit of ships through the passage known as the Narrows was strictly controlled. Whether entering or leaving, vessels were meant to keep to starboard, and also to maintain radio contact – taking independent evasive action if necessary.

As she made for the harbour mouth, the *Imo* found her passage blocked, so she moved over to the opposite channel – the channel that the *Mont Blanc* was using. The *Mont Blanc* signalled that she intended to hold her course and that the *Imo* should give way – but the *Imo* signalled that she, too, was maintaining her course. After a flurry of unresolved negotiations,

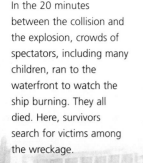

In the 20 minutes between the collision and the explosion, crowds of spectators, including many children, ran to the waterfront to watch the ship burning. They all died. Here, survivors search for victims among the wreckage.

the *Mont Blanc* saw only one option – to swing to port across the bows of the *Imo*. As soon as the *Imo*'s captain realised what was happening he signalled evasive action – 'full steam astern' – to his engine room. But the *Imo*'s propellers churning the water in reverse dragged her out into the middle of the channel. Her bow crunched into the *Mont Blanc* creating a shower of sparks which ignited vapour escaping from the drums of benzene on deck.

As soon as they saw the flames, the *Mont Blanc*'s crew knew that their cargo would explode within minutes. They lowered the lifeboats and rowed towards the far shore. Their screams of warning went unheeded – the people on the quay were enjoying the spectacle – and probably didn't understand French. As the ship burned, crowds of spectators gathered to watch. And the burning ship drifted towards the industrial north end of Halifax.

THE SHIP GOES UP

At 9.05 am the fire reached the explosives. In a blinding flash more than 1900 people were killed. Around 9000 more were injured and an area of half a square mile was flattened. Much of the area burnt to the ground, fuelled by overturned stoves and cellars stacked with winter coal. The explosion blew in every pane of glass for miles around. Shock waves were reported as far away as Sydney in Cape Breton, 270 miles to the northeast. The impact also triggered a tidal wave that washed up the shoreline, sinking small vessels and funnelling up Tufts Cove (due north of the explosion) where there was a tiny native American Mi'kmaq settlement. It was swept away by the man-made tsunami.

In Halifax, the bewildered survivors were in a state of shock. Most were convinced they were under German attack, so when the truth emerged there was some comfort in the knowledge that there would be no more explosions. Troops, sailors and hundreds of volunteers organised a huge relief effort. Much of the aid came from the people of Massachusetts, who shipped medical staff and supplies, food, clothing, transport – and even glass and glaziers – from Boston. Halifax still presents Boston with a giant Christmas tree as a thank you for their help in December 1917. And every year, at 9 am on December 6, a memorial service is held close to where the *Mont Blanc* exploded.

Escape from an underground tomb

The collapsed mine
workings at Lengede the
day after the accident.

In November 1963, eleven German miners were rescued
from a collapsed mine, having survived 14 days
underground. Their emergence, witnessed by more than
450 journalists, attracted worldwide media attention
and became known as the 'miracle of Lengede'.

On October 24, 1963, 129 men clocked on at the Mathilde pit at an iron mine at Lengede, northwest Germany. For some, it would be the longest shift of their lives. Others would never emerge.

The iron extraction process required a lot of water, so to cope with the demand, a number of artificial lakes had been created right above the underground workings. At 7.30 pm, close to clocking-off time, all the lights went out and the conveyor belts carrying the mined ore shut down. At first the miners blamed an electrical short circuit – irritating but not a major problem.

They had no idea that the base of one of the lakes above them had ruptured and tonnes of water and mud were cascading into the galleries and tunnels beneath. But as soon as they heard the unmistakable roar of floodwater, they knew they were in trouble. Frantically, the men looked for an escape route, climbing, crawling, wading and swimming – some even knocking together a makeshift raft. A few hours later, 79 men emerged safely. But 50 miners were still trapped.

A rescue team was assembled. Mining engineers and surveyors pored over maps and documents and ordered urgent delivery of specialist drilling and rescue equipment. They believed that there could be survivors near to where the water had entered the mine. Their first test bore was on target. Forty metres below ground, the team found and rescued seven miners.

THE FAINTEST SOUNDS OF LIFE

There was hope for others, too. Sudden flooding will push any remaining air up into the higher reaches of a mine, where it forms pockets and stops water from entering. Four men had been working in one such area. But two days after the flood, time was beginning to run out. The rescue team sank another borehole. There was jubilation when they detected the faint noise of someone tapping on the drilling rod. But the men would have to

Major pit disasters

China, 2005
On February 15, 2005, a gas explosion 250 metres below ground in a coal mine in the 'rust-belt' of north-east China killed at least 203 workers.

Germany, 1962
The worst catastrophe ever to hit the Saar coalfield in West Germany took place on February 7, 1962, at the Luisenthal pit near the town of Völklingen, when a firedamp explosion killed 299 miners.

Wales, 1913
An accident at the Universal Colliery, at Senghenydd in South Wales, took the lives of 439 miners on October 14, 1913. Just 12 years previously, 81 miners were killed in an incident at the same mine.

wait in the darkness for five more days before the drilling team could make a shaft wide enough to get them out.

It was essential for the rescuers to maintain pressure in the air pocket and prevent water from gushing in. This would happen as soon as the pressure was released, so throughout the operation, pressurised air was pumped in. Then a special device known as a Dahlbusch bomb was sent down to retrieve the trapped men. The narrow, torpedo-shaped steel capsule could hold one man at a time. Each man had to squeeze into the narrow tube before being hoisted to the surface. Three of the four came out alive. They then spent several hours in a de-pressurisation chamber before being released.

By November 1, 1963, eight days after the accident, the management of the mine was about to wind up the rescue operation – convinced that no one else could have survived underground for so long.

Rescue shaft

Supply shaft

c.57m

Initial shaft (aborted)

Water table

As quickly as possible, three shafts were sunk into the 'Old Man' pit to try and reach the men still trapped in one of its underground caverns.

LIFE IN THE 'OLD MAN' YET

But some men were still alive. On the night of the accident, 21 miners had taken refuge in the 'Old Man', a long-abandoned exhausted seam. The passageways were no longer propped up and were in danger of collapse, but the men had no choice. They inched cautiously upwards as the flood waters rose behind them, eventually reaching a dead end. Then they all squeezed into a cavern measuring just six metres by three. The air quality was so poor that breathing was difficult. All of the men developed headaches and became drowsy through lack of oxygen. They began to fall asleep; some were crushed and killed by falling rocks and boulders as they slept.

The survivors were woken by a gust of fresh air. A compressed air line somewhere in the mine had probably ruptured, allowing the men to breathe. Meanwhile, the lamps on their helmets had gone out, the matches they carried were wet and their cigarette lighters out of fuel. Though the miners could breathe they were still in total darkness. They gradually became unbearably thirsty. Although there was water all around them, it was undoubtedly contaminated by the putrefying bodies. In the end they were so desperate for water that they took the risk and drank. They then tried to make themselves heard by blowing a piercing whistle and yelling as loudly as possible. But when it became clear that nobody could hear them, they lapsed into silence.

A MIRACULOUS RESCUE

Ten days after the accident, 11 miners were still alive. But despite growing pessimism from the management team, not everyone on the surface had abandoned hope. Some of the miners were so insistent that, under similar circumstances, they would have tried to escape into the 'Old Man' that the mine's manager agreed to investigate the area. No accurate maps of the obsolete workings were available. Instead, a borehole was drilled in a spot based on an educated guess. When the drill hit the tracks of the mine railway they knew they must be in roughly the right area, so they moved the drilling operation over by a few metres.

Suddenly, the drilling team burst through to an underground cavern, 55 metres deep. From there, knocking sounds began to reach the surface – ten full days after the disaster. The rescuers lowered a small lamp down the hollow tube of the drilling rod, followed by a pencil and pad on which all the survivors wrote

The miners trapped at Lengede were rescued with the so-called Dahlbusch bomb. The device was named after the Dahlbusch colliery in Germany where it was first used in 1955 to rescue three miners from a depth of about 900 metres after an underground fire.

down their names. The tube, just 6cm in diameter, became a vital supply line for the trapped men. Articles of dry clothing were shoved down it, as well as tea and food in narrow containers and finally, a microphone.

Meanwhile, police stopped and turned back the lorries that had started to carry the heavy rescue equipment away from Lengede. The main drilling teams were also brought back on site. Even now, it was by no means certain that the men would be saved as the roof above them could collapse at any moment – but although the manager of the mine gave the operation only a 50-50 chance of success, the press was already talking excitedly about the 'miracle of Lengede'.

> *'We had a choice: either drown where we stood or get crushed to death in the "Old Man".'*
>
> FROM THE MEMOIRS OF BERNHARD WOLTER, A SURVIVOR OF THE LENGEDE PIT DISASTER.

At 6 am on November 7, the main rescue shaft reached the cavern. Two miners went down with the Dahlbusch bomb to help their colleagues out. When the 11 survivors emerged into the light after 14 days underground, they had to shield their eyes behind dark glasses. Photographs and television footage of their rescue were broadcast worldwide. But though the men were glad to be alive, none could forget their 29 dead colleagues – one of whom was never found and still lies buried somewhere in the depths of the mine.

The great North Sea floods of 1953

In 1953 a devastating storm surge swept through the North Sea, flooding the English and Dutch coasts, causing loss of life and widespread devastation. Both countries were ill-prepared for the impact of the storm, and even the elaborate Dutch sea defences were easily breached. In the aftermath of the disaster, new flood control programmes were rapidly put in place.

There seemed nothing particularly unusual about the storm that raged along the Dutch coast on January 31, 1953. For some people, including 10-year-old Ko van Oeveren, it even marked a welcome change from the previous day. In the village of Stavenisse, in southern Holland, the young boy cycled to the harbour on a stormy Saturday afternoon to ride his bike through the waves as they broke over the quayside.

On the morning of February 1, the flood tide retreated and the water level dropped. Some people were still trapped on the roofs of their houses and boats were used to paddle down flooded streets looking for survivors.

But by the evening, the inhabitants of Stavenisse noticed with alarm that the sea was encroaching ever closer to their houses. At around midnight, Ko's father made emergency preparations: as their house was situated on top of a dike he asked several relatives, who lived on lower-lying land, to spend the night with them. A total of 11 people, the family's six chickens and small pig, were holed up in the building as it was surrounded by a foaming tide. Finally, the water also reached their house, flooding the floor to a depth of 30 centimetres. To save the piglet from drowning, Ko's father had to hold the frantic animal's head above the rising water. On Sunday morning, the ebb tide brought some welcome relief.

Many other people living on the Dutch coast were less lucky. Zeeland, the low-lying area of islands and reclaimed land at the confluence of the Rhine, Meuse and Scheldt estuaries was worst hit by the storm surge. Without warning, the North Sea snatched back from the Dutch land they had taken centuries to reclaim.

TAMING THE NORTH SEA

The Dutch word for 'flood' is watersnood or 'water peril', a term that encapsulates the misery of those in the regions inundated by the surge. Throughout the history of the Netherlands, there had been catastrophic watersnoods caused by a sudden rise in

A low hill surmounted by a windmill turned out to be the last bit of dry land left as this small village on the Dutch coast was inundated. When the dikes broke at about 4 am on February 1, people awoke to thunderous noise and rushed to their rooftops. Just a few people saw the water coming and found a high spot before it reached them.

either the North Sea or the country's major rivers. The second St Elisabeth Flood hit the area around Dordrecht in southern Holland in November 1421, destroying 30 villages, while the All Saints' Day Flood of November 1570, claimed at least 20,000 lives in the affected regions.

By the winter of 1953 these devastating floods were ancient history. The entire Dutch coast – with no chains of dunes to act as natural high-water barrages – was protected by high dikes, built to exacting standards. The low-lying land, or polders, that lay behind the sea dikes had once been drained by windmills, now supplanted by efficient new diesel pumps.

A long-cherished dream of the Dutch, to dam the Zuyder Zee behind sea dikes, had been realised. The former sea inlet, created by storm surges in the Middle Ages, was now partly absorbed into the IJsselmeer, a shallow freshwater lake, and partly reclaimed as fertile polder land. It seemed that the North Sea had been tamed, and the Dutch were now far better equipped against its ravages. The Meteorological Service could detect the approach of deep lows while they were still far out in the Atlantic and raise the alarm in good time when a real emergency threatened. In general the Dutch felt secure behind the dikes; but on this occasion their confidence was misplaced.

Storm surges in the North Sea

Orford Ness, 1897
During a heavy storm one mile of the shingle spit at Orford Ness in Suffolk was washed away.

Thames Estuary, 1928
A northerly gale raised water levels in the Thames Estuary so high that London was flooded. In Southwark, Westminster and Hammersmith, the embankments were overtopped by water. When a section near Lambeth Bridge collapsed, water rushed into the basements of nearby houses so quickly that 14 people drowned.

Hamburg, 1962, 1976
315 people were killed, and a further 15,000 made homeless, in a storm surge that hit Hamburg on February 16–17, 1962. When the century's worst flood hit the same spot in 1976, although sea levels were higher than in 1962, there were no deaths – a result of improved sea defences.

AN UNDERESTIMATED LOW

On January 30, 1953, off the coast of Iceland, a marginal low developed. But it barely figured on meteorological charts, so a severe weather warning was not issued. Over the course of the day it shifted southeast and entered a zone where cold air from the Arctic and warm subtropical air from the south mingled as though in a whirlpool. The low quickly reached hurricane force, buffeting the northeast of Scotland on January 31 with winds at speeds of up to 112 miles an hour. As it crossed over the North Sea from the Shetland Islands and approached Denmark, the whirlwind pushed huge volumes of water southwards. As the water entered the relatively shallow waters of the North Sea, it created a tidal surge, which flowed in an anticlockwise direction.

> *'The waves were gigantic; I had never seen anything like them before.'*
>
> KO VAN OEVEREN

At 4 pm on January 31, the surge hit Scotland, reaching the coast of the Netherlands at 4 am the following day, where hurricane-force gusts at speeds of up to 90 miles an hour were measured. The extreme wind speeds were the lesser problem: the rising sea level, which hit a record high in the southern part of the North Sea where it funnels into a narrow strait, was far more serious.

AN UNPRECEDENTED CATASTROPHE

Across the North Sea, in England, the floods were the worst natural disaster ever recorded. A total of 307 people were killed the mainland with a further 224 at sea. At Felixstowe on the Suffolk coast, where hurricane force winds were recorded at 8 pm, 38 people died when their wooden 'pre-fabs' were flooded. Canvey Island in Essex was inundated with a loss of 58 lives.

Waves over 6 metres high swept over the Lincolnshire coast. The Stranraer–Larne railway ferry *MV Princess Victoria* was lost at sea in the North Channel east of Belfast with 135 fatalities and many fishing trawlers sank. Floodwaters even breached sea defences to reach London's East End, inundating 1000 homes. Flooding forced the evacuation of 30,000 people and 24,000 properties were seriously damaged. While many communities had emergency plans, gales had brought down telephone lines and the co-ordination required for a large-scale evacuation was not in place. There was almost no warning of the impending disaster.

At the Hook of Holland, the mean tide level was exceeded by more than 3 metres, while the water-level indicator at Amsterdam rose to almost 4 metres above its usual mark. Even the strongest dikes could not withstand such an onslaught. They were breached at several points on the morning of February 1, and such was the force of the floods rushing through them that they gouged holes up to 15 metres deep and flooded 1250 square miles. The consequences were terrible. In the Netherlands alone, more than 1800 people were killed; 70,000 people were evacuated, an estimated 200,000 animals drowned and around 4000 buildings destroyed, with 45,000 more badly damaged.

The Netherlands has spent huge sums on a massive hydraulic engineering project – including these flood barriers at Hagestein on the Rhine – to enable better flood control in the future. Three giant sea walls, called storm surge barriers, protect the fragile inlets and dikes. The barriers remain open in normal weather, but during a storm surge 63 hydraulic-powered sluice gates, each 6 metres tall, keep the rising waters out.

FUTURE PROSPECTS

In the UK the floods caused a national outcry. The Government implemented a programme to build and strengthen sea defences. Nearly 30 years later, in 1982, the Thames Barrier programme was finally completed, intended to protect London from any future calamity. An inquiry into the disaster recommended that a flood warning organisation should be set up, and the Storm Tide Forecasting Service was established, providing 24-hour forecasts of tidal surge and wave activity.

The 1953 storm surge shocked the Netherlands to the core. The first result of the disaster was that people completely lost confidence in their coastal defences. There was a determination to make the sea defences absolutely effective by implementing the Delta Plan on the estuaries of the Rhine, Meuse and Scheldt rivers. For more than 40 years, huge amounts of money were invested in this massive hydraulic engineering scheme, consisting of high dikes and ingenious storm flood weirs, which open and close automatically as required on the sea side when tidal currents are flowing. The opening mechanism is just as important as the closing mechanism that prevents sea water entering, since the danger of flooding often comes from Holland's rivers overflowing inland at times of storm surges.

Yet the greatest danger still comes from the sea. The level of the North Sea has risen inexorably for more than a century, and by the end of the 21st century, the water level could be 50–60 centimetres higher than it is today. The number of severe storm surges is increasing, and in places the coastline will recede by an average of more than 4 metres a year. Even with all the technology now at our disposal, there is no comprehensive and final defence against the forces of nature.

They changed the world

12

The legacy of a genius

Leonardo was not simply a painter, even though he was one of the foremost artists of the Italian Renaissance. In his parallel career as an inventive genius he anticipated a host of modern innovations, from the tank to the helicopter.

When Leonardo da Vinci died in 1519, contemporaries mourned the passing of a genius who had come to epitomise the spirit and ideals of the Renaissance. Yet this celebrated public figure was at the same time one of the most enigmatic and secretive characters of his day.

Leonardo was a brilliant painter, but he often became 'bored of working with the brush' and left many of his canvasses incomplete. Possibly because he found it hard to work for people in positions of authority, he seldom finished a commission successfully. His quick mind led him to make or foresee many important scientific discoveries, but he never published his ideas. A gentle vegetarian who loved animals, he despised war, yet spent a considerable part of his career devising weaponry that could maim or kill.

RISING TO GREATNESS

Born on April 15, 1452, in the small town of Vinci, just outside Florence, Leonardo was the illegitimate son of Ser Piero d'Antonio, an ambitious 25-year-old notary, and a peasant girl,

Caterina. Shortly after the boy's birth, his father took
legal custody of him and he was brought up by his paternal
grandparents for a few years until his father realised that the
woman he had married could not bear children of her own. He
then took Leonardo into his own home to raise and educate him.
Even as a young boy, Leonardo showed extraordinary talent. He
learned to play the lyre and sing beautifully, and was often found
sketching animals and plants.

A UNIVERSAL GENIUS

In 1468, when his grandfather died, Leonardo's family moved
to Florence. Leonardo's father realised that his son had unusual
artistic gifts and apprenticed him to Andrea del Verrocchio, a
renowned painter, sculptor and goldsmith, who was the most
sought-after Florentine artist of the day. The foremost artists and
thinkers in the city were habitués of his studio. Even as a humble

Leonardo da Vinci died
in the presence of King
Francis I of France, at
least according to this
romanticised 19th-century
portrayal of the scene. In
fact, Francis was away at
the time, celebrating the
birth of his second son.

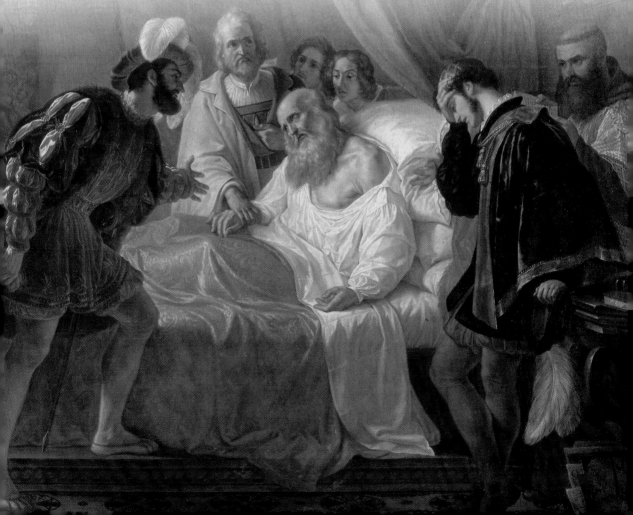

A wooden model of a bicycle was constructed on the basis of Leonardo's sketches, but few of his many inventions were made in his lifetime.

apprentice he was quick to demonstrate his phenomenal talents. He contributed an angel to his master's *Baptism of Christ*. The result was so superior to the rest of the painting that Verrocchio apparently resolved never to paint again.

In 1477, Leonardo decided to strike out on his own. In 1482 he applied for a post at the court of Ludovico Sforza, Duke of Milan, abandoning *The Adoration of the Magi*, his first important commission in Florence, when his application succeeded. In his letter, Leonardo stressed his military expertise, claiming that he could provide the Milanese forces with everything from 'bombards, mortars and fire-throwing engines' to 'catapults, mangonels, trabocchi or other unusual machines of marvellous efficiency.' In time of peace, he could give his master 'as complete satisfaction as anyone else in architecture, in the construction of buildings both public and private, and in conducting water from one

> '*There are some people…who leave nothing behind in this world except full privies.*'
>
> LEONARDO DA VINCI

place to another'. Finally, he could 'execute sculpture in marble, bronze or clay and also painting in which my work will stand comparison with that of anyone else whoever he may be'.

Leonardo mentioned his artistic talents almost as an afterthought. He obviously believed that his abilities as an engineer would count for far more in the duke's eyes. From 1485 until he returned to Florence in 1499, he delved into a host of subjects, including the workings of nature, flying machines, geometry, mechanics, canals and architecture, designing everything from churches to fortresses. The weapons included embryonic designs for a tank and ideas for the design of submarines. His interests, talents and abilities seemed limitless.

SCIENTIST AND INVENTOR

Leonardo's experiments in anatomy were truly revolutionary, as was much of the other work he undertook in fields as far removed as zoology, botany, geology, optics, aerodynamics and hydrodynamics. Starting while he was still in Milan and accelerating from around 1505, he became more and more wrapped up in his scientific investigations.

Leonardo would go to extreme lengths to ensure accuracy. Paolo Giori, his first biographer, wrote 'in the medical faculty, he (Leonardo) learnt to dissect the cadavers of criminals under inhuman, disgusting conditions...' Leonardo himself vividly described his ordeal 'living through the night hours in the company of quartered and flayed corpses fearful to behold'.

His insatiable curiosity pushed him onwards. The result was a vast collection of notes on a bewildering variety of topics, from the nature of the Sun, Moon and stars to the mysteries of flight. He nurtured a passionate dream of being able to ascend into the sky and gain a view over the whole external world. For years, he immersed himself in studying the anatomy of birds and the mechanics of their flight. His designs for parachutes and flying machines were a portent of the future, even though his ideas did not get beyond the drawing board. Not until 1783 was man's dream of flying realised with the Montgolfiers' hot-air balloon.

Leonardo's interest in human anatomy is evident in his famous drawing showing the proportions of the body. His biographer recalled that he dissected bodies 'because he wanted to draw the different deflections and reflections of limbs and their dependence on the nerves and joints. This is why he paid attention to the forms of even very small organs, capillaries and hidden parts of the skeleton.'

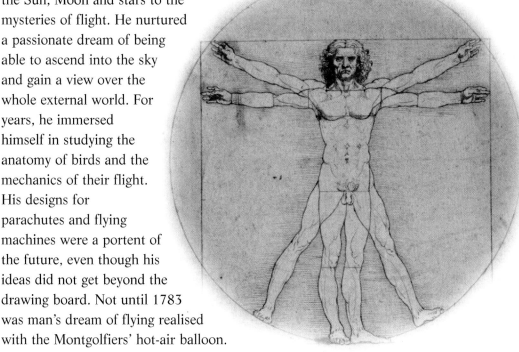

LEONARDO'S LEGACY

In 1516, following the death of his patron Guiliano de Medici, Francis I of France offered Leonardo the post of Premier Painter, Engineer and Architect of the King. Francis provided him with a generous stipend and a comfortable manor house near the royal chateau at Amboise. Although his right hand was partially paralysed as the result of a stroke, he could still draw, teach and theorise. He died in May 1519, leaving a remarkable legacy.

From the 1490s onwards, Leonardo had recorded his studies in meticulously illustrated notebooks. Some 13,000 drawings survived him. In his will, Leonardo left all his manuscripts, drawings, instruments and tools to Francesco Melzi, one of his surviving pupils. Melzi made it his life's work to conserve and archive his former master's legacy, not an easy task given his master's lack of organisation. In addition, fearing that spies might steal his ideas, Leonardo drafted all his notes in mirror writing and encrypted them in self-devised codes.

When Melzi died in 1570, Leonardo's effects passed to his son, who gradually realised what a treasure trove he had inherited, and turned it to his financial advantage. He sold off Leonardo's papers piecemeal – and as a result we now only know the whereabouts of around half of the notebooks. Most are in public collections around the world, while a few are in private hands.

By striving to combine the arts and the sciences, Leonardo sought to provide answers to the great, universal questions. At the same time, he was a compulsive perfectionist, who rarely saw anything through to completion. For the constant driving force behind everything he created was the conviction that he could never quite capture the essence of what he was trying to portray.

A catalogue of masterpieces

Mona Lisa
The enigmatically smiling *Mona Lisa* (c.1503) is the world's most famous painting.

The Last Supper
The fresco (1497) in Milan's Santa Maria delle Grazie has engendered endless debate as to its symbolism and meaning.

Designs for sculpture
Leonardo came up with bold, innovative solutions for his monumental *Equestrian Statue of Francesco Sforza* (c.1485–99). But the actual statue was never completed.

Architectural influence
Leonardo's designs for buildings helped shape the course of architecture throughout the 16th century.

Cartography
Leonardo's maps of Tuscany are some of the earliest examples of modern cartography.

Metal
war machines

New weapons, first the crossbow and longbow and later firearms and cannon, ended the days when armoured knights could charge to triumph almost at will.

The devastating hail of arrows loosed off by the English longbowmen rained down on the French knights as they ploughed across the mud, trampling their own advance guard of Genoese crossbowmen in their eagerness to charge. English arrows punched through the armour worn by the French, sending them plunging to the ground en masse.

Even warhorses were protected by plates of heavy armour.

As the contemporary chronicler Jean Froissart wrote, they 'fell like snow'. Edward III of England had wrongfooted the numerically superior French with his revolutionary tactics. His battle plan relied on the deployment of archers, who, firing from concealed positions, decimated the ranks of the French knights with wave after wave of deadly fire. Edward's force of 3000 skilled archers were each loosing between 10 and 20 arrows a minute. Charge after charge was repulsed until the French, who had come prepared for a conventional fight, man-to-man and knight-to-knight, were forced to withdraw in total defeat.

For the first time in history, bows and arrows had trounced a powerful mounted army. Philip VI of France was forced to flee the field, leaving as many as 1500 French noblemen dead, while countless others were captured.

A knight's apparel

Undergarments
Generally made of linen, they comprised the *braie*, a form of breeches worn by knights, leggings, and a shirt.

Extra padding
A thickly quilted garment known as a *gambeson* was worn beneath the armour; it insulated the wearer against cold and also served as padding.

Chain mail
The next layer was a slip and collar of chain-mail, made from hundreds of steel eyelets and rings linked together.

Protecting the extremities
The splints protecting the arms and legs, plus the *sabatons* (overshoes), the gauntlets, the breastplate, and the helm – which together formed the external pieces of armour – were all made of iron. These provided the knight with full protection against enemy weapons.

A MILITARY REVOLUTION

The battle of Crécy on August 26, 1346, marked the beginning of the end for knightly armour, at least as an effective mode of defence on the battlefield. It also signalled a decisive shift in battle tactics. After Crécy, the pendulum swung away from mounted knights in favour of infantry, supported by detachments of longbowmen and crossbowmen.

The change was revolutionary – not least because it happened so quickly. In the Crusades, in which knights had won glory championing Christianity in the Holy Land, the mounted knights were like invincible metal leviathans, impressing friends and foes alike. An early 12th century Muslim chronicler recalled: 'They were clad from head to toe in armour made from a material that appeared to be composed of linked iron rings. They seemed to form a single iron phalanx off which our blows glanced harmlessly.'

Although the French army was superior in numbers, it met disaster at the Battle of Crécy in 1346 when confronted by Edward III's longbowmen.

Even then, there were weapons to which armour was vulnerable. Not for nothing did the Second Lateran Council forbid Christians to employ longbows and crossbows in battle against their fellows in 1139, though, as things turned out, the ban proved ineffectual.

ARMED FOR COMBAT

Along with a suit of armour and an array of weapons, medieval knights needed at least three horses: a specially trained warhorse, a horse for journeying, and a packhorse to carry their gear. All this cost a fortune. At the end of the 11th century a chain-mail vest could cost between 20 and 100 oxen, a general purpose horse five to ten oxen, while a warhorse might cost 25 times that. Both on the battlefield and at tournaments, an opponent's horse and armour were highly prized items of booty.

As the penetrating power of weapons increased, armour became more extensive and costly. In the mid-13th century, with the more widespread use of crossbows, forged helmets and chain-mail vests were supplemented by pieces of armour made of sheet iron. Over time, this extra protection was itself augmented by breastplates and pauldrons (shoulder pieces), splints covering the arms and legs, and helmets with visors that could be opened when required. Full body armour for battle could weigh between 25 and 35 kilograms. A helmet alone weighed 3 kilograms. Jousting armour, worn for short periods, could weigh double this, so that the wearer had to be hauled onto his horse by a rope and pulleys, or manhandled into the saddle by a squire. Battle was physically demanding: when fighting in hot weather, knights wearing helmets might faint from lack of oxygen.

ARMOUR FOR POMP AND DISPLAY

The first tournaments were devised in the early 11th century to allow noblemen to engage in trials of strength with one another. Though the Church tried to ban jousting, just as knights were starting to become obsolete as a fighting force, tournaments were establishing themselves as an indispensable feature of courtly life.

The suits of armour created for tournaments were masterpieces of precision craftsmanship, of the kind centred on Milan, Augsburg, Nuremberg and Innsbruck from the 13th century onwards. They reflected the fashions of the time as well as trying to meet and beat developments in offensive weaponry.

DECLINE TO A STATUS SYMBOL

The widespread adoption of firearms in the mid-17th century saw most troops abandon iron armour, since it was so unwieldy to wear and of little practical use against the new weapons. Just as the knightly epoch was drawing to a close, however, armour for sheer display experienced a revival, with magnificent pieces of armour and accoutrements produced specifically for festivals and tournaments. What had once been practical protective clothing was now worn for prestige, as at the meeting of Francis I of France and Henry VIII of England at the Field of the Cloth of Gold in 1520. Tilts, jousts and other chivalric entertainments were the order of the day, and temporary fountains were plumbed to flow with red wine for the duration of the discussions.

On occasions like these, armour still had a value. What it no longer had to prove was its worth on any battlefield.

A miracle cure for malaria

When quinine was first brought to Europe in the 17th century its efficacy against malaria was hailed as nothing short of miraculous.

At the beginning of the 17th century malaria was widespread through much of Europe as well as the tropics. It was a much feared disease with no known cure. People did not know that the disease was caused by a protozoan parasite transmitted in the bite of the female *Anopheles* mosquito. But they had noticed that it was associated with marshes and stagnant water, and so called it 'marsh fever'. The illness began with flu-like symptoms and general malaise, progressing to bouts of nausea and high fever, often resulting in death. With no effective medicines at their disposal, all that physicians could do was try to alleviate the raging temperature.

> '*There is a tree growing in the vicinity of Loxa that the natives call the "Fever Tree".'*
>

Then in 1631 news arrived in Europe of a miracle cure from the high Andes of South America. Doña Leonor, the wife of the Count of Cinchon, Viceroy of Peru, had been terribly ill for several days, her body consumed first by a raging fever and then an icy chill. The Viceroy's personal physician told him that only a miracle could save his wife. But then a Jesuit priest arrived and administered a bitter-tasting white powder to Doña Leonor. One month later the Countess of Cinchon had made a full recovery.

The powder came from the bark of a tree found only in the Andes. In 1638 an Augustinian monk wrote: 'Its cinnamon-coloured bark, if ground to a fine powder with a weight equal to that of two silver coins and administered in a drink, can cure fevers, and has already achieved some marvellous results in Lima.' The Swedish naturalist Carolus Linnaeus, famous for his system for classifying plants and animals, later gave this genus of tree the name *Cinchona* in honour of the Countess.

MEDICINE FROM THE FOREST

Of course, Doña Leonor's recovery was no miracle. The ground-up bark contained quinine, which killed the protozoan pathogens. But how did that Jesuit priest arrive at the idea of giving quinine to the sick countess? One legend recounts how a man with malaria went to quench his raging thirst by drinking from a small pool. Two *Cinchona* trees had fallen into the pool, and so the man ingested the medicine as he drank. According to another theory, the people of the Andes had long used the bark as a remedy for fevers and it would have been an obvious choice to alleviate the symptoms of malaria. Whatever way it was discovered, it was the Jesuit missionaries who brought *Cinchona*'s anti-malarial properties to the attention of the Europeans.

A CATHOLIC MEDICINE

During the 17th century the Jesuits favoured distributing the remedy widely. The theologian and later Cardinal Juan de Lugo was charged by Pope Innocent X with the task of gathering information about the bark of the *Cinchona* tree. He had a sample examined by the Pope's personal physician, Gabriele Fonseca, who was impressed by the curative properties of the powder. Thereafter, Lugo became a powerful advocate for the use of quinine. His influence, and the Jesuits' monopoly of the drug, gave quinine its nicknames: 'Cardinal's powder' and 'Jesuit bark'.

But a medicine that was so strongly promoted by the Catholic Church soon aroused suspicions. A rumour was circulated in England that a dastardly Popish plot might be behind the bitter powder. When Oliver Cromwell came down with a high fever in 1658, he vehemently refused to take the 'Jesuit medicine' and died from the effects of malaria. But Charles II of England and the French king Louis XIV, were both cured by quinine.

SUCCESSFUL MONOPOLIES

In Europe demand soared and anyone who traded in quinine was assured of a healthy profit. Governments also became interested. The drug was crucial to European efforts to colonise malaria-infested regions. With all of the precious bark coming from South

The largest factory in Africa for the manufacture of quinine is in the Democratic Republic of Congo. Because exposure to large doses of the drug over a protracted period can lead to quinine poisoning, the workers at the plant have to wear protective masks when handling the fine powder.

America, Europeans began to ask why they shouldn't simply cultivate the valuable trees in their own colonies.

In the mid-19th century Dutch, French and English expeditions set off to the Andes on a mission to gather saplings and seeds from the *Cinchona* tree and smuggle them out of the country. If caught the smugglers faced certain death, since Peru, Ecuador, Colombia and Bolivia were desperate to retain their monopoly of the trade. Even so, many botanists took part and did manage to acquire some of the coveted saplings. But it was not easy to establish a profitable plantation on a commercial scale. The Dutch were the first to do so, on the Indonesian island of Java, and by the 1930s were responsible for supplying almost all the world's quinine.

QUININE IN WAR

Quinine was much sought after during the Second World War. In 1940, Hitler's armies overran the Netherlands and requisitioned the country's large quinine stocks. When the Japanese conquered Java and the Dutch East Indies two years later, they cut off the supply of quinine to the Americans and British. Thousands of Allied soldiers stationed in Africa, Burma and the South Pacific began dying of malaria. In response the US government sent tropical botanist Raymond Fosberg to the Andes to find bark. The *Cinchona* bark he managed to acquire was transported to America by plane and the Allies secured around 6000 tonnes of bark in the last years of the war.

After the war, the importance of *Cinchona* seemed to be on the wane, as various synthetic drugs for combating malaria came onto the market. But malaria-inducing pathogens have a tendency to quickly develop resistance to synthetic drugs, so doctors today still have frequent recourse to the proven natural medicine quinine.

Other miracle medicines

Vaccination against smallpox
In 1796, English physician Edward Jenner performed the first successful vaccination against smallpox.

Penicillin
In 1928, Alexander Fleming discovered penicillin, the first antibiotic. The drug was effective in combating all manner of infectious diseases such as septicaemia, pneumonia and puerperal fever.

Prozac
In 1988, Ray Fuller and the team at Eli Lilly launched Prozac (fluoxetine hydrochloride), a drug that would revolutionise the treatment of depression.

A
wonder drug
conquers the world

While trying to develop a
remedy for his father's
rheumatism, the chemist Felix
Hoffmann created aspirin.
The painkilling drug was
an overnight success and
remains one of the world's
most widely used medicines.

For millennia, herbalists the world over
have known about an effective cure for
a headache. From the ancient Egyptians
to Native Americans, healers swore by
the painkilling effect of the same remedy:
steep some willow bark in boiling water
and drink the liquid. As early as 400 BC,
the ancient Greek physician Hippocrates
recommended willow extract as a way
of reducing fevers (an antipyretic)

It is widely accepted
that Felix Hoffmann
discovered acetylsalicylic
acid (ASA), although in
1949 a colleague, Arthur
Eichengrün, claimed that
it was his idea to
synthesise the drug.

and relieving pain (an analgesic). But there was just one problem with the healing willow extract: it was extremely bitter and those who did manage to swallow it suffered intense nausea and an inflamed stomach lining.

A BITTER PILL

In 1859, while working at Marburg University in Germany, the chemist Hermann Kolbe discovered the chemical structure of salicylic acid, willow bark's active ingredient. He developed a process by which it could be synthesised and mass production of the drug began in 1874. But although the laboratory-made salicylic acid was considerably cheaper than the equivalent natural product, it retained the unpleasant side effects and bitter taste of the original.

The demand for aspirin went through the roof. By 1938 production lines churned out thousands of packets of aspirin a day.

One recipient of the synthetic salicylic acid was the father of Felix Hoffmann, a young German chemist. Afflicted with rheumatoid arthritis, Hoffmann senior relied on the drug, but had grown thoroughly fed up with its side effects. It was his constant nagging for an improved formulation that led Felix Hoffmann to make one of the most important pharmaceutical discoveries of the 19th century.

A METICULOUS CRAFTSMAN

Born in 1868, Felix Hoffmann began his career working in various chemists' shops before going on to study pharmacy and chemistry at the University of Munich. In 1894, armed with a letter of recommendation from Nobel Prize winner Adolf von Baeyer, Hoffmann secured a position at the pharmaceutical laboratory of Friedrich Bayer & Co in Elberfeld.

He quickly set about satisfying his father's request. They used the technique of 'acetylation', or causing a substance to react with acetic acid. In this process, an acetyl group bonds to the original molecule, thereby altering the chemical structure of the substance. The research team at Bayer had already used this method to create or improve a number of different medicines. Hoffmann suggested that they try making salicylic acid react with acetic acid. French chemist Charles-Frédéric Gerhardt had already succeeded in bonding salicylic acid with an acetyl group in 1853. But he had not managed to produce pure acetylsalicylic acid (ASA) and had given up on the idea. After studying Gerhardt's experiments, Hoffmann persevered and on August 10, 1897, managed to produce ASA in a pure form.

'America is the country where you can buy a lifetime supply of aspirin for one dollar and use it up in two weeks.'

JOHN BARRYMORE, AMERICAN ACTOR

In pharmaceutical terms, the process was a huge success. Even so, the Bayer pharmacologist responsible for testing new drugs was sceptical at first. The head of the laboratory is reputed to have been the first person to swallow the new powder to find out how palatable it was. He then conducted a series of experiments on animals and then on patients at a nearby hospital to investigate its efficacy and possible side effects. The results were unequivocally positive: the substance had analgesic, antipyretic and anti-inflammatory properties, while the side effects were noticeably less severe than those of salicylic acid. Felix Hoffmann's father was a happy man indeed.

ASPIRIN SPANS THE GLOBE

Bayer & Co felt sure they were on to a winner. But when the company tried to patent the drug in Germany, the application was refused on the grounds that ASA was not a new invention but merely a spin-off of Gerhardt's original work. The decision left Bayer with only one option: to register the painkiller as a trademark at the Imperial Patent Office in Berlin. In 1899, the drug was registered as 'Aspirin'. 'A' stands for acetyl; 'spir' comes from the former scientific name *Spiraea* for the meadowsweet flower; while '-in' is a commonly used ending in chemical names.

The painkiller was originally available only in powder form, and was sold in glass bottles. But as early as 1900 the first aspirin tablets appeared on the market. People all over the world began to take aspirin as an effective remedy for fever and headaches, inflammatory ailments and rheumatism. By 1909, the sales of aspirin accounted for a third of Bayer's total turnover.

IT WORKS – BUT HOW?

Aspirin was clearly an effective drug, yet for a long while no one had any idea how the drug actually worked. It was only at the beginning of the 1970s that the British pharmacologist John Robert Vane from the Royal College of Surgeons in London described aspirin's precise effect on the human physiology. For this research, Vane was awarded both the Nobel Prize for Medicine in 1982 and a knighthood. Vane discovered that ASA suppresses the body's production of prostaglandins. These chemicals have various functions within the body. They are involved in the development of fever, pain and inflammation in the body, regulate the expansion and contraction of blood vessels and influence the movement of platelets in the blood. Since Vane's discovery, ASA has also been prescribed in small doses for the prevention of heart attacks and strokes. If all the aspirin produced in one year was processed in the form of 500mg tablets, these would make a chain that stretched from the Earth to the Moon and back again.

Aspirin: a great success story

The record-breaking pill
In 1950, aspirin earned an entry in the *Guinness Book of Records* as the best-selling drug in the world. Bayer produced its ten-billionth aspirin tablet on September 15, 2000, at a facility in Bitterfeld, Germany. Today, patients worldwide take more than 40,000 tonnes of acetylsalicylic acid (ASA) annually.

Aspirin on the Moon
When the Americans made their Moon landing in 1969, mission commander Neil Armstrong's small first-aid kit aboard Apollo 11 contained aspirin.

On top of the world
Aspirin played its part in a successful ascent of Mount Everest in 1992, when it was used to alleviate headaches brought on by altitude sickness.

The bloody reign of the Catholic monarchs

Ferdinand of Aragon and Isabella of Castile conquered Granada, Spain's last Muslim stronghold, expelled the Jews, and financed the explorations of Columbus. Was their motive religious, or was religion just a convenient cover for their secular ambitions?

Under a clear winter sky, Isabella, sole surviving child of John II of Castile, rode in state through the streets of the city of Segovia, wearing a white brocade dress trimmed with ermine. Two servants held the reins of her grey mare, resplendent in a golden bridle. Ahead rode the Marquis of Moya, his sword held aloft, symbol of the monarch's absolute power of life and death.

Because of the power of Ferdinand and Isabella's joint kingdoms, their daughters, including Joanna of Castile and Catherine of Aragon, married with several European dynasties, setting the bases for the great heritage of their grandson Charles V.

In the centre of the market square a rostrum had been hastily erected. Around it, representatives of the nobility gathered. There on the morning of December 13, 1474, Isabella swore to uphold the laws of the Catholic Church, preserve the freedoms and privileges of the nobility, serve the common good of the realm, and to ensure that justice was administered fairly. Thereupon, she was proclaimed 'Queen and Protector' of Castile.

It was the second major political move that Isabella had made in her short life. Like its predecessor – her marriage to Ferdinand of Aragon – it was carefully conceived and skilfully executed. Even Ferdinand was taken by surprise by the speed with which she acted. He had been visiting his father's court when he learned of his brother-in-law's death and did not return to Castile in time for the coronation. When he finally did arrive, he discovered to his annoyance that he had been referred to as his wife's 'rightful consort', and had not been given any real power in the governing of the realm. Even though Isabella eventually agreed to give Ferdinand the title of 'king consort', she made it clear that this was an honorific concession and she remained the sole incumbent of the Castilian throne. After all, as she pointed out, she had fought tooth and nail to get there.

'I, the Queen.'

ISABELLA OF CASTILE'S CUSTOMARY SIGNATURE

A FIGHT FOR THE THRONE

Isabella was only three years old when her father died. Her mother, Isabella of Portugal, brought her up in relative seclusion until Henry IV, her half-brother, brought her to court at the age of 13, along with Alfonso, her full brother. Henry claimed that he wanted to supervise the closing stages of Isabella's education, but in reality his aim was to prevent the two royal children becoming rallying points for Castile's turbulent and discontented nobility.

Henry's machinations were unsuccessful. The nobles rose in an attempt to secure the crown for Alfonso. Defeat at the Battle of Olmedo in 1468 and Alfonso's death shortly afterwards – it was popularly believed that he had been poisoned – did not end their intrigues. Deprived of their first leader, they turned to Isabella as their new candidate for the throne. Although Isabella rejected their offer of the crown, Henry eventually gave into their pressure. In September 1468, he recognised Isabella as his sole heir and excluded Joan, his own daughter, from the line of succession. In any event, Joan was widely held to be illegitimate and, so her opponents argued, was unfit to be queen.

Then came the added complication of Isabella's marriage plans. Back in 1460, Henry had offered his half-sister's hand to Don Carlos, the eldest son of John II of Aragon and also heir to the kingdom of Navarre. John opposed the match, favouring instead her marriage to his younger son, Ferdinand. The fruitless negotiations dragged on, ending only on Don Carlos's death in 1465. Henry immediately turned to Alfonso V of Portugal as a suitable replacement. Other possible candidates were Richard, Duke of Gloucester, brother of Edward IV of England, and the Duke of Guienne, brother of Louis XI of France. Again he ran up against an insuperable obstacle. This time, it was Isabella herself.

Now 17, Isabella had a mind and will of her own. She knew what she wanted and was determined to get it. She defied her half-brother, telling him that she was determined to marry her cousin Ferdinand, now heir to the throne of Aragon. Furious, Henry threatened her with imprisonment in the Alacazar in Madrid, but she still stubbornly refused to fall in with his plans. But he did exact from her a promise that she would not enter into any matrimonial negotiations until his return from a campaign he was about to wage in Andalusia.

A CLOAK-AND-DAGGER MARRIAGE

Isabella had no intention of keeping her word and was swift to take advantage of the opportunity presented by Henry's absence. With the assistance of the Archbishop of Toledo and Don Fadrique Enriques, the High Admiral of Castile, she left the court under the pretext of visiting her mother. Eventually, she arrived in the city of Valladolid, where she waited impatiently for her husband-to-be to meet her.

When Isabella of Castile died in 1504, she had established Spain as a major European power, and through her sponsorship of Columbus paved the way for the expansion of Spanish influence throughout the Americas.

Ferdinand, too, took pains to conceal his tracks. With a great show of formality, he and his father left Zaragoza, the capital of Aragon, ostensibly to put down a revolt in Catalonia. No sooner were they out of sight of the city than father and son parted company. The latter, in disguise, set off towards Castile. Six days later, the bridegroom set eyes on his wife-to-be for the first time.

The marriage took place on October 19, 1469. The wedding was a low-key affair, held in the presence of just a few carefully chosen guests. There may well have been a good reason for this. Because Ferdinand and Isabella were cousins, Pope Paul II had to sanction the marriage, but the haste with which the ceremony had been arranged left no time to get his approval. The letter that purported to give his assent that the Archbishop of Toledo read out at the wedding was a forgery. Luckily for Ferdinand and Isabella, the Pope was happy to give his blessing retrospectively.

UNITING THE KINGDOMS

Even after her coronation, Isabella's hold on the Castilian throne was not secure. Before he died, the vengeful Henry had repudiated the agreement making her his heir. He reinstated Joan, by this time married to the Alfonso Isabella had spurned, as his rightful successor. The result was a five-year civil war, with Portugal supporting Joan. It ended with the defeat of the Portuguese and Joan's Castilian supporters in 1479 and her decision to retire to a convent the following year.

This 19th-century Spanish painting portrays the Catholic kings offering prayers of thanks at the scene of their greatest triumph – the capture of Granada, the last Muslim stronghold on Spanish soil.

By this time, Ferdinand had succeeded to the throne of Aragon. The way was clear for the two monarchs to achieve their ultimate ambition: the unification of Spain under strong monarchical rule. They agreed that they would hold equal authority in their respective countries and the motto coined to describe the new arrangement: *Tanto monta, monta tants – Isabel como Fernando* (As much as the one is worth so much is the other – Isabella as Ferdinand), summed it up succinctly. Their rule ushered in what came to be regarded as Spain's golden age.

Ferdinand and Isabella's first priority was to curb the power of the nobility and the priests, who had taken advantage of a series of weak rulers to become almost independent of the Crown. They set up the *Santa Hermandad* (Sacred Brotherhood), a permanent security force that could be called upon to support them whenever the need arose, and used every means at their disposal to bring them to heel.

Neither the king nor the queen would countenance any interference. They were determined to establish the absolute authority of the crown. They needed loyal administrators to help them keep order while they embarked on the last stage of the great *Reconquista*, the subjugation of the Moors in southern Spain,

The task took them a decade to complete. On January 6, 1492, Granada, the last Muslim stronghold on the Iberian Peninsula, finally fall. From a vantage point outside the city, Ferdinand and Isabella watched as the cross and the coat of arms of Castile were raised on the highest minaret of the central mosque. But the campaign had not been motivated purely by missionary zeal, even though Ferdinand and Isabella had been granted the title of 'Most Catholic' monarchs by Pope Alexander VI, himself Catalan by descent. First and foremost, it was a

The *Reconquista*

The *Reconquista* was the campaign by the Christians to wrest control of the Iberian Peninsula from the Moors, who had invaded the region in 711. The campaign had its first major successes in the 11th century under kings Sancho III of Navarre and Ferdinand I and Alfonso VI of Castile and Léon.

Steps on the road to *Reconquista*
Under Pope Alexander VI, key moves were made by the rulers of Castile in the interior, the kings of Portugal along the Atlantic coast (to 1297), and by the kingdom of Aragon along the Mediterranean coast.

A time of little progress
There was a stalemate between the sides for most of the 14th and 15th centuries.

Final success
With the capture of the Andalusian city of Granada by Isabella I of Castile and Ferdinand II of Aragon in 1492, the *Reconquista* was finally completed.

In 1492 Ferdinand and Isabella ordered the expulsion of the Jews from Spain. Although those who had converted to Christianity were allowed to remain, they were soon subjected to renewed persecution.

political stratagem to forge a strong bond between Aragon and Castile. Such a union, it was felt, would also instil in the Spanish people a feeling that they were participating in a defining moment in world history – Christianity's last great crusade.

DISCOVERING THE NEW WORLD

Among the cheering crowd witnessing the event was the Genoese-born explorer Christopher Columbus. Rejected in his native Italy and in England and Portugal, he had come to Castile to solicit Ferdinand and Isabella's support for his planned expedition across the Atlantic to seek out a new route to the Indies. His plea fell on fertile ground.

In the wake of the successful *Reconquista*, Ferdinand and Isabella were eager to spread the knowledge of Christianity to hitherto uncharted territories. The queen agreed to provide the necessary funding for Columbus' expedition. On August 3, 1492, three ships crewed by 87 men put to sea. They sighted land on the far side of the Atlantic just 36 days later – possibly the first Europeans to reach what was to become known as the New World. Before long, what had started as a daring voyage of discovery became a systematic campaign of conquest and colonisation as the Spanish began to carve out a vast empire in the newly discovered Americas. Two years after Columbus's epic voyage, Pope Alexander VI divided the whole of the unexplored world between Spain and Portugal in the Treaty of Tordesillas.

THE TERROR OF THE INQUISITION

At home, Ferdinand and Isabella were determined to
enforce strict religious conformity, which they saw as essential
to achieving national unity, particularly as the country was
home to two significant non-Christian communities. The first
of these to be put under the spotlight were the Jews, despite the
longstanding Spanish tradition of tolerance towards them. In
1492, a decree was issued ordering their expulsion. Those who
had converted to Christianity – known as *converses* (New
Christians) – were not left in peace for long. They were suspected
of secretly continuing to observe the rituals and customs of their
former faith.

Over time, the persecutions spread wider. In 1502, another
law required Muslims to convert to Christianity or to emigrate.
A vague suspicion or an anonymous tip-off was enough for
investigations to be launched and files to be opened. Torture
and the threat of burning
at the stake were favourite
methods of extracting
confessions. In this way, the
Spanish Inquisition became
established in the Iberian
Peninsula. With the

*'Destroyers of the Mohammedan
sects and extinguishers of all
heretical falsehood.'*

INSCRIPTION ON THE TOMB OF ISABELLA I AND FERDINAND II

infamous Tomás de Torquemada as its first Grand Inquisitor, it
reached a terrible crescendo. The Inquisition gained a foothold
as an instrument of royal power throughout the realm.

THE ROYAL LEGACY

Isabella died in 1504 and Ferdinand, who survived until 1516,
assumed the regency of the kingdom. Joanna, Isabella's elder
daughter and heir, had gone mad following the death of her
mother. His annexation of the kingdom of Navarre in 1512
fulfilled the dream he had shared with his wife. Spain now
stretched from the Pyrenees to the Rock of Gibraltar.

Working successfully together, Catholic monarchs laid the
seeds of future Spanish greatness. It was to be their successors –
bequeathed immense lands and seemingly limitless riches – who
squandered their great legacy.

Dutch scientist Christiaan Huygens took timekeeping to new levels of accuracy with his pendulum clock. His early clocks had an error of just a minute a day, later refined to just 10 seconds a day.

When time began to tick

The earliest civilisations had ways of measuring time but their methods were cumbersome and imprecise. When 13th-century monks developed the mechanical clock, timekeeping became more accurate, with a fundamental effect on the way people ran their lives. Clocks even inspired philosophers to come up with a completely new concept of the universe.

It is hard to imagine a world without clocks; they synchronise our lives, determine when we get up, go to bed and everything we do in between. Clocks have had a huge influence on the development of society and the world of work. Because they enabled precision of measurement, great leaps in scientific progress followed.

THE SUN AND THE MOON

Ancient astronomers – in Babylon, ancient Egypt, India, China and South America – divided time into days, months and years by following the movements of the Sun and Moon. To break the day into smaller units, a stick was placed in the ground. Over the course of the day, the length and angle of the shadow cast by the stick changed. A person could use it to tell the time either by the length of the shadow or by its position on a predetermined scale. Sundials of this type were used in ancient Mesopotamia, Egypt and Greece. The makers of the rudimentary instruments introduced many improvements over the course of the centuries. But sundials were useless at night and in bad weather.

WATER, FIRE AND SAND

Simple water clocks were an alternative. A container was filled with water, a small hole made in its base with a scale on the inside. As the liquid trickled through the hole, the time that passed could be read off from the water level as it went down the scale. The

'Everybody's got a watch, but nobody has any time.'

AUSTRIAN POET ERNST FERSTL.

ancient Greeks called such water clocks *clepsydra*, or 'water thieves'. Fire was also used to measure time. Passing time was calculated by observing tapers or joss-sticks as they burned down or the falling level of oil in a burning lamp. Or a candle with a scale marked on the side would be lit.

In the Middle Ages, two equally sized glass vessels were joined one above the other with a narrow tube and the top half was filled with fine sand. The sand would take a specific amount of time to trickle into the lower container. For several centuries, these hourglasses were used to measure the duration of jousts

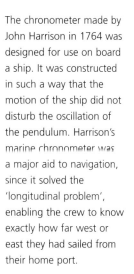

The chronometer made by John Harrison in 1764 was designed for use on board a ship. It was constructed in such a way that the motion of the ship did not disturb the oscillation of the pendulum. Harrison's marine chronometer was a major aid to navigation, since it solved the 'longitudinal problem', enabling the crew to know exactly how far west or east they had sailed from their home port.

and duels, court hearings and sermons. Their popularity waned with the arrival of mechanical clocks, although they are used today as egg-timers.

THE INVENTION OF TICKING

Monasteries were run according to a strict timetable, with prayers or 'offices' being said at certain prescribed times. Monks used sundials, water clocks and marked candles, announcing important times to the community by ringing bells. From the end of the 13th century, church records and other historical documents testify to the use of mechanical clocks in monasteries.

The basic principle of the clock had been known since the 9th century. A weight attached to a coiled rope was dropped so that the momentum it generated could be used to drive a system of gearwheels. In turn, the gears could drive a hand. The only component missing was a form of brake to control the rate of fall of the weight so that the mechanism and the hand attached to it could move forward in steps and at regular intervals. The solution was two metal plates, known as pallets, set at right angles to one another and mounted on a spindle known as a foliot that swung to and fro. Known as an escapement, this mechanism was used by the monks in their early clocks at the end of the 13th century. It controlled the motion of a gearwheel, arresting it for a moment and then releasing it so that the momentum of the weight could drive the mechanism forward a step. As it moved and the next tooth of the gearwheel hit the locking surface on the escapement, it produced a sound that still symbolises the passage of time: the ticking of the clock.

THE SEARCH FOR PRECISION

The new timepieces were displayed on the facades of cathedrals, monasteries and in grand houses. It was not long before the striking of the hour by the town hall clock signalled the start of the working day and meetings of the town council. People began to gear their lives to the hands of the clock. In the early 16th century, a German locksmith called Peter Henlein invented spring-powered clocks. Without heavy weights, clocks could be smaller and more portable, but they slowed down as the spring unwound. In 1657, Dutchman Christiaan Huygens built the first pendulum clock. It was known that a pendulum of a given length always oscillated at a regular frequency. Once this principle was applied to maintaining a steady rhythm in the motion of clockwork mechanisms, timepieces became more accurate.

A MECHANISTIC VIEW

The invention of the clock was so revolutionary it set philosophers' minds to work. Humans had built an 'automaton' – an instrument that could move itself – using not witchcraft but the principles of physics. Did the same physical laws that governed clockwork mechanisms also apply to the whole universe? Perhaps other unexplained phenomena had also arisen through this form of pure physics – and the universe was nothing more than a vast machine with God as the celestial clockmaker. Ideas such as this formed part of the 'mechanistic' view of the world that was popularised by philosophers such as René Descartes and physicists like Isaac Newton in the 17th century.

Advances in timekeeping

The pendulum clock
The most accurate pendulum clocks, produced in the 20th century, lost or gained only a few seconds over the course of a year.

The quartz clock
It was not until 1929 that pendulum clocks began to be surpassed in their accuracy by quartz clocks. These deviate from the real time by just half a second a day.

The atomic clock
The first atomic clock was developed in 1949. The most accurate atomic clock yet constructed is inaccurate to one second in three million years.

The
best deal
of all time

Colonised by the Russians at the end of the 18th century, Alaska was a source of valuable sea otter pelts. Stocks of sea otters rapidly declined and the vast region seemed little more than an encumbrance when it was sold to the USA for a song in 1867. But the territory turned out to be a goldmine.

Baron de Stoeckl (right), the Russian ambassador, and Henry Seward, the US Secretary of State (seated) negotiated the price to be paid for Alaska.

On July 20, 1741, the *Sviatoi Piotr* (Saint Peter), sailing from Kamchatka under the Russian ensign, dropped anchor off the southern coast of Alaska near Kayak Island. Vitus Bering, the ship's Danish captain, dispatched a landing party in two boats. Their mission was to replenish fresh water supplies from streams on the island. The expedition's German doctor and naturalist Georg Wilhelm Steller planned to conduct research in the new territory. His time was limited: the commander of the expedition allowed him just ten hours for a brief reconnaissance sortie – but he made a significant discovery – that of the sea otter. Bering, like many of his crew, had contracted a severe case of scurvy. He was critically ill and keen to embark on the return journey.

Vitus Bering and the discovery of Alaska

The first Kamchatka expedition
In 1724, Tsar Peter the Great sent the Danish explorer Vitus Bering to explore the eastern fringes of Siberia. This enterprise went down in history as the 'First Kamchatka Expedition'.

The discovery of the Bering Strait
In 1728, Bering proved beyond doubt that Asia was separated from America by a strait, subsequently named the Bering Strait in his honour.

The second Kamchatka expedition
From 1733, Bering commanded the 'Second Kamchatka Expedition'. It explored Siberia and Kamchatka and discovered the northwest coast of America – Alaska.

The expedition led by Bering and the Russian captain Alexei Chirikov, set out from St Petersburg in February 1733. Russian rulers had instigated a number of expeditions in the 18th century to find out more about the remote regions of Siberia and the northern Pacific coastline. The tsars' curiosity had political and economic motivation. The most precious commodities from the far east of the Russian empire were the pelts of animals such as sable and silver fox. On reaching the Pacific Coast, the explorers came across an intriguing new species. Steller described the mammal: 'A living sea otter is both graceful and beautiful to look at and has a lively, playful character. All in all, it is a very engaging and affectionate animal. When you see a sea otter running, the sheen on its pelt is more luxuriant than that of the blackest velvet.' His comments were to become the sea otter's death sentence.

MERCILESS HUNTERS
The onward journey of Bering and his crew from the Alaskan coast was plagued by ill fortune. It was not long before the men

Majestic Mount McKinley in Denali National Park in Alaska, is the highest peak in North America, at 6198 metres. Much of Alaska lies within the Arctic Circle, with perennially frozen ground, or permafrost. The region is still largely untamed wilderness, although there are concerns about the environmental impact of oil extraction on the North Slope oilfields of Prudhoe Bay.

on board the ship, who were weakened by the ravages of scurvy, had lost their bearings completely. They were forced to spend the winter on an uninhabited island, one of the Commander Islands that lie off Russia's Kamchatka peninsula. Many of the sailors succumbed to the disease, including Bering himself. A few finally managed to make it back to the far eastern seaboard of Russia in 1742, where they recounted how they had found an untapped resource of animals with superb pelts.

These observations stimulated the first 'rush' to affect the northwestern corner of America. As early as 1743, fur trappers appeared on the uninhabited island where Bering had died, by now named after him, and then proceeded east along the Aleutian Islands chain, reaching the mainland of Alaska by 1761. Their travels yielded rich spoils. Towards the end of the 18th century, well over 20,000 sea otter pelts were coming onto the market every year. The main market for the skins was found among the Chinese aristocracy.

In Russia, the tsars skimmed off their share in the lucrative fur trade by imposing excise duty on the indigenous hunters. In America the exploitation of stocks of fur-bearing animals was turned over to commercial societies that were granted a trading monopoly in return for a handsome fee. The Russians soon recognised that they would gain greater profits if they could convince skilled native hunters to work for them. They used highly questionable tactics to force Aleut hunters to bring them valuable sea otter pelts by taking women and children hostage. For the Aleuts, supplying the Russians with sea otter pelts was the only way of securing their families' safety.

The first commercial society was incorporated in 1781, and three years later the first permanent Russian settlement was established near the modern town of Kodiak. The Russian-American Company was founded in 1799, and determined Russian colonial policy in the New World up until 1867. Tsar Paul I conferred on the company the exclusive right to trade in North America north of the 55th Parallel and made it responsible for administering all settlements in Alaska, which was now given the official status of a Russian colony.

RUSSIAN AMERICA

Little now remains of the period of Russian control in Alaska apart from a few churches and numerous place-names. The actual number of Russian colonists in North America never exceeded 1000. Yet when the Russian trappers first set foot on the American continent, around 62,000 indigenous people were living in the territory, primarily Inuit, Aleut and other American Indian tribes. It soon became clear that it was not just the sea otters that were going to suffer under their new masters. The native inhabitants of Alaska were enslaved and forcibly relocated, and were banned from building the canoes that they needed for hunting. Diseases introduced by the newcomers killed the indigenous population in

396

The Inuit, one of the aboriginal peoples of Alaska, inhabited a vast Arctic region from the Bering Strait to Greenland. The Russians exploited their hunting skills, and their numbers were depleted by violence and by the European diseases they contracted from their unwelcome visitors.

their thousands. In a period of just 80 years, the Aleut population of Alaska fell from 16,000 to 2000, not least because the wholesale destruction of the sea otters deprived them of a vital source of food. Sea otters were not the only stocks of native fauna that were depleted by the relentless hunting. The Russians also pursued the Bowhead whale. In no time, they had decimated the population of this animal as well, inflicting terrible hardship on the traditional Inuit whale hunters.

Over the course of the 19th century the decline of the sea otters is clearly reflected in fur trading statistics: while around 20,000 pelts were still coming onto the market in 1820, by 1900 this figure had dropped to just about 600. In western Alaska, the sea otter was almost wiped out over the course of a few years. The Russian-American Company was forced to look for new hunting grounds, pushing south down the Pacific coast of America as far as present-day California. Here, the Russian-American Company encroached on territory already being exploited by Americans, Spaniards and Britons and conflict appeared imminent. As a foreign-policy expedient Tsar Alexander I was forced to curtail the influence of the company, which reverted simply to governing Alaska. But the territory was no longer turning a profit, and it was not clear what the rulers of Russia should do with it. Furthermore, holding on to Alaska might conceivably make them powerful enemies in the wider world.

THE TROUBLESOME COLONY

His successor, Tsar Alexander II had grown tired of pursuing ventures overseas. Maintaining his colony on the North American continent was proving a costly enterprise, and the income it generated had by now slowed to a trickle. The high cost of Russian defeat in the Crimean War (1853–56) had emptied the state coffers. But what was to be done with a colony of 585,000 square miles? The tsar decided to sell off the vast territory. The next question was to whom? The USA had already proved itself an eager and reliable purchaser. In 1803 it had acquired more than 772,000 square miles of land from France in the Louisiana Purchase. Half a century later it had bought almost 30,000 square miles from Mexico in the Gadsden Purchase. The tsar authorised the Russian Minister to the United States to enter into negotiations over the sale of Alaska.

'Seward's Icebox.'

POPULAR US NICKNAME FOR ALASKA IN THE LATE 19TH CENTURY

A GOOD BUY

The purchase negotiations between Russia and the USA began in 1866, during the term of office of Andrew Jackson, the 17th President of the United States. Across the table from the Russian ambassador to the USA, Baron Eduard de Stoeckl, the most senior negotiator on the American side was Secretary of State William Henry Seward. This was a lucky break for the Russians, for Seward, with his passionate commitment to the expansion of America, had a keen interest in acquiring Alaska for the USA. De Stoeckl was well aware that Seward was eager to strike a deal, and proved to be a skilful negotiator. In the course of the seemingly interminable discussions, which continued until the end of March 1867, de Stoeckl managed to drive the price up from the original offer by half as much again. Finally, on March 30, the price the two parties settled on was confirmed in Article VI of the signed treaty: $7,200,000, payable in the form of gold bullion. That worked out at five cents per hectare (two cents per acre) for the vast territory, or, at today's prices, around 30p per hectare. This still amounted to a very good deal for the Americans. They had paid France more than seven cents per hectare when concluding the Louisiana Purchase in 1803.

The deal provoked an outcry among the American public. Most citizens of the USA did not consider the purchase of Alaska to be a bargain. They regarded the region – which was out-of-the-way, completely undeveloped, and lay far to the north, separated from the rest of the Union by Canadian sovereign territory – as an utter waste of money. And so they dubbed the purchase 'Seward's Folly' and called Alaska 'Johnson's Polar-bear Garden'. Most delegates in the Senate and House of Representatives were opposed to the agreement. It took all of Seward's powers of persuasion and a degree of bribery to secure a narrow majority in favour of ratifying the treaty.

On April 9, 1867, the United States Senate ratified the treaty and on October 18 the stars and stripes was hoisted for the first time over the town of Sitka, founded by the Russians in 1804 as Novo Arkhangelsk. At the time of the handover it contained 116 small log cabins housing 968 residents. The Americans chose an Aleut name, 'Alaska', for the territory. It would be almost another century before Alaska was admitted to the Union as the 49th state, on January 3, 1959.

GOLD FEVER

To the great chagrin of the US government, the fears of citizens who were opposed to the purchase seemed to be borne out in the late 19th century. The new colony in the Arctic Circle generated almost no income. Some revenue came in from fishing, but the fur stocks, the 'soft gold' that had attracted the Russians to North America in the first place, were virtually exhausted.

All of a sudden the situation changed and a new sense of enthusiasm galvanised the territory. Gold was discovered under the permafrost-covered soil of the region's vast expanses. There had been a few isolated gold strikes previously, but no-one had paid them much heed. But when gold was found at Juneau in 1880, a new feeling of hope spread throughout the region. Prospectors went on to find gold in Nome in 1898, and at the Tanana River in 1903. Crowds of eager prospectors embarked on the long, arduous

'There are strange things done in the midnight sun By the men who moil for gold.'

ROBERT SERVICE
THE CREMATION OF SAM MCGEE

journey north, hoping to strike it rich overnight. It was only with this 'Gold Rush' that Americans became aware of the huge untapped potential of Alaska's mineral deposits. Secretary of State Seward died in 1872, but if he had lived to witness the development, he would surely have felt thoroughly vindicated.

The territory of Alaska, separated from Asia by a narrow strait, is also of great strategic importance. During the Cold War, it was a vital outpost of the United States in its trial of strength against the Soviet Union. During this same period other forms of mineral wealth were discovered, which nowadays generate huge revenues for major companies and the state alike: oil and natural gas. These energy resources were first found on the Kenai Peninsula, then at Cook Inlet, and, in the 1960s, along the coast bordering the Arctic Ocean. In 1969, a consortium of US oil concerns paid the state close to a billion dollars to secure the extraction rights. The state reviled as 'Seward's Icebox' had turned out to be a goldmine.

The scramble for white gold

A single cut in the bark releases a trickle of latex. The Indians of Central and South America had used latex for many centuries before Europeans discovered it in the 16th century. The Indian name for rubber, 'Caoutchouc', means 'weeping wood'. In Brazil *Microcyclus*, a fungal disease, has attacked the rubber tree. The plant has almost vanished from its native home, but still thrives in the Far East.

During the 19th century, precious sap tapped from Brazilian trees supplied almost all the world's growing rubber industry. In 1876 a British adventurer was persuaded to smuggle seeds of the tree, *Hevea brasiliensis*, out of the country. The transplanted Brazilian trees thrived in the British colonies of the Far East, eventually putting paid to the rubber boom that had made the Amazon rich.

For thousands of years, the Amerindian peoples of South America have haboured a secret – how to transform the sticky white sap exuded by the *Hevea* tree into an elastic material that could be used to make a variety of different objects. The sap, known as latex, was slowly coagulated on a pole turned over a smoky fire. The acid in the smoke caused the latex to harden. The crude rubber was formed into large balls, which were floated downstream to market. In the 19th century, Brazilian rubber 'barons' persuaded the Amazonian peoples to collect the latex, and through the indigenous people's expertise, the rubber tycoons were able to amass substantial fortunes.

RUBBER BOOM

The rubber barons were shrewd businessmen, determined to maintain their world monopoly of the product. The demand for the material, stimulated by the growing industrialisation of the west, sparked an unprecedented boom in Amazonia. In 1830, the production of natural rubber worldwide was just 130 tonnes. As demand increased towards the end of the 19th century, a pound of rubber cost nearly $3 on the world's commodity markets. Between 1890 and 1915 with increasing demand from burgeoning industries in the United States and Europe, enormous sums of money flooded into Amazonia and into the pockets of the businessmen.

Some of the money was invested in transforming Manaus, a settlement in the heart of the Amazon close to the source of the rubber, into a magnificently opulent city. Now the capital of the Brazilian federal state of Amazonas, Manaus lies on the Rio Negro, 11 miles from its confluence with the Amazon. Since the start of the boom, the town had an electric

The manufacture of rubber

Tree sap
Natural rubber derives from the milky sap (latex) of a genus of tropical plants that contains some dozen different species including *Hevea brasiliensus*.

Tapping the latex
A cut is made in the bark of the tree. Roughly every three days, the latex can be tapped for a total of two to five hours

Early uses of rubber
For centuries, the Amerindians of the Amazon used natural rubber to waterproof clothes and to make flexible water flasks.

Vulcanisation
Natural rubber became an enormously important raw material in 1839 when Charles Goodyear invented vulcanisation, a chemical process which turns uncured natural rubber into a smooth, malleable and versatile product.

power supply and boasted a tram network. Splendid public and private buildings were erected on streets laid out in a grid pattern. By the 1890s, Manaus had also acquired a racecourse, a bullring, 24 bars, 36 doctors, 11 fancy restaurants, and seven bookshops. Many Europeans contributed to the splendid architecture. The cast-iron framework for Manaus's covered market halls was commissioned from Gustave Eiffel, creator of the Eiffel Tower in Paris, while Waldemar Scholz, a German entrepreneur, built the showy Palácio Rio Negro, which today houses the Amazonas state assembly.

The rubber barons were able to indulge in the most outrageous luxuries. Waldemar Scholz was said to have a pet lion, a yacht, motorboat and elaborately liveried servants. Another tycoon, having commissioned a palace simply to house his race horses was so taken with it that he decided to move into part of the house himself. Others burned money to light their cigars and sent their laundry out to Europe.

The Teatro Amazon's exterior is a mixture of European architectural styles, surmounted by a prominent dome. Every fixture and fitting in the opera house, opened in 1896, is of the highest quality: crystal chandeliers from Venice, silk wall hangings from France, and precious hardwoods from the surrounding Brazilian tropical rainforests.

The Teatro Amazon is the city's crowning glory. Fitted out in a luxurious and eclectic style, the opera house is a testament to the dream of an eccentric adventurer. The story of the genesis of the Teatro inspired the film, *Fitzcarraldo*. In the film, an opera lover becomes obsessed with the idea of building an opera house in the jungle – a dream that ultimately turns to madness

> '*Manaus had actually become El Dorado. Gold flowed like water through its streets.*'
>
> VICTOR VON HAGEN

and despair. In real life, Manaus bears witness to the fact that his dream was realised, though only briefly, in the city's heyday at the end of the 19th century.

THE END OF THE RUBBER BOOM

Yet the rubber barons were soon to see their fortunes dissipate. British entrepreneurs were showing an increasing interest in the lucrative rubber trade. For decades Britain's Asian colonies had attempted to produce latex, spurred on by growing demand from an expanding manufacturing industry. But Asian latex did not match the quality of the Brazilian material; the Amazonian *Hevea* tree simply produced a better quality raw material.

In 1876 Henry Wickham, a British adventurer who had spent time in Amazonia, wrote to Kew Gardens, giving a glowing account of the properties of a plant native to the Amazon Basin – *Hevea brasiliensis*, or the rubber tree. His brief report excited Sir Joseph Hooker, the director of Kew; he wondered if Wickham's account held the key to solving a pressing economic and strategic problem. Hooker commissioned Wickham to collect 70,000 *Hevea* seeds from the Amazon Basin, smuggle them out of the country and ship them to Britain. It was a highly risky enterprise, since Brazil was prepared to execute anyone who tried to take even a single seed across her borders.

SEED SMUGGLER

That same year, Wickham embarked upon his daring quest. With the help of Amerindian guides, he gathered the seeds, packed them carefully between banana leaves and shipped the precious cargo to the botanists at Kew. The excitement among the plant experts was enormous. Could the seeds be the key to wresting the rubber monopoly from Brazil? Only around 4 per cent – 2800 – of the seeds eventually germinated. They were raised in the tropical greenhouse at Kew and shipped first to the island of Ceylon. From there seedlings were taken to Singapore. Recently developed bud grafting techniques enabled large numbers of identical trees to be produced. From 1898 onwards, *Hevea* trees formed the nucleus of large plantations, mostly in Malaya.

In 1888, Dunlop's invention of the pneumatic tyre had contributed to a seemingly insatiable worldwide appetite for rubber. As early as 1914, British horticulturalists developed ways of obtaining higher yields from the *Hevea* tree. British production soon surpassed that of Brazil and Asian plantations eventually supplied more rubber than all of South America. Malaya quickly became the main source of rubber for world industry, and as the raw material became more plentiful, the price fell dramatically. The Amazon's rubber boom was fatally damaged. In 1920, the price of rubber on the world's markets slumped almost overnight from $3 a pound to less than 20 cents.

At times, rubber was worth more than silver.

In 1920, Henry Wickham was knighted and given an *ex gratia* payment of several thousand pounds for his services. He was known to his close friends as the 'Father of the Rubber Industry' but to his enemies as the 'Executioner of Amazonia'.

Front cover t 1953 floods in Holland **357**
b Whale-hunting in the Arctic **255** l to r Buffalo Bill **261**
Aztec stele at temple of Quetzalcoatl **98** Inuit hunter **396**
Ché Guevara **55** Alexander the Great **278** Isabella of
Castile **383**
Back cover t Hun victory over the Alans in **372 114**
Cleopatra **297** l to r Sioux Chief Sitting Bull **261**
Muslims versus Crusaders **315** Chinese emperor Pu Yi **39**
Templar knight **73** Robert Capa **164** *Portrait of A
Grotesque Old Woman* by Quentin Massys **167**
Title page as for front and back covers
Introduction Czech explorer, Franz Behounek stranded
on the Arctic ice following the crash of the airship *Italia* **232**
Contents Chapter 1 Woman about to be drowned as a
punishment for murdering her child **25** Chapter 2 Orson
Welles and Joseph Cotton in *Citizen Kane* **66** Chapter 3
Still from the series *Roots* **94** Chapter 4 David Livingston
being carried by bearers **119** Chapter 5 Phoolan Devi and
her gang **130** Chapter 6 Dying Spanish soldier
photographed by Robert Capa **162** Chapter 7 The palace
at Knossos **197** Chapter 8 Julius Caesar and Vercingetorix,
leader of the Gauls **208** Chapter 9 The airship *Italia* **229**
Chapter 10 Cleopatra **297** Chapter 11 The destruction
of Halifax, Nova Scotia **350** Chapter 12 Leonardo da Vinci
on his deathbed **364**
12 and 13 Sipa/Koden **16** Corbis/Roger Ressmeyer
19 picture-alliance/akg-images **20** Interfoto/Karger-Decker
23 picture-alliance/akg-images/Erich Lessing **25** akg-images
26 Interfoto/Archiv Friedrich **29** Interfoto/Archiv Friedrich
31 akg-images **32** Interfoto/Archiv Friedrich **34** ullstein
bild/Archiv Gerstenberg **36-37** Corbis/Patrick Ward
39 picture-alliance/akg-images/Goldschmidt
40-41 Corbis/Yang Liu **43** Interfoto/Sammlung Karl Steiner
45 picture-alliance/akg-images **47** picture-alliance/dpa/
Abaca Ammar **49** picture-alliance/akg-images
53 Interfoto/Karger-Decker **55** picture-alliance/dpa/Peter
Endig **57** picture-alliance/dpa/epa **59** Corbis/Bettmann
60 ullstein bild/Nowosti **63** Look/Uli Wiesmeier
66 picture-alliance/akg-images **68** picture-alliance/dpa/UPI
70 Interfoto/Daniel **71 and 73** picture-alliance/akg-images
74 picture-alliance/dpa **76** picture-alliance/akg-images
78-79 and 82 akg-images **85** picture-alliance/akg-images
88 Interfoto/Archiv Friedrich **88-89** picture-alliance/dpa/
Chad Ehlers **91** picture-alliance/akg-images **93** dpa/Dieter
Klar **94** kpa **96** Corbis/Bettmann **98** Corbis/Paul Almasy
100 picture-alliance/akg-images **102** Corbis/Underwood
& Underwood **105** Corbis **107** ullstein bild/AP
109 l picture-alliance/akg-images/Erich Lessing
r SV-Bilderdienst/Scherl **111** Corbis **112** Interfoto/Zeit Bild
114 picture-alliance/akg-images **116** Wildlife/A. Visage
119 mauritius images/Steve Bloom Images **120** akg-images
123 ullstein bild/Granger Collection **124** Interfoto/D.H.
Teuffen **126** Ricardo Funes/AP/Empics **130** Sipa/Rex
Feature/Dieter Ludwig **132–135** Corbis/Sygma/Kapoor
Baldev **136** ullstein bild/Archiv Gerstenberg **138** Bridgeman
Giraudon **140** t Wildlife/D. Harms b ullstein bild/Granger
Collection **142** Interfoto/D.H. Teuffen **145** ullstein bild
146 Topfoto.co.uk **150** dpa/UPI/Joel Landau
151 Corbis/Bettmann/G.B. Kress **155** picture-alliance/dpa
157 picture-alliance/akg-images **158** akg-images

161 Interfoto/Victor Radnicky **162-164** Robert Capa 2001
by Cornell Capa/Magnum Photos/Agentur Focus
165 picture-alliance/dpa **167** The National Gallery
168 akg-images/Erich Lessing **170** t akg-images
b dpa/dpaweb/Jens Büttner **172** Superbild/Graefenhain
174 akg-images **177** akg-images **178-179** ullstein
bild/Leone **180** akg-images **184** ullstein bild/Archiv
Gerstenberg **184-185** mauritius images/age
186 Superbild/Incolor **188-189** Bilderberg/Rainer Drexel
191 action press/Oy Lehtikuva **192** action press/Christian
Augustin **195** t akg-images b Picture Press/camera press
196 Bilderberg/Wolfgang Kunz **199** Picture Press/camera
press **201** picture-alliance/Okapia/Willi Rolfes
202 laif/Christian Kaiser **208** Bridgeman Giraudon/
Musée Crozatier, Le Puy-en-Velay **211** Interfoto/Alinari
213 Corbis/Bettmann/Alexander Gardner
216 Corbis/David Muench **219** akg-images **221** Corbis
223 Avenue Images/Index Stock/David Carriere
226 and 229 akg-images **231 and 232** SV-Bilderdienst/
Scherl **232** Corbis/Bettmann **235** ullstein bild
236 picture-alliance/akg-images **239** b r Corbis/Bettmann,
background image mauritius images/Stock Image
240 and 242 Corbis/Bettmann **244-245** picture-alliance/
akg-images/Erich Lessing **247** Interfoto/Archiv Friedrich
248 Interfoto/Karger-Decker **250** picture-alliance/akg-
images **252** Corbis/Bettmann **255** akg-images
257 b Corbis/Bettmann, background image PhotoDisc
258 Corbis/Bettmann **261** Corbis/D.F. Barry
264-268 akg-images **270** akg-images/Cameraphoto
272 Interfoto/Baptiste **275-280** picture-alliance/akg-images
282 picture-alliance/dpa/Keystone/Alessandro Della Valle
284 picture-alliance/akg-images/Gilles Mermet
286 akg-images **289** Fan & Mross/Michael Schindel
290 akg-images/Gilles Mermet **292** akg-images
295 f1 online/Felix Agel **297** Corbis/Christie's Images
299 akg-images/Erich Lessing **301** picture-alliance/dpa
302 picture-alliance/akg-images **305** action press/Rex
Features **307 and 309** Corbis/Christel Gerstenberg
312 Bridgeman Art Library **310** Corbis/Araldo de Luca
313 b ullstein bild/Archiv Gerstenberg, background
image picture-alliance/akg-images/Tarek Camoisson
315 akg-images **318-319** Corbis/Dorothea Lange
321 Corbis/Bettmann **322** Corbis/Bill Stormont
324-325 Corbis/The Mariners' Museum **327** dpa
329 dpa/UPI **331 and 332** Corbis/Bettmann **335** dpa
338 dpa/epa/Victor Drachev **341** ullstein bild/ddp
343 ullstein bild/Reuters **344** ullstein bild/Chaperon
346 AP **349 and 350** Corbis/Bettmann **352** ullstein
bild/dpa **357** action press/Zuma Press Inc. **358** AP
360-361 akg-images **355** dpa/APA/Hans Techt
365 akg-images/Rabatti-Dom **366 and 367** akg-images
369 Corbis/Jonathan Blair **371** Corbis/Bettmann
373 t argus/Pasieka, b ullstein bild/Höfer
375 laif/Ulutuncok **377 and 378** Bayer AG
381 and 383 ullstein bild/Granger Collection
384 akg-images/Erich Lessing **386-390** ullstein bild/
Granger Collection **392** ullstein bild **396** ullstein bild/
Granger Collection **394** Wildlife/M. Breiter **400** Okapia/
Dr. Klaus Heblich **402** Corbis/Wolfgang Kaehler
Illustrations 80-81, 153, 220 and 354 Ralf Krischok

Amazing Tales from Times Gone By
was published by The Reader's Digest
Association Limited, London
from material first published as
Geschichten aus der Geschichte by
Reader's Digest, Stuttgart

First edition copyright © 2006
The Reader's Digest Association Limited
11 Westferry Circus, Canary Wharf,
London E14 4HE
www.readersdigest.co.uk

We are committed to both the quality
of our products and the service we
provide to our customers. We value your
comments so please feel free to contact
us on **08705 113366** or via our website
at **www.readersdigest.co.uk**

If you have any comments or
suggestions about the content of
our books you can contact us at
gbeditorial@readersdigest.co.uk

Project editor Lisa Thomas
Designer Kate Harris
Editors Liz Clasen, Celia Coyne, Helen Spence,
Elizabeth Wyse
Translator Peter Lewis
Proofreader Ron Pankhurst
Indexer Michael Dent
Authors Dr. Irmela Arnsperger, Berit Lina Barth,
Jonathan Bastable, Dr. Birgit Gläser, Dr. Peter Göbel,
Jeremy Harwood, Guido Huß, Dr. Roland Knauer,
Sylvia Krümpelmann, Dr. Frauke Lätsch, Dr. Alwin
Letzkus, Frank J. Müller, Prof. Dr. Boike Rehbein,
Dr. Andrea Schleipen, Prof. Dr. Holger Sonnabend,
Susanne Straub, Kerstin Viering

READER'S DIGEST GENERAL BOOKS
Editorial Director Julian Browne
Art Director Nick Clark
Head of Book Development Sarah Bloxham
Managing Editor Alastair Holmes
Picture Resource Manager Sarah Stewart-Richardson
Pre-press Account Manager Sandra Fuller
Product Production Manager Claudette Bramble
Senior Production Controller Deborah Trott

Origination Colour Systems Ltd
Printed and bound in Europe by Arvato Iberia

Book code: 400-290-01
ISBN-10: 0 276 44208 3
ISBN-13: 978 0 276 44208 7
Oracle code: 250009742H.00.24